TAMING JAPAN'S DEFLATION

A VOLUME IN THE SERIES

Cornell Studies in Money

Edited by Eric Helleiner and Jonathan Kirshner

A list of titles in this series is available at cornellpress.cornell.edu.

TAMING JAPAN'S DEFLATION

The Debate over Unconventional
Monetary Policy

Gene Park, Saori N. Katada,
Giacomo Chiozza, and
Yoshiko Kojo

CORNELL UNIVERSITY PRESS   ITHACA AND LONDON

First published 2018 by Cornell University Press

Printed in the United States of America

Library of Congress Cataloging-in-Publication Data

Names: Park, Gene, author. | Katada, Saori N., author. | Chiozza, Giacomo, author. | Kojo, Yoshiko, 1956– author.
Title: Taming Japan's deflation : the debate over unconventional monetary policy / Gene Park, Saori N. Katada, Giacomo Chiozza, and Yoshiko Kojo.
Description: Ithaca [New York] : Cornell University Press, 2018. | Series: Cornell studies in money | Includes bibliographical references and index.
Identifiers: LCCN 2018007696 (print) | LCCN 2018021284 (ebook) | ISBN 9781501728181 (pdf) | ISBN 9781501728198 (epub/mobi) | ISBN 9781501728174 (cloth : alk. paper)
Subjects: LCSH: Monetary policy—Japan. | Deflation (Finance)—Japan. | Nihon Ginkō. | Banks and banking, Central—Japan. | Japan—Economic policy—1989–
Classification: LCC HG1275 (ebook) | LCC HG1275 .P27 2018 (print) | DDC 339.5/30952—dc23
LC record available at https://lccn.loc.gov/2018007696

This book is dedicated to our families

Contents

Figures and Tables

Figures

Tables

Preface and Acknowledgments

This book is the culmination of four years of work. Over that time, we have accumulated enormous debts. While we cannot monetize these debts, we would like to acknowledge all the people and institutions who made this project possible. We would first like to thank those who took time from their busy schedules to meet with us for interviews. We interviewed well over forty scholars and policymakers for this book. It is no exaggeration to say that without their help, this book would simply not have been possible since much of what they conveyed, while central to monetary policymaking, is simply not accessible in any other form: transcripts, minutes, existing scholarly works, or news accounts. Some of these people prefer to stay anonymous. The others we list here in alphabetical order:

Ben Bernanke, Danny Blanchflower, Jess Diamond, Robert Feldman, Yoshihiro Fujii, Yoshinori Hayashi, Eiji Hirano, Etsurō Honda, Kazuhito Ikeo, Nobuo Inaba, Takatoshi Itō, Kentaro Katayama, Masahiro Kawai, Yasunori Kishiro, Donald Kohn, Hideo Kimano, Hideo Maeyama, Yoshitaka Murata, Nobuyuki Nakahara, Takumi Nemoto, Kiyohiko Nishimura, Kunio Okina, Kōhei Ōtsuka, Adam Posen, Isaya Shimizu, Masato Shimizu, Sayuri Shirai, Shigenori Shiratsuka, Masato Shizume, Miyako Suda, Lars Svensson, Shinji Takagi, Hirobumi Takinami, Kazuo Ueda, Masanobu Umeda, Anders Vredin, Hirohide Yamaguchi, Kōzō Yamamoto, Takeshi Yamawaki, Kaoru Yosano, and Hiroshi Yoshikawa.

A book is a form of dialogue with an audience. The quality of the conversation that we would like to start with this book was enhanced enormously by the numerous interactions we had with leading scholars and policymakers. Our conversations with these experts occurred over the course of several years in a variety of gatherings that include a book manuscript workshop on September 9, 2016, at the University of Southern California (USC), the International Studies Association Annual Meeting, American Political Science Association Conference, Stanford Summer Juku, the Journal of International Money and Finance—USC Conference, as well as numerous other individual presentations in Japan, Germany, Sweden, and the United States. We would especially like to thank Joshua Aizenman, Brock Blomberg, Lawrence Broz, Jeffry Frieden, Kōichi Hamada, Mitsuhiro Fukao, Takeo Hoshi, Jacques Hymans, Joe Gagnon, William Grimes, Kenji Kushida, Ryūnoshin Kamikawa, Azusa Katagiri, Masanaga Kumakura, Phillip Lipscy, Masao Mabuchi, Benjamin Nyblade, Ayako Saiki,

Cheryl Schonhardt-Bailey, and Derek William Valles. Two anonymous reviewers for Cornell University Press provided extensive feedback. Their contribution cannot be understated. As they will notice upon seeing the book, their feedback led to substantial improvements.

We could not have completed this project without the generous support from the Center for Global Partnership of the Japan Foundation (CGP). CGP's financial support allowed us, among other things, to hire research assistants and hold the aforementioned book manuscript conference. We thank Lisa Wong at CGP for her patient and effective support for this project.

The School of International Relations and Center for International Studies at USC supported our project intellectually, financially, and administratively. We are especially grateful to the institutions' leaders: Dave Kang, Patrick James, and Robert English. The latter two made arrangements to host Giacomo Chiozza at USC for a year, and that invitation contributed to our serendipitous partnership. Linda Cole, Gina Hakim, Cort Brinkenhoff, and Madeline Brown also provided excellent administrative support. The Department of Advanced Social and International Studies and Graduate School of Arts and Sciences at the University of Tokyo and Loyola Marymount University provided valuable supported for the project as well. We would also like to express our gratitude beyond our own institutions. Special thanks to Markus Heckel at the Institute for Management and Microeconomics at Goethe-Universität, Eisaku Ide at the Faculty of Economics at Keio University, Marie Söderberg, director of the European Institute of Japanese Studies (EIJS) at the Stockholm School of Economics, and Masayuki Takahashi at Saitama University's Graduate School of Humanities and Social Sciences.

We would be remiss not to acknowledge our excellent research assistants, who took valuable time away from their own endeavors to help with this project: Gabi Cheung, Edith Conn, Yūki Fujii, Mayumi Itayama, Meredith Shaw, Scott Wilbur, Mingmin Yang, Naomi Yoshida, and Xinlin Zhao.

Finally, we would like to thank the editors at Cornell University Press. We reached out to Cornell University Press's acquisition editor, Roger Haydon, at an early stage, and he provided guidance before we had completed a draft of the manuscript. After benefiting from his early hands-on approach throughout the process, we have come to understand why his name has shown up in the acknowledgments sections of so many excellent books. Roger put us in touch with the series editors for "Cornell Studies in Money," Eric Helleiner and Jonathan Kirshner, and they kindly reviewed parts of the manuscript long before it was sent out for formal review. The manuscript benefited significantly from their substantive feedback and the rigorous review process they oversaw.

We are grateful to so many people who helped us along the way to understand the complexities of the changing monetary policy landscape. We have entered an era where policies that were scarcely imaginable a generation ago have now become the mainstream. Yet the literature on the subject has not fully caught up with this new reality. While at times hard to follow for nonspecialists, the stakes of monetary policy have been and continue to be high. We hope this book stimulates a broader dialogue about the factors that drive the political choices over these policies.

Acronyms

ABCP	Asset-Backed Commercial Papers
ABS	Asset-Backed Securities
BIS	Bank for International Settlements
BOE	Bank of England
BOJ	Bank of Japan
CBI	Central Bank Independence
CME	Comprehensive Monetary Easing
CP	Commercial Papers
CPI	Consumer Price Index
DICJ	Deposit Insurance Corporation of Japan
DPJ	Democratic Party of Japan
DSGE	Dynamic Stochastic General Equilibrium Model
ECB	European Central Bank
ETF	Exchange-Traded Funds
FILP	Fiscal Investment Loan Program
FOMC	Federal Open Market Committee
FRB	Federal Reserve Bank
FSA	Financial Service Agency
GDP	Gross Domestic Product
GFC	Global Financial Crisis
GSE	Government-Sponsored Enterprise
IMES	Institute for Monetary and Economic Studies
IMF	International Monetary Fund
J-REIT	Japanese Real Estate Investment Trust
JGB	Japanese Government Bond
LDP	Liberal Democratic Party
MBS	Mortgage-Backed Securities
MOF	Ministry of Finance
MPC	Monetary Policy Committee
NPL	Nonperforming Loan
OECD	Organisation for Economic Co-operation and Development
PBC	Political Business Cycle
QE	Quantitative Easing

QQE	Quantitative and Qualitative Easing
RFB	Reconstruction Finance Bank
SCAP	Supreme Commander for the Allied Powers
SMP	Securities Markets Programme
WPI	Wholesale Price Index
ZIRP	Zero Interest Rate Policy

Currency and Foreign Exchange Rates

We cite figures throughout this book in Japanese yen. We also include the approximate value in US dollars. The dollar conversions are based on the average annual exchange rate for the specific year for which the conversation is estimated. A list of the conversion rates used in this book is provided in an appendix.

Japanese Names

Japanese names in the main text are cited with the family name first, following the Japanese convention. One exception is the acknowledgments and references, where names are listed following Western convention for consistency.

Interviews

We conducted over forty interviews for this book. The majority of these interviewees are based in Japan although we also reached out to experts outside of Japan as well. These experts expressed a wide spectrum of views on monetary policy. We conducted most of the interviews with the condition of anonymity. Unless individuals explicitly gave us approval to identify them by name, we quote them in our book without identifying their names.

TAMING JAPAN'S DEFLATION

Chapter 1

IDEAS, NETWORKS, AND MONETARY POLITICS IN JAPAN

Deflation and stagnation are the threats of our times.

—Lawrence Summers, 2016

Since the end of World War II, deflation had been a rarity, with only a handful of countries experiencing temporary episodes. Indeed, the defining postwar problem for monetary policymakers and economists had been how to curb inflation, particularly in the aftermath of the oil shocks in the 1970s. Then, starting in the latter half of the 1990s, Japan's economy slid into recession and prices began to decline, and the economy entered a pernicious deflationary spiral, a trend that largely continued for more than fifteen years and from which Japan has not yet clearly emerged as of late 2017. The economic and social costs of this deflation have been high. Once seemingly an oddity and cautionary tale, Japan now has new company. In the wake of the global financial crisis of 2008, other countries are experiencing low inflation and in some cases outright deflation. One prominent economist, Lawrence Summers, has proclaimed that deflation is now one of the central "threats of our time."[1]

Yet despite the widespread awareness of the potential dangers posed by deflation, Japan's central bank—the Bank of Japan (BOJ)—was surprisingly complacent. Economists and policymakers articulated new theories and suggested "unconventional" monetary policies (also referred to as nonstandard monetary

---

1. "Larry Summers Warns of Epochal Deflationary Crisis If Fed Tightens Too Soon," *The Telegraph*, January 22, 2016, http://www.telegraph.co.uk/finance/financetopics/davos/11362699/Larry-Summers-warns-of-epochal-deflationary-crisis-if-Fed-tightens-too-soon.html, accessed on January 23, 2016.

policy) to combat deflation. Many central banks across the globe have tapped these policy instruments in their battle against deflation. These policies have now become a part of a new lexicon—quantitative easing (QE), price-level targets, forward guidance, negative interest rates, helicopter money, etc.—that shows up daily across the media.

Even though Japan's economy was mired in deflation for longer than any other major economy, the BOJ was slow to embrace these unconventional measures despite an early experiment with quantitative easing. Japan's economy dipped into deflation in the mid-1990s and again more seriously in the late 1990s; this period was followed by a prolonged period of deflation from the end of the 1990s through the mid-2000s. With the start of the global financial crisis (GFC) in 2008, economic growth dropped sharply, as did prices. While the Federal Reserve Board (FRB) and Bank of England (BOE) raced ahead with radical measures to avoid financial collapse and deflation, the BOJ remained cautious, largely staying the course. Then the Japanese economy suffered another blow with the devastating triple disaster of 2011: earthquake, tsunami, and nuclear crisis. Despite these challenges and seemingly unshakeable deflation, the BOJ remained reluctant to embrace aggressive unconventional monetary policies.

Policy then shifted sharply at the end of 2012 under Prime Minister Abe Shinzō during his second term. Abe promised aggressive monetary measures to reflate the economy as part of his "Abenomics" package of economic revitalization policies. In early 2013, he appointed a new governor of the BOJ—Kuroda Haruhiko—who promised to do "whatever it takes" to overcome deflation and embarked on an unprecedented antideflationary monetary policy.

How can we understand the seemingly long resistance to sustained reflationary measures? More broadly, in the context of uncertainty, as central banks shift from battling inflation to deflation, what influences the spread of new ideas and policies?

The Argument

In this book, we contend that Japan's longer commitment to its monetary orthodoxy reflects entrenched *policy ideas*—a set of shared beliefs about policy goals, priorities, and causal relationships—within Japan's monetary policy-making network. Central to the network was the BOJ itself (not just the Policy Board but the larger bureaucratic organization), which developed a relatively coherent *worldview* (which we use interchangeably with policy ideas) over the course of its previous experiences. This view included placing a premium on price stability (even in the context of very low inflation), skepticism about the efficacy of monetary policy to spur economic growth, a belief that monetary easing could have adverse side effects, and an interpretation of independence that made it suspicious of acting in concert with the executive and the Ministry of Finance (MOF).

The establishment of legal independence for the BOJ in 1998, right as Japan was tipping into recession and deflation, established policymaking authority in a new independent board with members nominated by the executive and confirmed by the legislature. Despite this formal structure, an informal monetary policy network influenced monetary policy choices as well as appointments to this board. The relatively closed nature of the monetary policy network, and the BOJ's strategic position within it, shaped the circulation of pre-existing policy ideas and made the Policy Board less receptive to unconventional monetary policy by limiting the impact of processes of ideational change highlighted in the literature.

The monetary policy network remained stable for the first fifteen years after the BOJ's de jure independence, but the political underpinnings grew less secure as economic stagnation and deflation persisted. The dominant policy ideas then went through a radical policy paradigm shift. This ideational shift was triggered by policy failure and BOJ intransigence, which invited greater political intervention to reframe deflation as a critical economic problem that could be addressed through monetary policy. As the conviction in policy failure strengthened, electoral competition pushed the major parties to challenge the BOJ orthodoxy and embrace new ideas in the run-up to the election at the end of 2012. Abe Shinzō and his party, the Liberal Democratic Party (LDP), declared deflation a top priority and demanded the boldest reflationary measures as part of its campaign manifesto.

Once in power after his party won a landslide election, Prime Minister Abe deliberately circumvented the existing monetary policy network. Consulting his own advisers, who had been highly critical of the BOJ, he appointed a new governor and two deputy governors. He then eventually replaced every other member of the Policy Board. Once a laggard in pursuing bold reflationary policies, the BOJ Policy Board has gone to extreme lengths to raise inflation, deploying policies that have not been tried by other central banks. Prime Minister Abe, his advisers, and the new BOJ governor, Kuroda, did not act in isolation; the larger global context was critical to the ideational shift in Japan. By the end of 2012, new monetary policy ideas had already diffused to the BOE, FRB, and European Central Bank (ECB), in part through their more porous policy network structures. These central banks (as well as others) had deployed unconventional policies, and the FRB, an early mover, was already on its third round of QE. The actions of other central banks not only framed deflation more clearly as a major economic problem but also suggested that the unconventional policies, which the policy network had viewed with skepticism, could be used to combat deflation without many of the feared adverse consequences.

Monetary Policy and Policy Ideas

More broadly, this book makes the case that to understand central bank monetary policy choices, we need to consider the ideas that shape how central bankers view the world. A rich literature, which we discuss in more detail in chapter 3, has explored how policy ideas, particularly in the realm of economic policy, diffuse and influence policy choices. In the case of monetary policy, there are particularly compelling reasons for considering the role of policy ideas. Central bankers, unlike politicians or political parties, do not have obvious material interests that would influence their monetary policy choices. Furthermore, it is questionable to view central bankers as merely agents of political principals. With the diffusion of central bank independence, central banks have a legal basis for at least partial autonomy. Of course, elected officials grant this independence and delegate responsibility, and thus this independence is contingent. Even so, central bankers have a degree of slack from their principals. The bar to removing officials before their terms end is high. Their autonomy is enhanced by the highly technical and complex nature of monetary policy and deference to policy expertise. Furthermore, the norm that central bank independence is positive and should be preserved provides additional insulation. Despite political backlash against central bank policies—e.g., the painful interest rate hikes under Paul Volcker in the early 1980s or controversial QE policies since the GFC—de jure independence remains intact.

Thus, to understand monetary policy we need to move beyond theories that are based on assumed material interests and preferences to consider the ideational factors that shape how central bankers view the world. This study focuses on the impact of ideas on the BOJ's monetary policy, but the relevance of the point is broader. In some ways, the BOJ is not unique. Policy ideas with similarities to those of the BOJ circulate outside of Japan as well, and in some contexts they have been well institutionalized. The Bundesbank is widely known for its monetary conservatism shaped by hyperinflation during the Weimar Republic, and the ECB was created in a way that reflected this view: a narrow mandate to focus on price stability, strong independence from government, and a prohibition on financing government debt. Indeed, one can speculate that if the Bundesbank still controlled its own monetary policy, it might have acted similarly to the BOJ in the face of the GFC. Alternatively, if the Bundesbank had had fuller control over the ECB's monetary policy decisions, all indications suggest that the

ECB would have been much slower to adopt unconventional monetary policy or perhaps might have avoided it entirely; we discuss this point more fully in our conclusion. While not a central bank but rather an international financial organization, the Bank for International Settlements (BIS), based in Basel, is known for its "BIS view," which includes a strong commitment to price stability, a belief that macroeconomic austerity can facilitate recovery, and the view that monetary easing, including QE, can have a host of negative side effects.

Central bankers belong to institutions with different national histories, different internal practices, and different ideas. Central bankers may adhere to different economic theories or be trained in different ways. Even in a context where policy ideas are more diverse and less coherent than they were with the BOJ, they still matter fundamentally since they define the terms of the debate; in this deeper sense, policy ideas *constitute* the politics of monetary policy.

That ideas are so central to the politics of monetary policy suggests a need to move beyond the conventional notions of central bank independence and principal-agent models that underlie rationalist approaches to monetary policy. This framework draws attention to the relationship between political agents with preferences based on their material incentives and technocratic central bankers shielded by varying levels of de jure independence. One basic conundrum for these theories, with the notable exception of the work by Adolph (2014), is that they discount the role of central bankers themselves even though policy boards have formal authority over monetary policy. This parsimonious perspective ignores that central bankers are embedded in a wider set of institutions and influences ranging from the professional field of economics to memberships in hierarchical organizations with long histories and distinctive practices. To ignore these influences and how they shape broader policy ideas is to miss much of what drives the debates over monetary policy. This is particularly true since the GFC, given the uncertainty about how to respond to deflation.

Studying Ideas: The Approach of This Book

The study of ideas presents a number of challenges to researchers. Ideas are difficult to measure and to connect to outcomes in a rigorous way. Furthermore, it is also hard to explain how and why specific ideas become coherent and win out over other ideas. In the context of monetary policy, even if we accept that monetary policy ideas matter, one faces the challenge of making them tractable to social scientific inquiry. Policy boards, which are vested with monetary policy authority, are composed of individuals. These individuals may have different training and may adhere to different economic assumptions and theories. Furthermore, they may have been appointed at different times and by different people from different parties. One can fairly ask if any generalizations can be made at all. To address these challenges, we use a mixed methods approach that combines data from interviews, quantitative content analysis, and qualitative case studies. We believe our approach can be used to study the impact of ideas on policy in other contexts as well.

One of the central challenges of ideational approaches is to explain the conditions under which certain ideas prevail. To ground our account, we focus on the institutional conditions that enabled specific ideas to be reflected in the Policy Board deliberations and decisions. We conducted a detailed analysis of the formal and informal monetary policymaking institutions—what we refer to as the monetary policy network—based on more than forty interviews with elites. We show how the closed nature of this network perpetuated a specific policy view. As part of our analysis, we also compare the BOJ to other central banks to illustrate the ways in which the policy network in Japan was comparatively closed until Prime Minister Abe disrupted it.

To measure ideas and to study their impact on actual policy outcomes, we use content analysis. Ideational approaches have been critiqued for lacking rigor, but there are increasingly sophisticated methods for measuring ideas and sentiment. One of these is content analysis, which increasingly utilizes computerized statistical techniques. This approach has already been applied in the study of monetary policymaking. Schonhardt-Bailey (2013) takes advantage of computer-aided content analysis to examine the monetary policy discourse in the United States.

The advantage of computer text analysis is that it can handle large amounts of data and in some cases can identify patterns not apparent to the researcher. The disadvantage is that the statistical methods behind computer text analysis still cannot capture all the nuances of natural language. We strike a middle ground. We use software to extract complete sentences that contain key words and then use human coders to code the sentiment in these sentences. Specifically, we analyze the minutes of the BOJ's Policy Board meetings to broadly measure central bankers' attitudes toward price stability. On the basis of this coding, we create a quantitative index to measure the sentiment of the BOJ Policy Board. Then, going a step further, we test statistically the impact of this sentiment on actual monetary policy.

We conduct detailed case studies of key monetary policy choices since 1998 to look more directly at the politics of monetary policy. Drawing on interviews, written records, news accounts, and secondary sources, we examine (1) how the BOJ's ideas were reflected in policy deliberations, and (2) how the role of ideas interacted with other factors such as growing political pressure and changing economic circumstances. This allows us to provide a more nuanced analysis that can take into account that the BOJ's policy ideas did not always win out; in several key cases, the Policy Board capitulated to political pressure. The case studies allow us to distinguish between policy changes that were due to such pressure versus policy changes that reflected a shift in the ideas about monetary policy.

Plan of the Book

We develop our argument over the subsequent chapters. Chapter 2 introduces in greater detail the question motivating this study and then considers a series of alternative explanations for the BOJ's reluctance to try bolder measures to reflate the economy. In this chapter, we lay out the reasons that deflation and low inflation can be harmful, the new economic ideas for tackling both, and the policy instruments that can be drawn upon to fight deflation. The chapter then reviews how the BOJ and other central banks have experimented with these ideas in different ways. We also highlight the larger context that makes Japan's relatively slow uptake of aggressive, unconventional policies so surprising. The chapter concludes by evaluating two types of alternative explanations: those based on policy grounds and explanations based on the academic literature.

Chapter 3 develops our theoretical approach. The chapter reviews existing work on monetary policy and makes the case for why we need an ideational approach to monetary policy. The chapter also articulates our framework, analyzing how the policy networks around monetary policy influenced the circulation and salience of specific policy ideas. The book then explains in chapter 4 the evolution of specific ideas about monetary policy within the BOJ organization, including the formative experiences that shaped the worldview of the BOJ. Chapter 5 explains the formal monetary policy process specified by the Bank of Japan Law (New BOJ Law). The chapter then lays out the central actors in the monetary policy network—the BOJ, the MOF, the Prime Minister's Office, and others—and compares the BOJ's monetary policymaking institutions to other central banks. Focusing on both formal and informal processes, the chapter elucidates how the monetary policy network, prior to Abe's intervention, allowed the BOJ worldview to be reflected in the formally independent Policy Board, both through influencing Policy Board nominations and monetary policy decisions.

To test the impact of the BOJ worldview on monetary policy, in chapter 6 we present the results of an empirical test. We use text analysis of the Policy Board's deliberations to measure central bankers' attitudes toward inflation and deflation. We then use a statistical test to estimate the impact of this sentiment on monetary policy choice, specifically the level of monetary base expansion. The finding supports our claim that central bankers' relative concerns about inflation and deflation help explain monetary policy decisions above and beyond objective economic measures and standard political explanations. To develop further support for our argument, we then present in chapter 7 findings from qualitative research drawn from a review of the policymaking deliberations, legislative deliberations, elite interviews, and other sources to show how ideas and institutions shaped several key monetary policy choices. Chapter 8 then shifts focus to the sharp break with the pre-existing monetary policy orthodoxy. The chapter covers how Prime Minister Abe circumvented the monetary policy network by changing the membership of the Policy Board and how he reoriented monetary policy to reflect his reflationary priorities. The chapter also assesses the outcomes of monetary policy under Governor Kuroda. Chapter 9 then revisits the book's main findings, compares the diffusion of unconventional polices in other contexts, and draws out the larger implications.

Chapter 2

DEFLATION, MONETARY POLICY RESPONSES, AND THE BOJ

> The fact that no responsible government would ever literally drop money from the sky should not prevent us from exploring the logic of Friedman's thought experiment, which was designed to show—in admittedly extreme terms—why governments should never have to give in to deflation.
>
> —Ben Bernanke (2016)

The high inflation of the 1970s and early 1980s was one of the defining challenges for monetary policy; it influenced economic theory, institutions, and policy. After learning from this tumultuous period, central bankers—aided by luck and structural economic changes (e.g., technology and globalization)—were regarded as having tamed inflation and paved the way for the "Great Moderation," which lasted roughly from 1987 to 2007 (Bernanke 2004). The period saw the steady decline of inflation and volatile fluctuations in the business cycle. As figure 2.1 shows, inflation fell steadily for the thirty-four OECD countries.

Soon after celebrating success in combating inflation, though, concerns shifted to the risks from low inflation and deflation. Japan was the first major economy to experience sustained deflation, starting in the late 1990s. Then, with the start of the GFC, many parts of the world began to look a little more like Japan. Inflation remains low, and at the time of this writing, deflation remains a concern in Japan and western Europe.

The Problem of Deflation

Deflation, when the price of goods and services declines, is attributable to a number of causes.[1] Not all forms of deflation are necessarily pernicious. Deflation can

---

1. Different schools of thought offer different explanations. Monetarists, such as Milton Friedman, largely see prices (and by extensions) as a function of the money supply. New classical economists view episodes of deflation as part of the natural business cycle.

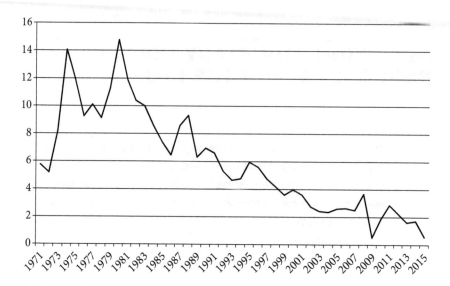

FIGURE 2.1.   OECD annual inflation rate (all items), 1971–2015

Source: OECD, accessed April 20, 2016, http://stats.oecd.org

result from supply-side improvements such as enhanced productivity and thus can coincide with economic growth. This was partly the case during the nineteenth century when deflation was relatively mild.[2]

Deflation can also occur through demand-side shocks. These shocks can be the result of policy mistakes, such as the decline in the money supply that contributed to a collapse in demand in the United States, Sweden, and Japan during the Depression, or recession as Japan experienced in the late 1990s.[3] Under such circumstances deflation can have potentially damaging economic consequences.[4] If prices are declining, then consumers may defer purchases, weakening aggregate demand, and companies may be reluctant to invest until prices recover. Reductions in investment can further lower aggregate demand, leading to a deflationary spiral. Deflation may also lower spending and investment by increasing the real burden

---

2. Even so, the periods of deflation are correlated with lower economic growth as well as greater social and political unrest. See Baig et al. 2003 for an overview of this work.

3. Ibid.

4. McKinnon and Ohno (2001) offer an interesting structural explanation for Japan's deflation. They argue that deflation results from the trade imbalance with the United States and legacy of US intervention in pressuring Japan to resolve it through yen appreciation. The expectation and concern about yen appreciation dampens private domestic investment.

of debt repayment; furthermore, the erosion of the value of collateral can reduce the ability of firms and consumers to continue to borrow and invest. While creditors may benefit in some instances from deflation, if deflation is serious, the value of collateral may fall as well, and if assets are liquidated, asset values may decline further, leading to a debt-deflation trap (Fisher 1933; Baig et al. 2003). Given that credit, including long-term credit, is now much more widely used, the negative effect of deflation on balance sheets is more harmful than in the past (Bernanke 1999). Deflation may also be damaging to the economy, since wages tend to be sticky. If wages do not adjust downward, profits will decline, which may lead to employment reduction and shrinking aggregate demand (Akerlof, Dickens, and Perry 1996). Prolonged deflation can also be hard to exit. A deflationary mindset can take hold as firms engage in deflation-oriented pricing strategies and financial institutions adopt deflationary investment strategies that further exacerbate the deflationary spiral (Shirai 2017).

Beyond the economic consequences, deflation also poses another serious risk: it can render conventional monetary policies ineffective. Central banks typically conduct monetary policy by targeting short-term interest rates. By buying and selling short-term debt securities, such as government bonds, they can influence their price and the interest rate. Increasing purchases of such bonds, for instance, raises their price, resulting in lower interest rates, while selling bonds has the opposite effect. By using such "conventional" (sometimes referred to as orthodox or standard) monetary policy, central bankers can influence asset prices, consumption, and investment decisions.[5] Under deflation, however, conventional monetary policy is constrained by the zero lower bound. Even if central bankers lower short-term nominal interest rates to zero percent, under deflation the real interest rate (the nominal interest rate minus the rate of inflation) will remain positive and potentially high depending on the severity of the deflation. Additional short-term debt purchases cannot lower short-term interest rates below zero.

The risk of low inflation is also heightened by the fact that inflation measures tend to overstate inflation (Boskin et al. 1996; Lebow and Rudd 2003); thus, an economy with very low inflation may in fact already have no inflation or be in

---

5. For instance, the effect of monetary policy on housing investment and prices has been found to be contingent on national mortgage market characteristics (Calza, Monacelli, and Stracca 2013). Monetary policy has different effects on asset classes (Mishkin 2001); moreover, financial innovation and regulation, some argue, mediates how monetary policy works through different transmission channels (Kuttner and Mosser 2002; Boivin, Kiley, and Mishkin 2010; Borio and Zhu 2012). We thank an anonymous reviewer for recommending that we reference this research.

deflation. Given that deflation can be hard to exit, the risks posed by deflation are asymmetrically greater than inflation, for inflation can be controlled through conventional monetary policy (Baig et al. 2003).

Not all periods of deflation are equally deleterious. As alluded to above, during the nineteenth century, deflation was relatively mild and reflected in part supply-side changes. Even so, those periods of deflation are correlated with lower economic growth as well as greater social and political unrest.[6] In the case of the Great Depression, there were more severe episodes of deflation that were driven by a collapse in demand in the United States, Sweden, and Japan, and economists have attributed this collapse to monetary policy mistakes and other factors.[7]

From the end of World War II until the GFC, there were only a few short-term episodes of deflation among the industrialized economies—Canada, Norway, Sweden, Germany, and Japan. Japan was the first and thus far only country to experience a prolonged period of recurring deflation.

Using Monetary Policy to Fight Deflation

John Maynard Keynes recognized the problem of the zero lower bound during the Great Depression. An economy can fall into a liquidity trap if aggregate demand is falling and short-term interest rates can no longer be lowered. In such a case, a government can intervene through expansionary fiscal policy (e.g., a boost in public spending, a tax reduction, or some combination) to boost aggregate demand. One of the implications of Keynes' work is that fiscal policy, rather than monetary policy, should be the key instrument for battling deflation.

More recently, economists have emphasized that monetary policy can still be used under deflation even if the key policy instrument of a central bank, short-term interest rates (typically the overnight interest rate banks charge each other in the money market), becomes ineffective. At the end of the 1990s and 2000s, economic theories emerged, inspired in part by the experience of Japan, that suggested how "unconventional" monetary policies—discussed in more detail further below—might be used to overcome deflation. These theories as well as specific policies have had diverse intellectual influences and arguably do not neatly fit into economic camps such as monetarism, New Classical, or New

---

6. See Baig et al. 2003 for an overview of this work.
7. Ibid.

Keynesian.[8] Indeed, Ben Bernanke, who came to see his views as close to those of the New Keynesians, has also acknowledged the influence of the monetarists Milton Friedman and Anna Schwartz.[9]

Forward Guidance

Forward guidance is a policy of communicating the future policy stance of the central bank, in order to shape future market expectations. Even if short-term interest rates are near or at zero, longer-term interest rates tend to be higher, as investors typically demand a term premium for holding a longer-maturity asset. Through forward guidance, central banks can signal that they will keep short-term interest rates lower into the future and thus shape expectations about future interest rates, thereby bringing down longer-term interest rates. For instance, a central bank can publicly announce that it will keep short-term interest rates at zero well into the future. As part of forward guidance, central bankers can also articulate clear metrics—such as employment, economic growth, or inflation rates—that will determine how long monetary easing will continue. Central banks can also make "unconditional" commitments to keep interest rates low for specific periods of time.

The theory behind forward guidance is the flip side of the theory of central bank independence: the challenge facing central bankers is that they must establish credibility to end *deflation* (Krugman, Dominquez, and Rogoff 1998; Svensson 2001, 2006; Kuttner and Posen 2004; Eggertsson and Woodford 2004; Ito and Mishkin 2006). The problem is that "markets believe the central bank will target price stability, given the chance, and hence that any current monetary expansion is merely transitory" (Krugman, Dominquez, and Rogoff 1998, 139). Central bank independence and a reputation for being hawkish on inflation thus make it harder to establish the credibility needed to end deflation. Forward guidance, by indicating the future path of monetary policy, can alleviate this credibility problem by committing to future monetary easing.

A central bank can use forward guidance in conjunction with *inflation targeting* to signal its intentions. The publicly announced target sets a goal for prices

---

8. In some cases, monetarists and new Keynesians have agreed on policy instruments, such as QE, but disagreed about the transmission mechanisms. In other cases, new Keynesians and monetarists have disagreed among each other. New Keynesians Eggertsson and Woodford (2004), for instance, have suggested that QE by itself is not effective.

9. On Bernanke's identification with new Keynesians, see his book, *The Courage to Act* (2015). On his acknowledgment of the influence of Friedman and Schwartz, see his remarks "On Milton Friedman's Ninetieth Birthday," November 8, 2002. Available at https://www.federalreserve.gov/BOARDDOCS/SPEECHES/2002/20021108/.

that central bankers are delegated to achieve. While inflation targets were initially suggested and used as a way to control inflation (such as in New Zealand), they can also be used as means to exit deflation by helping shape inflation expectations. A variation of forward guidance working in conjunction with inflation targets involves having a central bank commit publicly to overshooting its inflation target in an effort to induce a further increase in inflation expectations. Some economists have suggested that a *price-level target* also might be a more useful tool for overcoming deflation (Svensson 1999). A price target sets a numerical price level over the medium term as a goal, whereas an inflation target focuses on the forward-looking rate of change. In the case of a decline in prices, then, the gap between price level and the price-level target would increase, thus requiring greater intervention to make up the difference.

Quantitative Easing (QE)

Another policy instrument to overcome the limits of the zero lower bound is quantitative easing (QE). Rather than targeting the short-term interest rate, a central bank targets a large-scale quantitative expansion in the monetary base. A central bank can do so by expanding its balance sheet through the purchase of assets, such as government bonds, or through direct lending to targeted credit markets. Both policies effectively increase the currency and bank reserves in the economy. In principle, QE can work through several channels. One is the portfolio channel. As banks sell assets to the central bank in exchange for cash as part of QE, banks will rebalance their portfolios through the purchase of other assets. If banks rebalance by buying longer-term assets, this can drive down longer-term interest rates. A central bank can also choose to buy a mix of different assets to influence the respective longer-term interest rates of these assets directly. For example, if a central bank purchases longer-term government bonds, it can increase prices for longer-term bonds, thereby lowering long-term interest rates. Central banks can also change their portfolios without changing the size of their balance sheet—as they buy assets they can sell other assets—which is not strictly speaking QE since the monetary base does not increase. The influence on interest rates from such intervention is likely to be more limited (Bernanke and Reinhart 2004).

QE can also work through the asset-price channel. QE can boost the prices of assets such as stocks or housing, which in turn can stimulate consumption and investment. QE, ceteris paribus, can also lead to currency depreciation, thereby increasing domestic production by lowering the relative price of exports and increasing the price of imports. If profits increase, this in turn can increase asset prices through higher valuations. Such policies are expected to be more effective if the central bank indicates that the changes are likely to be permanent, signaling a long-term commitment to QE (Ito and Mishkin 2006).

Interest Rate Targeting

In addition to a target for a quantitative increase in the expansion of the monetary base, a central bank can also target an interest rate, a policy also referred to as "yield curve control." While under deflation, short-term interest rates may already be near or at zero, longer-term rates tend to be higher due to the term premium. Under QE, as discussed above, portfolio rebalancing or targeted purchases of longer-maturity assets can bring down these longer-term interest rates. Interest rate targeting, though, works through an explicit target interest rate. A central bank, for instance, may commit to keeping the ten-year sovereign bond rate to 1 percent. The central bank then would have to purchase whatever quantity of these bonds necessary to maintain this rate.

Negative Interest Rates

The constraints of the zero lower bound assume that central banks cannot lower interest rates below zero. As we now know, central banks can and have introduced negative interest rates.[10] A central bank can do this by levying a charge on banks for holding reserves at the central bank. By doing so, the central bank creates incentives for banks to invest in other assets to avoid the fee. Through shifting funds into different assets, negative interest rates via the portfolio rebalancing channel can drive down longer-term interest rates, which should encourage borrowing, spending, and investment.

Helicopter Money

The term "helicopter money" is a really a broad idea that could be implemented in a number of ways. The idea is attributable to Milton Friedman (1969), who once suggested a scenario where a helicopter drops $1,000 from the sky; more recently, the idea has been revived, in large part growing out of the discussion about how Japan could escape deflation.

In 2002, Bernanke publicly revived the idea by mentioning it in a speech as a Federal Reserve Board governor. Subsequently he has fleshed out his version

---

10. Economic philosopher Silvio Gesell, in the early twentieth century, actually suggested a version of negative interest rates. A currency would need stamps that would have to be purchased to stay valid, thus as time passed the growing cost of stamps would lower the real value of the currency.

of how it would work. Rather than literally dropping money from a helicopter, Bernanke has suggested two methods. A government could deliver a tax cut to the people or increase government spending (Bernanke 2016). Either could be directly financed by the central bank. Doing so would increase demand and raise inflation expectations. Also crucially, market actors would not expect such spending to result in future tax increases since the tax cut or spending would be financed by the central bank. Such a policy, in particular in Bernanke's version, is in reality a combination of fiscal and monetary policy. Given that central banks have authority over monetary policy and treasury departments oversee fiscal policy, a new governance framework for implementing such policy would likely be needed; Bernanke (2016) suggests that this institutional hurdle can be overcome by spelling out how such a system might be structured in the United States.

Another means to execute helicopter money policy would be to transfer funds directly to households and finance these transfers through the creation of new money (Lonergan 2014). Households would stimulate demand without having to worry about future tax hikes. Lonergan (2014) argues that the policy makes better sense than QE from a distributional perspective as well as in terms of effectiveness. Transfers would lead directly to demand and would channel cash to households rather than to the financial sector.

It is important to note three critical points. First, the above unconventional policies are far from exhaustive, and economists are constantly generating new policy options. Second, some of the options above, in particular helicopter money, have been discussed but remain on the fringes of serious policy debate. That more radical redistributive measures—such as cash transfers to households—are more or less off the table is a reflection of how the underlying politics determines the range of ideas considered. Thus the range of what are seen as serious or realistic policy options is at its core a political construction. Yet as politics change so too can the plausible range of options under consideration.

Third, most central bankers and economists do not believe that monetary policy (conventional or unconventional) is a magic wand. Most would agree that monetary policy cannot change the underlying potential for economic growth. Potential output—the output when the economy is at full capacity—is determined by factors such as demographics, technology, productivity, and human capital that are beyond the reach of central bankers. In the case of Japan, a declining and aging population and the fact that it is already a mature, technologically advanced country mean that the real potential growth level cannot easily be raised. The point of monetary policy, though, is not to raise potential output but rather to use monetary policy (conventional and unconventional) to manage aggregate demand to close the output gap (the gap between actual output and potential output). Economists have advanced arguments that suggest that unconventional policy can help overcome the limits of the zero lower bound in order to close this gap. As with all theories, these arguments have been and likely will continue to be debated even as empirical evidence accumulates. Under what conditions these ideas are translated into practice (or not), however, is a different question.

Japan's Response to Deflation in Comparative Perspective

The puzzle motivating this project is why the BOJ was reluctant to embrace unconventional monetary policy even after Japan had experienced deflationary spells for a longer time than other industrialized democracies. While the period after the GFC shows the starkest contrast in monetary policy between the BOJ on the one hand and BOE and FRB on the other, one should bear in mind that Japan had experienced deflation for nearly a decade longer than the United Kingdom or United States. Indeed, Japan experienced a recession and deflation during the mid-1990s. Then, after a short economic recovery around 1996, from 1998 the economy was in deflation (or occasionally periods of very low inflation) for more than seven years; see figures 2.2 and 2.3. While the deflation was mild, over time the trajectory of Japan's level of prices contrasts sharply with the United Kingdom, United States, and Euro area.

Reluctance to embrace unconventional monetary policy does not mean that the BOJ did not experiment with some unconventional monetary policy instruments. Indeed, the BOJ was the first country to experiment with QE from 2001 to 2006. In a larger sense, though, the BOJ has been resistant to unconventional monetary policy. As discussed further below and in other chapters of this book, the BOJ undertook its first QE unwillingly, pushed to wind it down at the earliest possible sign of recovery (which many believed was premature), and questioned the effectiveness of the experiment afterwards.

Although there were forceful calls by a number of prominent economists for the BOJ to try bolder action, one must bear in mind that beyond the BOJ's reluctance to try QE, the cautiousness of the BOJ also likely reflects the novelty of the experiment and limited empirical research at the time on how QE works. More surprising is the BOJ's aversion to employing bolder measures in the wake of the GFC, when Japan experienced a large output gap and steep deflation. Even as the BOE and FRB moved more decisively with unconventional policies, the BOJ remained comparatively conservative even though it had virtually no room to lower its key policy rate, which was 0.5 percent at the onset of the crisis; by contrast the target

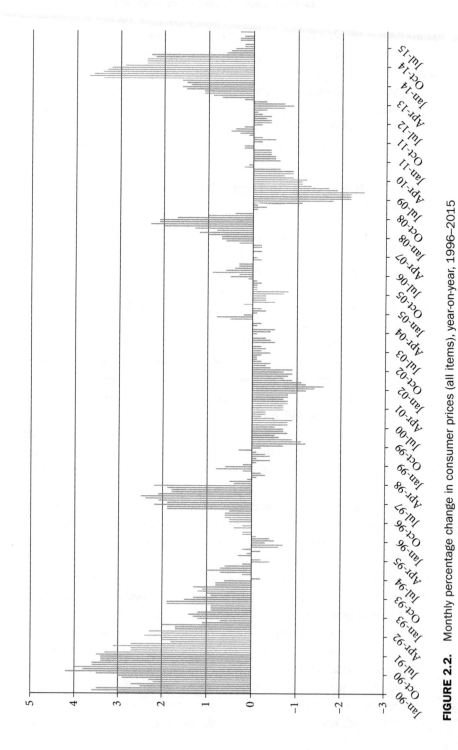

FIGURE 2.2. Monthly percentage change in consumer prices (all items), year-on-year, 1996–2015

Source: OECD, accessed April 20, 2016, http://stats.oecd.org

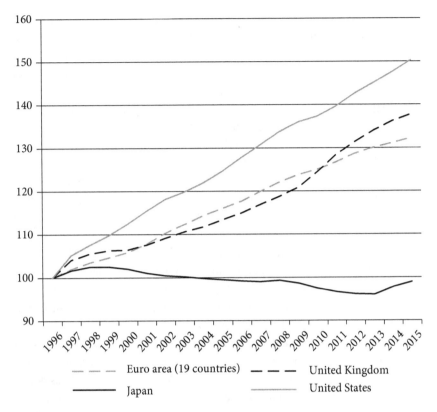

FIGURE 2.3.   CPI trend (all items excluding food and energy), 1996–2015

Source: OECD, accessed April 20, 2016, http://stats.oecd.org

policy rates for the BOE and FRB were at 5 percent, and as the crisis spread, both central banks rapidly lowered these rates.

The BOJ only shifted course at the end of 2012 with the election of Prime Minister Abe, who campaigned on the basis of a reflationary monetary policy. After coming to power, Prime Minister Abe forced the hand of the BOJ by moving to appoint three new executives to the Policy Board (chapter 8). The sections below discuss Japan's monetary policy choices and put the BOJ's responses in comparative perspective.

Japan's Early Experiment with Unconventional Policy

Japan in some ways was an early innovator in the arena of monetary policy. At the end of the 1990s, Japan's economy experienced a sharp downturn due to a confluence of factors: the collapse of several major financial institutions, the onset of the Asian financial crisis, and an ill-timed increase in the consumption tax. After the onset of deflation, the BOJ Policy Board experimented with new measures. From February 1999, Japan adopted a zero interest rate policy (ZIRP). The BOJ, despite strong opposition from the government and the Ministry of Finance (MOF), then lifted ZIRP in August 2000, a move that many have viewed as pushing the Japanese economy back into recession. As deflation resumed, the BOJ backtracked due to intense political pressure for its perceived policy mistake and began its experiment with QE, which it had previously considered but rejected. From March 2001 to March 2006, the BOJ shifted its target from the short-term interest rate (the uncollateralized overnight call rate) to a quantitative target for monetary base expansion (i.e., targeting an expansion of the "BOJ account balance"); the BOJ also purchased public and private debt. The BOJ expanded the goals of QE, gradually including the expansion of BOJ monthly purchases of Japanese government bonds (JGBs) from ¥400 billion (March 2001) to ¥1.2 trillion (October 2002) and raising the BOJ account balance target from ¥5 trillion (March 2001) to between ¥30 and 35 trillion (January 2006).[11] The BOJ then began to wind down the policy in March 2006. In addition to this shift in focus from the short-term interest rate to an expansion of the monetary base, the BOJ also experimented with a version of forward guidance, albeit with highly conservative parameters. The BOJ announced it would continue with QE until prices were stable at zero percent or higher. At the time, the BOJ was deeply resistant to introducing an inflation target, which some have argued to be one of the most effective monetary policy instruments against deflation (Ito 2004).

Central Bank Responses to the Global Financial Crisis

Despite struggling with deflation for much longer than other countries and the early experiment with unconventional monetary policy, the BOJ was reluctant to embrace aggressive monetary policy with the onset of the GFC (Katada 2013). With the collapse of Lehman Brothers in September 2008, the major central banks lowered their respective policy rates sharply; given their higher initial starting point, the magnitude of the interest rate cuts was much greater for the BOE, ECB, and FRB

---

11. Koike 2006, table 2. Also see Ito and Mishkin 2006, 147. ¥400 billion of JGBs was about $3.3 billion in 2001, while ¥35 trillion of the BOJ account balance target in January of 2006 was roughly $320 billion using the annual average of the yen-dollar exchange rate for the year 2001 (¥122 to a US dollar) and 2005 (¥110 to a US dollar).

(figure 2.4). These central banks also increased their monetary base through asset purchases more aggressively than the BOJ did, as figure 2.5 indicates.

The BOJ announced a program of QE after the Lehman bankruptcy in September 2008, but the monetary base expansion was modest in relative terms. As economic conditions worsened in the fall of 2010 in the face of the economic shock from Dubai and the US economic slowdown, the BOJ announced a new comprehensive set of policies that articulated criteria for exiting the ZIRP and created a new program that allowed the BOJ to buy a wider range of assets such as exchange-traded funds (ETFs) and Japanese real estate investment trusts (J-REITs), but the size of the QE intervention remained quite limited comparatively. Then, even after the devastating events of "3–11"—the date of Japan's magnitude 9.0 earthquake that triggered a devastating tsunami and nuclear crisis—the BOJ remained relatively cautious. As the economy went into a tailspin, the BOJ announced unsterilized asset purchases several days after the earthquake,

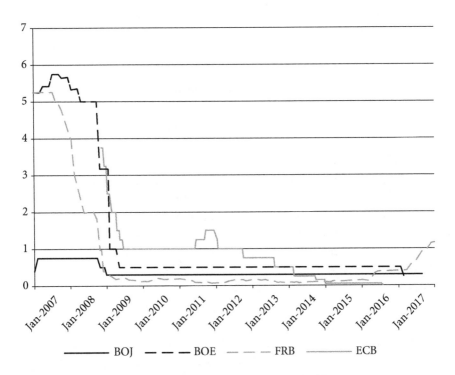

FIGURE 2.4. Main policy rates of FRB, ECB, BOJ, and BOE

Source: The data for the period up to September 2012 were retrieved from Fawley and Neely 2013. After September 2013: FRB (http://www.federalreserve.gov/newsevents/default.htm), ECB (https://wwww.ecb.europa.eu/mopo/decisions/html/index.ed.html),BOE (http://www.bankofengland.co.uk/monetarypolicy.Pages/default.aspx), BOJ (http://www.boj.or.jp/en/mopo/outline/index.htm).

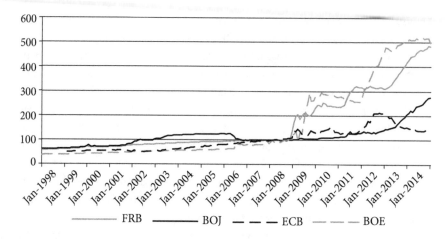

FIGURE 2.5. Monetary base expansion in the US, UK, Euro area, and Japan

Notes: (1) Reference point (index=100) is December 2007. (2) In May 2006, the BOE ceased the publication of M0, its main measure for monetary base. BOE's monetary base data is thus calculated by combining "Weekly amounts outstanding of Central Bank sterling notes in circulation total" and "weekly amounts outstanding of Central Bank sterling reserve balance liabilities.

Source: FRB, BOJ, ECB, BOE

but as figure 2.4 shows, the magnitude of the expansion of Japan's monetary base was still comparatively small.

This all changed sharply when Abe Shinzō came to power as prime minister at the end of 2012. The government and the BOJ soon agreed on an inflation target of 2 percent and a time frame of two years for achieving it. To do so, the BOJ announced in April 2013 a large-scale program referred to as QQE (quantitative and qualitative easing). The BOJ announced annual purchases of assets of ¥50 trillion (about $750–$875 billion) and an intention to double the monetary base in two years (see figure 2.4 to see the sharp increase). Through a two-pronged "qualitative easing," the BOJ targeted longer-maturity assets, including forty-year bonds, to lower long-term interest rates, with the goal of doubling the average maturity of its holdings. Then in the fall of 2014, as the economy slowed in response to a consumption tax hike, the BOJ announced an increase in the pace of risk-assets (riskier private assets) purchases to ¥80 trillion per year, a plan to increase the average maturity of holdings an additional three years, and a tripling of purchases of ETFs and J-REITs. Not having been able to achieve the 2-percent inflation goal, the BOJ then in January 2016 introduced a negative interest rate—a charge of –0.1 percent—on a small share of deposits at the BOJ to further lower interest rates and increase bank incentives to lend.

Federal Reserve Bank

By contrast, the FRB acted quickly. The FRB launched a large QE program (referred to as QE1) in November 2008, and more than doubled the monetary base by the end of 2008. The QE program targeted long-term assets in order to bring down interest rates via the portfolio balance channel. In addition to attempting to stimulate the entire economy, the FRB's QE1 also focused on reviving housing credit and the credit market more generally. Accordingly, the FRB purchased GSE (government-sponsored enterprise) debt (e.g., Fannie Mae and Freddie Mac), mortgage-backed securities (MBSs), and long-term treasuries (Fawley and Neely 2013). After financial stability was restored, the FRB wound down QE1 at the end of 2009. The economy remained sluggish, however, and inflation dipped below 1 percent.[12]

QE2 was announced in February 2010. Unlike QE1, which focused on averting financial collapse, QE2 aimed to stimulate growth and avoid deflation. As part of QE2, the FRB used large-scale purchases of treasuries to lower long-term interest rates. Then in 2011, the FRB announced "Operation Twist," a program to sell shorter-term securities and then use the proceeds to buy longer-term securities. While this measure did not increase the monetary base since assets were being sold, the rebalancing was intended to lower longer-term rates.

Then the FRB announced a third round of quantitative easing—QE3—in September 2012, committing to a set amount of monthly asset purchases, which it then ratcheted up in subsequent months, purchasing treasury bonds and MBSs. Unlike earlier rounds of QE, the FRB committed to a set amount of monthly asset purchases rather than a total target. The FRB also signaled for the first time that the QE would be open-ended and would continue until there were significant improvements in the labor market. Then in December 2013, the FRB began reducing purchases of securities as part of QE and finally concluded its QE program in October 2014. The FRB eased the transition by indicating that interest rates would remain near zero and that proceeds from its holdings would be recycled back into new asset purchases thereby keeping the monetary base level constant. At the end of 2015, the FRB then increased its target interest rate—the federal funds rate—to a range of 0.25 percent to 0.50 percent, and then in the fall of 2017, FRB began the process of tapering, that is, allowing the level of the monetary base to decline very slowly.

---

12. This overview is based on work by Fawley and Neely (2013) and supplemented by other work as needed.

The Bank of England

The BOE sets its policy in a slightly different context. The BOE is expected to pursue a monetary policy that will allow it to approximate an inflation target set by the government, which since 2003 has been 2 percent. In cases where the inflation rate is off from the target by more than 1 percent, the governor must write a letter to the chancellor of the exchequer to provide an explanation.

With the onset of the financial crisis, the BOE responded by slashing interest rates. Initially, the BOE, in conjunction with Her Majesty's Treasury, was more reluctant to use QE, but once it did in March 2008, the BOE's action was dramatic. The BOE more than quadrupled the monetary base through purchases that focused on medium- and long-term gilts—British government bonds—in order to bring inflation in line with its target of 2 percent. Subsequently, the BOE continued to expand its QE program in 2009 by £125 billion in asset purchases focusing on securities with maturities between three and five years or more than twenty-five years (Fawley and Neely 2013). In February 2010, the BOE paused its QE policy, but in October 2011, the BOE resumed QE by raising its asset purchase ceiling. Over subsequent months, the BOE announced further increases, eventually raising the ceiling to £375 billion. In addition to QE, then-new governor Mark Carney embraced forward guidance in 2013 by committing the BOE to not raising interest rates until unemployment dropped to 7.0 percent.

European Central Bank

The ECB reacted more incrementally after the collapse of Lehman Brothers, but it has since embraced more activist unconventional policies in response to the European sovereign debt crisis (late 2008 to 2012) and the subsequent economic slowdown and low inflation. Unlike the FRB and the BOE, the ECB did not initially announce the amount by which it would expand its monetary base. Also, the ECB relied initially more on direct lending to banks and purchases of covered bonds (bonds that are effectively backed by collateral). The ECB chose this policy to avoid purchases of national sovereign debt.[13] From 2008 on, the ECB increased the length of the loans from several weeks to up to three years. ECB loans to Eurozone banks were then used to buy such debt, a compromise brokered by then-French president Nicolas Sarkozy. As the European sovereign crisis escalated, the ECB created a program in 2010—the Security Market Program (SMP)—to buy

---

13. The ECB is not allowed to finance government debt directly. This restriction can be circumvented (and it was eventually) through government purchases of bonds on the secondary market. At the time, there was opposition to indirect financing over government as well.

government debt on the secondary market. Because many of these purchases were largely sterilized and thus did not expand the monetary base, this measure was not considered a QE policy.

In 2013, the ECB employed a version of forward guidance. ECB governor Mario Draghi announced that rates would be at "present or lower levels for an extended period of time" (Rodriguez and Carrasco 2014). The announcement was viewed as a weak version of forward guidance, however, since it did not indicate clear targets or thresholds that would determine the length of the easing policy, and it has been viewed as less forceful for this reason (Rodriguez and Carrasco 2014).

From 2014, the ECB intensified its antideflationary efforts. It expanded asset purchases by €10 billion a month, and it employed negative interest rates on deposits at the central bank. The ECB also launched a larger-scale unconventional policy in 2015 when it announced a program to increase asset purchases by €60 billion a month, the majority of which are assets held by the individual national central banks and can include national sovereign debt. The ECB also signaled that the asset purchases would be open-ended and would continue through at least September 2016.

The BOJ's Monetary Policy in Context

The first round of aggressive QE by the BOE and FRB reflects their circumstances. The United Kingdom and the United States were initially more exposed to the GFC, and there was a pressing need to restore credit, especially to the housing market. At the same time, after the financial system was stabilized, both central banks pursued further rounds of QE to deal with economic stagnation and low inflation. Compared to the United Kingdom and the United States, Japan's economic conditions during the GFC were more acute in a number of respects. Most importantly, Japan's economy had been experiencing declining prices since the late 1990s and was seen by many as caught in a deflationary trap (Krugman, Dominquez, and Rogoff 1998; Svensson 2001, 2006); indeed, Japan's experience became a cautionary tale about how difficult it is to end deflation. Furthermore, after the onset of the GFC, Japan actually suffered both a more severe drop in economic output and deep deflation. Japan's economic growth plunged from 2.2 percent in 2007 to −1.0 percent in 2008 and then −5.4 percent in 2009, a more dramatic drop than that of the United States or the Eurozone; see below (figure 2.6). Similarly, by 2009, Japan's inflation rate fell to −1.3 percent, much lower than the US rate of 0.4 percent. Japan's inflation rate stayed below the Eurozone, the United Kingdom, and the United States through 2013 (figure 2.7).

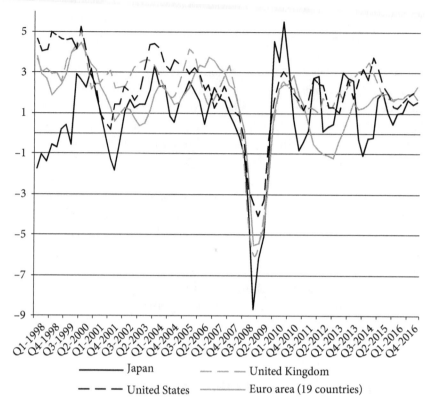

FIGURE 2.6. Seasonally adjusted real GDP growth rate by quarter, year-on-year: Japan, US, UK, Euro Area

Source: OECD, accessed on January 5, 2017, http://stats.oecd.org/Index.aspx#

Japan also faced economic challenges that the United Kingdom and the United States did not. In addition to the GFC, Japan also experienced the devastating events, discussed above, stemming from a massive earthquake in March 2011. Over the second quarter of 2011, the economy was shrinking at an annual rate of –5.5 percent, and Japan's economy fell back into deflation. Yet even with this shock, the BOJ still resisted a bold embrace of unconventional policy.

The Japanese economy also faced appreciation of the yen against the major reserve currencies, which dampened export competitiveness. The yen strengthened against the dollar, the pound, and the euro. This appreciation had numerous causes. With the move toward global capital mobility, central banks face a trade-off between independence in monetary policy and exchange rate stability,

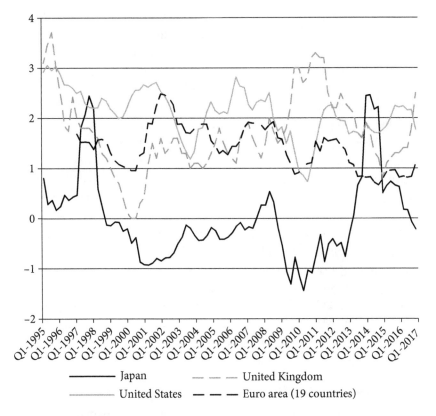

FIGURE 2.7. Change in Consumer Prices Index, excluding food and energy by quarter, year-on-year

Source: OECD, accessed on September 20, 2017, http://stats.oecd.org/Index.aspx#

as captured by the "impossible trinity."[14] With a floating exchange rate, Japan has ceded control over its exchange rate. With the onset of the crisis, the FRB and BOE pursued QE much more aggressively than did Japan, which had the effect of depreciating their domestic currencies relative to the yen. From this perspective, the Japanese economy bore the brunt of the unconventional monetary policies of other central banks via exchange rate appreciation, which made the relative price of imports cheaper and exports more expensive. This appreciation also reflected the flight to safety of the yen as a reserve currency and, at various points, the unwinding of the carry-trade, the investment in low-interest loans obtained in

---

14. The impossible trinity asserts that it is impossible to have free capital movement, a fixed exchange rate, and an independent monetary policy.

Japan into higher-yield foreign markets. After 3/11, the yen strengthened further against these currencies, reportedly in part due to the market speculation and also under the expectation that Japanese funds abroad would have to be repatriated to cover the costs of rebuilding (an expectation that ultimately was not borne out).

The effects on Japan's exchange rate were not trivial. From the start of the crisis in the second half of 2007 to about November of 2012, the yen appreciated by nearly 35 percent against the dollar, 50 percent against the pound, and 43 percent against the euro.[15] In trade-weighted terms, the yen did not experience an appreciation;[16] this was due in part to the continuing appreciation of the Chinese yuan over this period, since China is now Japan's largest trading partner. Still, compared to the baseline counterfactual of no yen appreciation against the major currencies, the effects were sizeable. Even small moves in the yen-dollar rate have a large impact on the bottom lines of Japan's large exporters. For instance, a ¥1 appreciation against the dollar is reported to reduce Toyota's annual operating profit by about ¥40 billion.[17] During the period mentioned above, the yen appreciated, with the dollar-to-yen exchange rate dropping by about ¥43 yen to the dollar. In addition, Japan's stock market tends to slump with yen strengthening due to the decline in the value of Japanese companies' sizeable overseas assets.

Policy and the Political Environment

Beyond economic stagnation, the environment was conducive in other ways for the embrace of unconventional monetary policy, particularly by the time of the GFC. As discussed above, economists articulated new theories of how unconventional policy could be used to help end deflation. Well-known economists across the world, including several from Japan, encouraged the BOJ to embark on a bolder reflationary monetary policy and advocated inflation targets, price-level targets, more reflationary monetary easing, and better coordination with fiscal policy.[18] These calls started as far back as the late 1990s (Krugman, Dominquez, and Rogoff 1998; Bernanke 1999) and steadily increased in subsequent years. In 2000, renowned economists from around the world presented ideas for ending deflation at a conference sponsored by the BOJ.[19] The economists urging more action included two Nobel laureates—Paul Krugman and Joseph Stiglitz—and

---

15. Authors' calculations based on data from the BOJ, the ECB, and the BOE.

16. We thank Greg Noble of Tokyo University for making this point.

17. Cooper and Matsuda 2016.

18. A partial list includes Ben Bernanke, Kōichi Hamada, Takeo Hoshi, Takatoshi Itō, Kikuo Iwata, Paul Krugman, Frederic Mishkin, Bennett McCallum, Adam Posen, Joseph Stigliz, and Lars Svensson.

19. Takatoshi Itō, Paul Krugman, Ben McCallum, Lars Svensson, and others.

numerous economists with experience as central bankers.[20] In some cases, economists openly challenged the BOJ's policy decisions. Even as Japan embarked on its first tentative experiment with QE, Ben Bernanke (2003), then a member of the Board of Governors of the FRB, called for bolder measures and shared these frank thoughts with the Japan Society of Monetary Economics in his speech:

> The sometimes frustratingly slow pace of change in Japan is all the more reason, however, for this nation's economists to speak out and present clear, persuasive arguments that will help guide the policy debate and urge leaders to effective action. At stake is not only the economic health of your country but also, to a significant degree, the prosperity of the rest of the world. Although Governor Fukui and his colleagues have so far not made radical breaks with previous BOJ policies, there is reason to hope that they will be open to fresh ideas and approaches.

There was also growing political pressure on the BOJ to embrace a more reflationary policy. Indeed, in Japan there were more vigorous calls for a policy change than in any other major economy; by way of contrast, in the United States, the FRB faced much criticism for having undertaken *excessive* unconventional monetary policy. Within the LDP, the party largely in power during the period of this study, there was serious dissatisfaction with the BOJ for not having done enough to combat inflation. In 2000, the BOJ decided to end its ZIRP despite strong resistance from the government and the Finance Ministry. The BOJ move sparked discussion within the LDP and led to the drafting of legislative proposals to change the BOJ Law. Some LDP lawmakers advocated, among other things, increasing the government's voice in monetary policy and establishing inflation targets.[21] The BOJ interest hike also drew widespread criticism from the largest business confederation, economists, and the IMF as well.[22]

Politicization and criticism of the BOJ picked back up from 2005 when the BOJ announced that it would taper its first modest QE program. Prime Minister Koizumi publicly indicated his displeasure, arguing that the economy was still in deflation and needed additional stimulus; his finance minister too viewed the tapering as premature. The chair of the LDP's powerful Policy Research Council went one step further, commenting that the government might have to consider revising the BOJ Law so that the BOJ would be more responsive to the government's view.[23] Later, he ordered the chair of the LDP's monetary policy

---

20. For instance, Ben Bernanke, Frederic Mishkin, Adam Posen, and Lars Svensson.

21. "Bank of Japan Gets Earful over Policies, Legal Proposals—Critics Slam Central Bank for Interest-Rate Revisions, Call for Clear Price Targets," *Nikkei Weekly*, March 19, 2001.

22. "BOJ Faces Rate-Change Aftershock," *Nikkei Weekly*, August 14, 2008.

23. "BOJ Feeling Political Heat on Easing," *Nikkei Weekly*, November 21, 2005.

subcommittee to look into the possibility of an accord with the BOJ in which targets—for both inflation and growth rate—would be jointly agreed upon.[24] Abe Shinzō, who was the chief cabinet secretary at that time, was also strongly critical of the BOJ's tapering.

The other parties as well expressed their dissatisfaction. One of the most visible examples was the Democratic Party of Japan's (later just the Democratic Party) Anti-Deflation League, which grew from twenty to about 150 members and which openly advocated for a more aggressive unconventional monetary policy. One of its proposals included setting an inflation target, adding an employment mandate (in addition to price stability) to the BOJ's objectives, and reforming the process of selecting Policy Board members. Other proposals directly referred to using monetary base expansion, through expansion of the BOJ's balance sheet, in order to fight deflation and yen appreciation (Dwyer 2012, 189).

Other minor parties joined in the calls for reform and a new monetary policy. Your Party included the issue in their platform and also introduced a bill, which failed, that called for an inflation target of 2–3 percent, limiting the central bank's legal independence, and allowing for the removal of three BOJ Policy Board executives if policy targets were not achieved. The party leader, like the Anti-Deflation League's, also publicly supported adding an employment mandate. The former People's New Party added a twist by calling for fiscal stimulus through deficit spending that the BOJ would directly underwrite (Dwyer 2012, 190–91).

This politicization was driven by a number of factors (Dwyer 2012). First, the perception of economic failure drove calls for more active monetary policy. Second, the difficulty of implementing other economic policies—such as fiscal policy and structural reform—increased the focus on monetary policy as the sole remaining viable economic instrument. Third, electoral reform shifted politicians' incentives to focus more on public goods, like economic growth, over targeted goods, such as public spending, and administrative reforms centralized decision making, making the government more accountable for its policy. Nonetheless, Dwyer (2012) contends that until Abenomics, this pressure had relatively little influence on policy.

Other Possible Explanations

Considering the state of the economy, the growing criticism of the BOJ, and the increasing politicization of the BOJ's monetary policy, in retrospect the monetary policy of Abenomics seems virtually inevitable. Less clear is why the BOJ's

24. "Nakagawa Torn among Loyalties—LDP Policy Chief Must Weigh Debts to Former Colleagues Koizumi, Takenaka," *Nikkei Weekly*, February 27, 2006.

Policy Board was so reluctant, particularly in the wake of the GFC, to embrace a bolder unconventional policy. We argue that the closed monetary policy network helped lock in pre-existing policy ideas and that this explains the Policy Board's resistance to adopting unconventional monetary policies. It is worth considering a few alternative explanations, though, before we move on to this argument. In this section, we consider several alternatives. The first four are explanations based on policy grounds, and the remainder are drawn from the scholarly literature.

Explanations of the BOJ Policy Board Choices on Policy Grounds

UNCONVENTIONAL POLICIES DON'T WORK

It could be that central bankers at the BOJ did not want to use bold, unconventional measures because they did not believe they would be effective. Before the BOJ tried its first modest experiment with QE in 2001, despite the existence of theoretical models, there was little contemporary empirical support for the idea that unconventional policies such as QE would work. Nonetheless, the BOJ modestly experimented with QE from 2001 and wound it down in 2006. The reluctance to try QE again, one could argue, might have been rooted in the conclusion that this experiment was unsuccessful. Indeed, former Governor Shirakawa himself argued that Japan's first QE did not work (2008).

The basic problem with this explanation is that the conclusion about QE is endogenous to the BOJ's worldview, which we discuss in more detail in chapter 4, in two key ways. First, the BOJ's skepticism about QE explains why the BOJ was tepid and unenthusiastic about its first QE undertaking. Indeed, the Policy Board had voted against numerous proposals for QE in 1999. One vocal member, Nakahara Nobuyuki,[25] introduced the proposal at every single Policy Board meeting from February through the end of the year—eighteen meetings in all—but every other board member present at each of these meetings voted against these proposals. The minutes indicate that the board did not see unsterilized intervention as an effective measure (Ito and Mishkin 2006, 144). The BOJ's Policy Board was forced into taking action by the political backlash from an interest hike (the lifting of the ZIRP) that many had criticized as poorly timed; not only was inflation still very low, but the economy was slowing with the bursting of the IT bubble in the United States.

---

25. Nakahara is an interesting case, as we discuss later. He was appointed due to his personal friendship with Fukui, who later became BOJ governor. Once becoming a board member, he was a perpetual dissenter who grew quickly suspicious of the BOJ's view. He frequently reached out to many other economists including Ben Bernanke, Lars Svensson, and others.

Some have argued that the Policy Board's tepid use of QE reduced its effectiveness. For instance, Baig et al. (2003) find that the BOJ's first QE experiment was not large enough to influence expectations. Japan's first QE was relatively small, and although the BOJ expanded its balance sheet by purchasing some longer-term assets, the overall share was relatively low. Svensson (2006) suggests there is evidence that the BOJ was not expected to maintain its QE, thus dampening its effect. Ito and Mishkin (2006) suggest that the central bank managed expectations poorly and that its commitment to overcoming deflation lacked credibility. Particularly during the first phase until 2003, the BOJ did not provide clear support for the policy, which they needed to do in order to influence expectations that the BOJ would not quickly wind it down.

Second, the conclusion that subsequent research showed that the BOJ's QE policy was ineffective reflected the BOJ's pre-existing bias. Papers written by BOJ researchers or published by the BOJ's internal think tank, Institute for Monetary and Economic Studies (IMES), did reach the conclusion that QE was ineffective.[26] This issue of perceptual bias is compounded since some of the research published on the effects of Japan's first QE was published by the BOJ itself, which carefully vets what is released. But more broadly, there was not a *clear* evidentiary basis for reaching the conclusion that the BOJ's QE policy was ineffective. In 2004, before the QE program had even concluded, Bernanke and his coauthors came to a conclusion that was essentially the opposite of the BOJ view: the BOJ's attempt at forward guidance was ineffective, but QE had a positive effect in lowering yields even though "many consider the manner to which it [QE] has been employed to have been relatively restrained and limited" (Bernanke, Reinhart, and Sack 2004, 5). Others subsequently found a variety of positive effects. Several studies conclude that Japan's first QE did in fact lower long-term interest rates (Fukunaga, Kato, and Koeda 2015; Lam 2011). Berkmen (2012) finds that QE had a positive effect on a number of economic variables, including output and inflation. A study by Bowman et al. (2011) suggests that QE improved the flow of credit. Researchers have debated the effects of QE and in some cases reached different conclusions. What is clear, however, is that the evidence on Japan's first experiment with QE did not provide unambiguous grounds for rejecting the efficacy of QE. As we discuss in chapter 8, research on QE in Japan and other contexts subsequent to the GFC has grown tremendously; on balance the work has largely found positive effects.

---

26. Some have found that the BOJ's ZIRP, particularly the commitment to keep interest rates low, had an interest rate effect, but that QE did not influence medium and longer-term interest rates (Baba et al. 2005; Oda and Ueda 2007; Ugai 2007).

JAPAN HAS HIGH PUBLIC DEBT AND LARGE DEFICITS

A second alternative explanation worth considering is that the BOJ was more hesitant to use QE because of the country's fiscal position. Japan currently has the highest gross government debt of any OECD country, and at the start of the GFC in 2008, its gross debt was more than twice as high as that of the Eurozone or the United States (see figures 2.8 and 2.9 below). Due to sizeable assets, its net debt is significantly lower, but it is still higher than the United States and the United Kingdom. As we will discuss in more detail later in this book, the issue of Japan's debt in fact has been a main concern of central bankers and policymakers more generally. There have been two primary concerns. One is that an expansion of the monetary base through large-scale QE effectively monetizes debt; with few external constraints over debt financing, the government will have less pressure to pursue fiscal consolidation. Another concern is that if inflation does increase, so will interest rates, which will make managing Japan's massive stock of debt more difficult.

The issue of high debt and how it relates to unconventional monetary policy is not clear-cut, however. Indeed, the high level of debt can be viewed as grounds

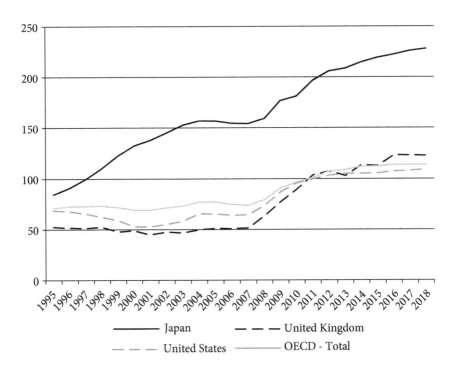

FIGURE 2.8.   General government gross financial liabilities as percentage of GDP

Source: OECD, accessed on September 20, 2017, http://stats.oecd.org/Index.aspx#

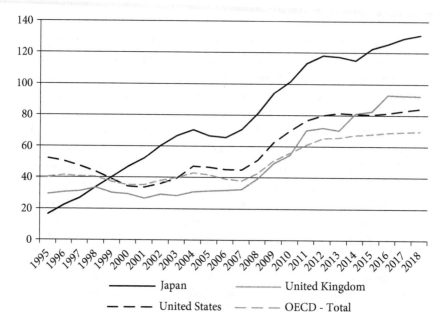

FIGURE 2.9. General government net financial liabilities as percentage of GDP

Source: OECD, accessed on September 20, 2017, http://stats.oecd.org/Index.aspx#

for *greater* use of unconventional policy. Japan's severe fiscal position has limited the government's scope for using fiscal policy. Arguably, this means that policy-makers may have more incentive to rely on unconventional monetary policy. Indeed, FRB chairman Ben Bernanke and the ECB reacted in part to the political paralysis that led to inadequate fiscal stimulus in the early phase of the GFC. Politically speaking, as Dwyer (2012) has noted, the lack of fiscal space in Japan focused politicians' attention onto monetary policy.

Moreover, stimulating inflation can have positive effects on the fiscal balance, particularly if the economy is in deflation. Deflation can hinder achieving budget balance by reducing revenue. Deflation can lead to "reverse bracket creep" as incomes fall and push people into lower income tax brackets, and lower prices can reduce the yield from consumption taxes. Moreover, with deflation, even low interest rates for government borrowing may still be high in real terms. One estimate suggests that for the three-year period between 2000 and 2003, deflation increased the real debt level by 3 percent of GDP (Baig 2003). Hoshi and Kashyap argue that in Japan "higher inflation would have reduced the true cost of borrowing."[27]

27. Takeo Hoshi and Anil K. Kashyap, "Where Is the BOJ's Accountability?" *Wall Street Journal*, March 9, 2011, http://blogs.wsj.com/economics/2011/03/09/the-bojs-critics-hit-back/, accessed on December 5, 2015.

Bernanke (2017b) estimates that an inflation rate of 2 percent in Japan would lower its debt-to-GDP ratio by 21 percent. Bernanke and Reinhardt (2004) also note that QE can also have an expansionary *fiscal* effect: by reducing the interest costs of the government, it can potentially reduce the need for a future tax hike.

One additional consideration is that due to the large stock of government debt, a larger-scale monetary base expansion may be needed to influence bond prices. As Gagnon (2016, 4) notes, "Japan has a much larger government bond market relative to GDP than the other countries studied, which may suggest that QE effects operate in proportion to the size of the targeted bond market rather than the size of the economy." From this perspective, high debt calls for an even bigger monetary base expansion.

JAPAN'S MONETARY BASE IS ALREADY HIGH

Finally, one additional situational factor that should be considered is the level of Japan's monetary base. While Japan's rate of increase was slow compared to the FRB and the BOE, as shown earlier, the level of the monetary base relative to the size of GDP has been higher in Japan, even prior to the launch of Japan's QQE policy in 2013. Some have pointed to this figure to suggest that Japan's monetary policy has been highly accommodative since by this measure the monetary base is already very high.[28] QE alone, however, does not account for Japan's high monetary base; historically, the monetary base as a share of GDP has been higher in Japan than in the United States or the United Kingdom even prior to the first QE. Also, the effect of QE should work through *relative* change, making the index we use in figure 2.4 a more appropriate measure of monetary easing.

Another problem with using monetary base as a share of GDP is that the figure can shift even without an expansion of the monetary base; for instance, if the economy goes into a recession, the denominator—GDP—will shrink, pushing up the value of the ratio. Thus, one can argue that the figure is endogenous to economic growth and arguably monetary policy as well. Between 1997 and the first quarter of 2017, the GDP of the United States increased by more than 126 percent, while Japan's GDP grew by less than 2 percent over the same period. If the Japanese economy had grown at the same rate as the US economy, the monetary base as a share of GDP would be less than half of what it is now, going from about 85 percent to 38 percent. Given Japan's different demographic profile,

---

28. This point is commonly cited in the press and was also mentioned by a number of the officials we interviewed. One recent example is the following article that mentions the high ratio: "BOJ assets swell to 90 percent of Japan's GDP," *Nikkei Asian Review*, May 3, 2017, https://asia.nikkei.com/Markets/Capital-Markets/BOJ-assets-swell-to-90-of-Japan-s-GDP, accessed on September 16, 2017. Wakatabe (2016, 38) also makes this point.

Japan does not have as high a potential growth rate as the United States, but the comparison illustrates some of the potential problems of using monetary base to GDP.

UNCONVENTIONAL POLICIES COULD GENERATE LOSSES FOR A CENTRAL BANK

When a central bank expands its balance sheet through asset purchases, it is exposed to financial risk. If, for instance, the price of bonds it has purchased declines, then a central bank could accrue losses. Many central banks in fact generate profits, which are typically transferred to the treasury. This is the case in Japan as well. One argument against QE is that if the losses are large, these profits would shrink or in the worst case scenario the central bank may require transfers from the treasury.

In principle, though, a central bank does not have to realize these losses as long as the asset stays on its balance sheet. If a central bank did have to sell these assets, losses would have to be realized. This might occur as a central bank exits from QE. Thus far, no major central bank has yet accrued losses due to QE policies. In fact, the net income for the FRB doubled on an annual basis compared to the years before QE policies were undertaken, and if the FRB were forced to sell off assets, losses would have only a moderate effect that would be unlikely to exceed the amount of increased remittances from previous years (Labonte 2014).

The risk for a central bank, however, depends on the type of assets purchased as well as the maturities. Thus it is possible that, depending on the nature of the intervention, large losses could accrue. If losses were realized, the cost to the government could be weighed, though, against the fiscal gains from inflation on the budgetary side. Some have even suggested that QE purchases of sovereign debt could allow a government to simply cancel those debts (Lonergan 2014). Once a central bank takes on government bonds, in reality it is just one branch (a treasury) of the government owing another branch (a central bank) money. Thus, the obligation ceases to exist in a meaningful sense.

Alternative Explanations Based on the Scholarly Literature

A well-developed literature has explored the political determinants of monetary policy. It should be noted that this literature does not focus on explaining when central banks use unconventional monetary policy. Still, the literature is a useful starting point that articulates a logic that in some cases can be extended to understanding when central banks might or might not resort to unconventional policy as a means of monetary easing.

CENTRAL BANK MANDATE AND SENSITIVITY TO INFLATION

According to Copelovitch and Singer (2008), a central bank's sensitivity to inflation is a function of its institutional mandate, in particular whether or not it has responsibility for bank regulation. They find that central banks that regulate banking tend to be less hawkish toward inflation. Since such central banks must worry about financial stability, they tend to prefer easing that can help the financial position of banks. The effect is conditional on the size of the banking sector; the larger the relative size of the sector, the greater the effect. By this logic, one might argue that the BOJ had an institutional orientation toward stronger inflation control since it did not oversee regulation of the financial sector. In Japan, the financial sector, as Copelovitch and Singer note, is overseen by other agencies, specifically the Financial Services Agency (FSA) and Deposit Insurance Corporation of Japan (DICJ).

While plausible as a hypothesis, this argument does not fit the Japanese case well. First, while the FSA has primary responsibility for banking regulations, the BOJ also has responsibilities, which should make it sensitive to the banking sector. Indeed, the New BOJ Law specifies that the BOJ has responsibility to maintain financial stability *and* price stability. More concretely, the BOJ carries out on-site inspections of financial institutions (*kōsa*) in accordance with Article 44 of the New BOJ Law. Indeed, the MOF first granted the BOJ a role in inspecting banks in 1928 so that it would have a stronger sense of responsibility in maintaining their financial health. In more recent years, the BOJ's role has been expanding. In 1999 the BOJ and the MOF conducted a version of bank stress tests together, and since the early 2000s, the BOJ has been responsible for macroprudential supervision to assess the overall risk to the financial system. This analysis has grown increasingly sophisticated, and since 2005 the BOJ has issued a biannual financial system report that reviews its findings. Second and relatedly, the size of the banking sector in Japan is very large, indeed the relative size as a ratio of GDP is by far the largest of all of the countries for which Copelovitch and Singer (2008) have data. According to their own theory, the huge size of the banking sector in Japan should make central bankers more attuned to the banking sector, thus less hawkish on inflation.

Even more fundamentally, there is room for debate over what kind of monetary policies will most effectively promote financial sector stability. Since the collapse of its asset bubble at the start of the 1990s, the BOJ repeatedly discussed the issue of financial stability as it deliberated monetary policy, but in a way that suggested it had preferences that were the opposite of those suggested by Copelovitch and Singer's theory. From the perspective of the BOJ, maintaining financial stability, at least until Abe became prime minister in 2012, required avoiding excessive easing that might produce an asset bubble and ultimately destabilize the financial sector.

CENTRAL BANKER MATERIAL INCENTIVES AND MONETARY POLICY PREFERENCES

Another alternative explanation focuses on the preferences of central bankers, which as we discuss in the next chapter, is largely ignored in much of the literature on monetary policy. Adolph (2014), to his credit, develops a theory of central banker preferences. Preferences, he argues, can be driven by material incentives in securing post-central-bank tenure positions, in particular in the financial sector. Thus the preferences of such central bankers reflect not what their political principals demand, but rather those of "shadow principals," more specifically the financial sector firms to which they supposedly hope to parachute after their service as central bankers. Assuming that financial firms prefer low inflation, central bankers signal their loyalty to the sector through their votes for price stability.

In a general sense, the assumption about the preference of financial firms is potentially problematic. As we can see from the above discussion, Copelovitch and Singer (2008), in contrast to Adolph (2014), argue that financial firms prefer monetary easing. More specifically with respect to Japan, Adolph's theory of a shadow principal does not apply since virtually none of the executives of the BOJ's Policy Board follow the trajectory that he describes. From 1998 up until Kuroda, the governorship went to former BOJ officials at the ends of their careers. At the end of his tenure, Hayami was seventy-eight, Fukui was seventy-three, and Shirakawa was sixty-three. Governor Kuroda himself is as of the time of this writing seventy-three. None of the retired governors went into finance, but instead went to academia and various research institutes. Of all the governors and deputy governors combined, no one has gone onto a lucrative career in finance.[29] Thus, Adolph's shadow principal argument sheds little light on the Japanese case. He does also suggest, however, that beyond material incentives, career socialization can shape preferences too. This is closer to our approach, which we discuss more fully in the next chapter.

PARTISAN POLITICS AND MONETARY POLICY

One of the classic political theories of macroeconomic policy advanced by Hibbs (1977) and refined by Alesina (1987) contends that the party in power pursues macroeconomic policies that reflect their social bases of support. Left parties pursue more accommodative economic policies to stimulate employment, while right parties focus more on controlling inflation. By this logic, partisan differences in the government should account for some of the variation in monetary

---

29. Some headed think tanks (Fukui, Fujiwara, Yamaguchi H., and Iwata K.) and others became academic (Nishimura and Shirakawa) or went into public service (Mutō).

policy. The partisan politics approach can be extended to how price changes have differential impacts on creditors and debtors. Since creditors tend to be rich while debtors are less so, price changes have varied distributional consequences for different classes (Blyth 2013). Inflation benefits debtors since the value of their obligations is lowered in real terms; conversely, inflation hurts creditors since it reduces the real value of repayments. Furthermore, the wealthy are more threatened by the prospect of inflation, while wage earners worry more about unemployment from slow growth (Kirshner 1998, 75). Thus these differential effects should reinforce the partisan logic of the original theory, suggesting that left parties would have additional reason to pursue monetary easing and right parties would prefer tighter monetary policy.

The partisan politics model, however, cannot explain the rise of Abenomics that made reflation a top priority and the embrace of much bolder monetary policies to do so. According to the partisan politics model, the LDP center-right party should have been more committed to price stability than the center-left DPJ (Democratic Party of Japan). In fact, the LDP controlled the government during periods when the BOJ did seem to prioritize price stability, even when Abe himself first served as prime minister from 2006 to 2007. Yet the same party and even the same prime minister shifted with Abe's second term in office. Indeed, by the time of the general election at the end of 2012, the LDP took a more aggressive reflationary position than the DPJ. Still, it is plausible, excluding Abe's dramatic break, that partisan control over government might account for some of the differences in monetary policy. We revisit this issue in our analysis presented in chapter 6.

THE POLITICAL BUSINESS CYCLE

Nordhaus (1975) advanced one of the earliest political models of monetary policy, the political business cycles (PBCs). According to his theory, incumbents use fiscal and monetary policy prior to an election to increase their chances of staying in power. Thus one would expect election cycles to create incentives for greater easing. While elegant as a theory, the majority of research finds little empirical support for PBC.[30] In the Japanese case specifically, where the prime minister can choose the timing of the elections, the findings have been mixed. Cargill and Hutchison (1991) and Kohno and Nishizawa (1990) find some support for the view that the government manipulates policy as elections approach. On the other hand, Ito and Park (1988) and Ito (1990) find no support for this claim.[31]

---

30. See Drazen 2001 and Franzese Jr. 2002 for reviews of this extensive literature.

31. There is stronger evidence that the government calls for elections when economic conditions are favorable.

As with the partisan politics model, we visit this argument in our quantitative analysis in chapter 6.

VETO POINTS AND MONETARY POLICY

Scholars have also explored the role of veto points in the political system in shaping the extent of influence that a government can have on legally independent central bankers. A government can exert pressure on central banks by indicating its displeasure with policy choices, including threatening to change the central bank's mandate or limit and possibly take away legal independence. In the United States, for instance, the House of Representatives passed resolution HR133 in 1975 to express its displeasure with the FRB, nudging the central bank to give more weight to price stability (Meltzer 2010, 986–90). Researchers have found that when there are fewer veto points, threats to take action against a central bank are more credible, thus increasing the level of influence over central bankers (Lohmann 1998; Keefer and Stasavage 2003).

From this perspective, Japan's political institutions should be conducive to government influence on monetary policy. Japan has a parliamentary system that fuses the legislative and executive. Thus there are fewer veto points than with the more fragmented political institutions of the United States. But unlike the United Kingdom's Westminster system, to which it has been compared, Japan's parliament has a stronger upper chamber that can block legislation and appointments. Thus, there is the possibility of partially divided government if the two chambers are controlled by different parties, a situation referred to in Japan as a "twisted Diet" (*nejire kokkai*) and which existed periodically during the period under study. This condition affected the BOJ governor appointment in 2008 (chapter 5). In chapter 6, we revisit these arguments and test quantitatively for the effect of varying veto points (whether there was divided government or not).

THE ROLE OF US POWER AND INFLUENCE

Realist explanations in international relations focus on the role of power in influencing economic policies. In the security realm, Japan has had an asymmetric dependence on US power, while in terms of economic relations, Japan's trade surplus has been a frequent source of friction between the two countries. The United States has applied pressure on countries to pursue economic policies to address trade imbalances and to attempt to preserve the Bretton Woods monetary regime (Gilpin 2001). The United States led international efforts to pursue adjustment on its terms, for example the Bonn Summit (in 1978) and the Plaza Accord (in 1985). Scholars working on the Japanese political economy have noted that such foreign pressure from the United States (*gaiatsu*) has often influenced actual macroeconomic policy (Calder 1988; Suzuki 2000). Extending this logic, one can hypothesize that the BOJ might not have adopted aggressive unconventional policy due to potential US opposition since such policies might have led to depreciation of the yen relative to the dollar, which would further exacerbate the trade imbalance.

While plausible, this argument has several problems. First, as discussed above, Japan faced intense yen appreciation after the GFC. After the tragic events—the triple disaster—of March 2011, the G-7 in fact coordinated a currency intervention to drive the yen down. Second, the US government has not in fact complained about the BOJ's unconventional policies. The US Treasury monitors the exchange rates and reports its findings to Congress, but QE is not viewed by the Treasury as exchange rate manipulation. Besides, in Japan, the MOF, not the BOJ, has authority to decide on exchange rate market intervention. In fact, the US Treasury has been supportive of monetary easing even after these policies contributed to a depreciation of the yen to the dollar and under a much more protectionist president. The Treasury's 2017 report notes, "Given that the weakness of domestic activity and demand growth are contributing to Japan's trade imbalances, it is critical that the authorities complement accommodative monetary policy and flexible fiscal policy" (US Treasury Department 2017, 2). Thus the Treasury has reiterated the US's long-standing position dating back to the 1970s that monetary policy easing—via conventional or unconventional policy—would help Japan reduce its balance of payment surpluses with the United States.

This chapter situates the BOJ's monetary policy in a broader perspective. The economic, policy, and political contexts were conducive to more aggressive experimentation with unconventional monetary policy, especially by the time of the GFC. One should recognize still that even by 2007 the empirical support for unconventional policies remained relatively thin. The context was one of high uncertainty for all central bankers. Since the GFC, there has been more research on the effects of QE and other unconventional policies. On balance, this research finds support for the notion that QE can have positive effects on long-term interest rates, inflation, and the economy.[32] The BOJ's policy since 2013 had some immediate impacts—on asset prices, on interest rates, on the exchange rate, and, according to some, on economic growth—but some see QE as having diminishing effects for Japan.[33] As we discuss in chapters 8 and 9, the debate over the

---

32. See Gagnon 2016 for a detailed literature review.

33. Paul Krugman: Meeting with Japanese officials, March 16, 2016, https://www.gc.cuny.edu/CUNY_GC/media/LISCenter/pkrugman/Meeting-minutes-Krugman.pdf, accessed on March 25, 2016.

effects of the BOJ's monetary experiments under Governor Kuroda and at other central banks continues.

Given the uncertainty at the time about the right course of action and empirical debate over how effective unconventional policies are, we would expect the role of ideas to be more influential than ever. It is to this topic that we turn in the next chapter.

Chapter 3

MONETARY POLITICS
Interests, Ideas, and Policy Networks

Printing more money to play politics at this particular time in American history is almost treacherous, or treasonous, in my opinion.

—Rick Perry, former Governor of Texas, 2011

Are the BIS's methods unsound? I don't see any method at all. Instead, I see an attitude, looking for justification.

—Paul Krugman, 2014

You can't think about what is happening in the economy constructively, from a policy standpoint, unless you have some theoretical paradigm in mind.

—Janet Yellen, 2014

There have been two broad approaches to studying the politics of monetary policy: rationalist explanations focus on the role of material interests, while social constructivist and sociological approaches emphasize the role of ideas, norms, and identity. This study falls in the latter camp. To explain the BOJ's reluctance to accept unconventional monetary policy, we focus on the role of policy ideas entrenched within the larger BOJ organization (as opposed to only the Policy Board, whose members are appointed) and the larger policy network around it in sustaining these ideas. This chapter lays out the case for taking such an ideational approach through a critical review of the literature, then turns to the specific challenge of studying ideas, and, finally, explains how this book seeks to address these challenges.

Rationalist Approaches to Monetary Policy

The earliest accounts of monetary policy, and economic policy more broadly, were rationalist in orientation. Arguably, this approach remains dominant,[1] although as we discuss further below, a rich and growing body of work explores

---

1. Abdelal, Blyth, and Parsons (2010) argue that rationalist approaches have dominated international political economy.

the role of ideational factors. At a general level, rationalist approaches infer actor preferences from what are assumed to be their material incentives. Some working in this vein further examine how institutions, primarily formal ones, influence the ability of different actors to realize these preferences. Early examples of this work include the PBC literature and theory of partisan politics, both discussed in the previous chapter, that are based on the electoral incentives of governments and parties. With the spread of central bank independence, scholars have paid greater attention to how institutional factors influence monetary policy within this rationalist framework. The common assumption is that politicians are influenced by electoral incentives, but that different institutional arrangements give them varying degrees of influence over technocratic agents, that is, central bankers, who prioritize price stability (another critical but problematic assumption discussed below). Indeed, this is the key assumption behind granting legal independence to central banks in the first place.

According to the theory of central bank independence (CBI), while there may be a long-term desire to limit inflation, governments may face shorter-term political incentives to use monetary policy to stimulate the economy, thereby giving rise to the time-inconsistency problem (Kydland and Prescott 1977; Barro and Gordon 1983). If private-sector actors come to expect the government to behave this way, this can raise their inflationary expectations, thereby introducing an inflationary bias. Even if central banks publicly commit to limiting inflation, they may face a credibility problem if politicians are able to intervene. To solve this dilemma, a government can tie its own hands by delegating monetary policy to an independent central bank (Rogoff 1985; Alesina and Tabellini 1988; Neumann 1991). According to the theory of CBI, the enhanced credibility from central bank independence should deliver lower inflation, bring interest rates down, and spur economic growth, a claim that, as we discuss below, has faced serious challenges.

Based on the expectations from the theory of CBI, scholars, particularly economists, have attempted to measure the impact of the degree of legal independence—by looking at a variety of dimensions of independence from legal statutes[2] and other measures—on monetary policy and economic outcomes. As further discussed below, the empirical results have been mixed, and the theory has been challenged on other grounds as well. Others have examined how the effect of legal central bank independence on monetary policy is contingent on additional factors, such

---

2. Measures look at legal statutes covering appointment and protection of governors, the resolution of conflict between the executive and central bank, provisions covering lending to the government, stated policy goals, role in banking supervision, etc. See Cukierman 1992 and Grilli, Masciandaro, and Tabellini 1991 for two well-known indexes of CBI.

as the labor market structure, openness to trade, government partisanship, union density, and so forth (Hall and Franzese 1998; Iversen 1999; Franzese Jr. 1999).

Researchers have also studied the avenues by which political agents can influence monetary policy given the delegation of authority and establishment of de jure independence. The work on delegation looks broadly at the issue of how political agents can control bureaucratic agencies (Epstein and O'halloran 1999; McCubbins, Noll, and Weingast 1989; Huber and Shipan 2002). The literature has highlighted a number of ways that principals can monitor and exercise control over such agents. In the case of legally independent central banks, principals face a number of specific constraints. A new government does not necessarily have the opportunity to appoint a new head of a central bank or other policy board members unless the term of the official happens to expire during the tenure of the government. Policy board member terms are fixed and in most cases the institutional barriers to replacing a member are relatively high. In many cases, the government also has limited control over the budget of a central bank, one of the powerful instruments that a political principal can use to influence bureaucratic behavior (Chang 2003). Central bankers also tend to have informational advantages due to the technical complexity of monetary policy.

At the same time, a government still has avenues of influence. If the timing is serendipitous, an executive may have the opportunity to select nominees to a central bank policy board. Governments can also pressure central banks by threatening to use legislation to curtail a central bank's independence. Recently, for instance, some vocal Republican members of Congress sharply criticized the FRB's large monetary stimulus at the onset of the GFC, and several legislative proposals to reform the FRB have been discussed. The work on veto points, discussed in chapter 2, contends that the nature of political institutions determines how credible such threats might be and ultimately the degree of influence on monetary policy that a government has (Lohmann 1998; Keefer and Stasavage 2003).

Challenges to Rationalist Approach to Monetary Policy

There are several grounds for critiquing rationalist explanations. On empirical grounds, some of the most extensively tested theories have mixed support. In the case of the PBC, the majority of research finds little empirical support.[3] While there is stronger empirical evidence for the effect of partisan politics—left

---

3. See Drazen 2001 and Franzese Jr. 2002 for reviews of this extensive literature.

governments have been found to be associated with higher output and lower unemployment (Alesina and Tabellini 1988; Alesina, Roubini, and Cohen 1997)—others have found that these outcomes are *not* the result of monetary policy (Faust and Irons 1999). One interesting extension of the partisan politics argument has looked specifically at the effect of the ideological composition of US congressional committees overseeing finance on money growth. Here too the evidence has been mixed.[4]

More fundamentally, rationalist explanations face a number of theoretical problems stemming from their narrow conception of preferences, institutions, and ultimately power. Preferences are read off of material incentives, typically derived from the position of different actors. This view of preferences underestimates the extent to which ideas can be an intervening factor that defines and gives meaning to policy preferences, as noted by a wide body of literature (Goldstein 1993; Katzenstein 1996; McNamara 1998; Schmidt 2002, 2010; Blyth 2003). This is particularly true in the realm of economic policy since it is economic ideas that attempt to pin down and specify causal relationships in a complex social world (McNamara 1998; Kirshner 2003; Abdelal, Blyth, and Parsons 2010). These ideas provide actors with a cognitive map that defines preferences and the appropriate means for pursuing these preferences. Even a basic question, such as whether inflation is good for workers or not, requires some understanding of the effects of inflation, an issue that remains contested among economists.

Another example pertinent to this book is the effect of monetary policies on the financial sector. Several rationalist theories are based on assumptions about the material interests of the banking sector although different scholars, such as Copelovitch and Singer (2008) and Adolph (2014), have made the opposite assumption of what bank preferences should be. In each case, there is an implied causal connection between a policy and the outcome for a bank. In the case of QE more specifically, many assume that QE benefits banks, but even this causal connection is contested—see Lambert and Ueda (2014)—illustrating how preferences are contingent on prior ideas. As some of the classic work on economic ideas demonstrated, the Keynesian revolution flipped on its head the conventional thinking about the right response to recession (Hall 1989) and in doing so reshaped political preferences, making possible new coalitions between business and labor (Gourevitch 1986). In the case of Sweden, for instance, these new ideas led the left-wing Social Democrats (SAP) to shift away from classical economic ideas toward a reflationary economic policy (Blyth 2002).

---

4. Grier (1991) found that a more liberal Senate Banking Committee predicts greater money growth, although Chopin, Cole, and Ellis (1996) claim that the effect is reversed when political control of committees of the House of Representatives is accounted for.

Rational institutionalists imagine a stable world with clear preferences and rules. In a deeper sense, though, ideas *constitute* the social reality of markets. One distinctive aspect of macroeconomics is that the belief in certain ideas creates market sentiment based on those ideas (Kirshner 2003). Economic theories are not just analyses but become constitutive of the economic processes themselves. Economic models, as they spread, lead market actors to behave as the model itself specifies (MacKenzie 2006, 2008). Monetary policy is quite literally a discursive exercise where policymakers use language in an attempt to coordinate economic activity through creating intersubjective understandings (Hall 2008; Holmes 2013). Using a concrete example, Bernanke (2016) had this reflection as he discussed hypothetical options for the United States:

> To be clear, I think it is unlikely that exotic policy tools like negative rates or targeting longer-term interest rates will be used in the U.S. in the foreseeable future. So why waste electrons discussing them? One reason is that public beliefs about these tools may influence expectations. For example, if the public and financial market participants are confident that government action will always be capable of returning inflation to the central bank's target, then long-term inflation expectations are more likely to be "anchored," which in turn makes attaining the inflation target easier. Consequently, and somewhat paradoxically, educating the public and market participants about more-radical monetary policy alternatives might help ensure that those alternatives are never needed.

The world does not always cooperate with this enterprise, however, which renders the economic concepts unstable and introduces new uncertainty (Abdelal, Blyth, and Parsons 2010). The onset of deflation in the wake of the GFC is a relevant example. While governments have an incentive to avoid or limit downturn and if possible sustain economic growth, conventional guides for monetary policy offer less insight into how to proceed. One such guide—the Taylor rule—generates a target interest rate adjustment based on the inflation, output, and other economic variables (Taylor 1993).[5] Under low inflation and deflation, however, economists have pointed out several limitations with the Taylor rule (Kuttner and Posen 2004; Ito and Mishkin 2006; Kohn 2007). As short-term interest rates approach zero, the Taylor rule fails to take into account the risk of hitting the zero bound (i.e., a zero interest rate) where conventional monetary policy will no longer be effective. The Taylor rule also does not factor in other risks, such as that posed to the

---

5. The inflation gap is the difference between the short-term nominal interest rate (federal funds rate in the United States or the call rate in Japan) and the desired inflation rate, and the output gap is the difference between actual output and potential output.

financial system at the onset of the GFC. Additionally, under deflationary conditions, the Taylor rule can produce negative values for interest rates, an option that only recently was considered and used by central bankers.

Under such uncertainty, policymakers had to grapple with basic questions: what is the likelihood of falling into deflation, how costly would it be if that happened, would unconventional monetary policies actually have the positive effects that some economists claimed, and might such policies have negative side effects, perhaps even stoking runaway inflation? Although some central banks, such as the FRB, had experimented with short monetary base expansions during the Great Depression in the 1930s,[6] for the most part unconventional policies were largely untested at least until the GFC. Therefore, empirical research on the efficacy of these policies was relatively thin, although it has increased subsequently. It is precisely during such periods of uncertainty that researchers have found that ideas are most likely to guide decisions (Goldstein and Keohane 1993; Berman 2001; Blyth 2001, 2002, 2007; Campbell and Pedersen 2014; Nelson and Katzenstein 2014).

Rationalist approaches also fail to acknowledge the power of ideas. Ideas legitimate some actions and delegitimate others, often in ways that elide the distributional issues. Indeed, it is this technocratic aspect of economic ideas that enhances their influence. By appealing to abstractions such as aggregate macroeconomic outcomes, economic ideas, such as the theory of CBI or importance of low inflation, obscure the distributional consequences of economic ideas (Kirshner 2003). As Blyth (2013) argues, the idea of austerity has had profound and negative distributional consequences. The treatment of the accumulating government debt in the wake of the GFC as a sovereign debt problem shifts the responsibility for fixing the problem onto those that can least afford it, those who will suffer from cuts in government spending in the name of austerity. Yet the debt problem Blyth (2013) points out stems not from government overspending but as a consequence of measures to save banks.

Ideas do not merely reveal causal relationships, since these theories themselves are subject to normative, theoretical, and empirical contestation. The theory of CBI is a case in point. It has been challenged on a variety of theoretical grounds, such as that CBI is endogenous to the groups that support it, in particular the financial sector (Posen 1995). The theory has also faced empirical challenges. According to the theory of CBI, it should deliver both lower inflation and higher

---

6. In 1932, the FRB purchased US Treasuries worth about $16 billion in current US dollars. The intervention was relatively small at 2 percent of gross national product. There was no quantitative target announced. Still, Bordo and Sinha (2016) find that it stimulated output growth and if maintained could have helped the economy recover more quickly.

real growth. While there is support that CBI is correlated with low inflation, the finding only applies to developed countries, and there is little evidence that CBI delivers stronger growth (Alesina and Summers 1993; Cukierman 1994).[7] Moreover, whether low inflation has positive economic effects is also unclear on empirical grounds.[8] Even more to the point, Posen (1998a) finds no evidence for a "credibility bonus" from legal independence. Yet the theory of CBI continues to have wide support.

Economic ideas gain influence as much through social acceptance as through evidence. McNamara (2002) observes that the theory of CBI is largely a cultural process. In the case of Japan, Grimes (2002) observes that the government adopted central independence in 1998 despite comparatively low inflation. Similarly, Chwieroth (2010, 46) finds that the consensus on the desirability of capital account liberalization within the IMF was more a reflection of internal norms than specific knowledge. Conti-Brown (2016, 148) nicely captures the position of the central bankers, specifically those at the FRB, and how they arrive at a consensus to guide policy:

> Without question, central banking practice is plagued by uncertainty, model failures, imperfect data, and even central banker ideology. But central bankers at the Fed aren't throwing darts at a decision tree, nor is there any evidence of venality and corruption. Instead, they are adjudicating between conflicting views of that uncertainty, those failures, these ideologies. To judge against those competing concepts, central bankers at the Fed are using the technical apparatus of empirical and theoretical macroeconomics to reach a consensus that creates a policy conclusion.

The rationalist literature also has tended to privilege the role of formal institutions and the actors operating within these institutions. From the rationalist perspective, the question motivating the research on monetary policy is seen through the lens of the preferences of voters and interest groups, how politicians respond to these preferences, and ultimately how politicians work within institutional constraints to attempt to influence monetary policy. Following the perspective of the work on delegation, much of the research focuses on how political principals attempt to influence and control agents, that is, central bankers.

This perspective largely ignores the embeddedness of central bankers in other social institutions and how a wider multitude of forces might influence them. This is ironic since central bankers are the ones with formal authority over monetary policy in countries with legally independent central banks.

---

7. For a discussion of this work, see Eijffinger and De Haan 1996 and De Haan and Kooi 2000.
8. See Kirshner 2003 for a review of these debates.

Moreover, central bankers themselves do not have any obvious material incentives in their own right. Rather, rationalist accounts for the most part—Adolph (2014) is an exemplary exception—assume central bankers have a greater preference for price stability than do politicians; the assumption is essentially a sociological claim that central bankers as a group are trained to have this worldview. This assumption, though, fails to acknowledge the range of views that central bankers might have. It says little about where on the spectrum of price stability central bankers might be or what they might view as the wider role of monetary policy in financial stabilization, controlling for asset bubbles, monetizing debt, or encouraging the government to pursue structural or fiscal reforms. In short, it says little about their larger worldview that animates how they think about monetary policy. As Forder (1996) notes in his pointed critique, an institution like central bank independence says nothing about how central bankers will behave.

By contrast, scholars in the sociological institutionalist and constructivist vein recognize that informal institutions and practices in which actors embedded are conduits for influence and the transmission of ideas. The literature on global governance in international relations has made this point explicit; as Rosenau (1995, 4) notes, governance "is more encompassing than government. It embraces government institutions, but it also subsumes informal, non-governmental mechanisms. . . . Governance is thus a system of rule that is as dependent on intersubjective meanings as on formally sanctioned constitutions and charters." Hall (2008) has applied this concept to understanding the emergence of monetary governance where authority is distributed across multiple levels—national, supranational, and transnational—and across private and public actors.

Sociological institutionalists have drawn attention to the role of professional fields (DiMaggio and Powell 1983, 1991). Others drawing on this perspective have linked a wide variety of outcomes to the professional field of economics, including the spread of neoliberalism (Domínguez 1997; Babb 2001; Ban 2016), pattern of IMF loans (Chwieroth 2013; Nelson 2014), capital account liberalization (Chwieroth 2010), and the spread of central banking norms and practices (Johnson 2016). More and more central bankers have formal training in economics, and a growing number have advanced graduate degrees (Adolph 2014; Wendschlag 2016). The field of economics thus arguably has a greater influence on monetary policy than ever. As an example, the emergence of the theory of CBI in the 1970s influenced central bank behavior in the United States *without* any institutional change. From the 1950s to the early 1970s, the FRB often coordinated policy with the government on economic policy under FRB chairman William Martin and then Arthur Burns despite legal independence. With the emergence of the theory of CBI in the late 1970s, the FRB reinterpreted its role to act more independently in order to keep inflation low (Schonhardt-Bailey 2013, 16–19).

Researchers have also pointed to organizations as sites of learning and socialization (Kaufman 1967; March and Olsen 1983; Carpenter 2001). Barnett and Finnemore (1999) argue that international organizations create social knowledge that define tasks, the relevant actors, and ultimately their interests, and these insights have been applied to monetary affairs. A growing body of work also suggests that central bankers have preferences that are shaped by organizational structure and experience. Adolph (2014) also challenges simplistic assumptions of central banker preferences. He contends that preferences develop through career socialization as well as through material interests based on career incentives. Central bankers working in a finance ministry or as a central bank staffer come to develop policy preferences that reflect their experience in those organizations. Similarly, Chwieroth (2010) and Nelson (2014) explore how organizational practices within the IMF socialize staffers into a specific worldview. Moreover, Chwieroth (2013, 2010) shows how informal practices can give these staff members a high degree of influence on decision making on major policy issues (loan packages and capital controls) despite their lack of formal power.

The Approach of This Book

This book builds on the work of sociological institutionalism and constructivism to explain the BOJ's reluctance to embrace unconventional policy. An approach that emphasizes the role of ideas provides a much broader view of the forces influencing central bankers. Specifically, we build on the work on *policy ideas*. Research has shown how policy ideas have shaped trade policy (Goldstein 1993), approaches to economic regulation (Vogel 1996; Blyth 2001), and macroeconomic policy (Hall 1989, 1993; Weir 1989; McNamara 1998; Kirshner 2003; Schonhardt-Bailey 2013).

Scholars have defined policy ideas as a set of shared beliefs about specific cause-and-effect relationships (Goldstein 1993; McNamara 1998). Policy ideas shape the interpretation of facts and evidence, and define policy options and their perceived trade-offs, thereby shaping how actors arrive at their own preferences (Goldstein 1993; McNamara 1998). We broaden the definition of policy ideas, following others (Blyth 2007; Campbell and Pedersen 2014), to include not just beliefs about causal relationships but also beliefs about goals and priorities. Thus, in the realm of monetary policy, policy ideas determine goals—price stability, financial stability, and the role of the central banking in financing debt—and also suggest various paths to achieving these goals.

The Challenge of Studying Ideas

Policy ideas are challenging to study, and this is true in the case of monetary policy as well. On the one hand, central bank independence provides a relatively stable institutional environment since policy board members are appointed and cannot easily be removed. On the other hand, there is no reason to assume that central bankers appointed to a policy board have a shared worldview. Within policy boards, competing policy ideas may be at play, particularly as new circumstances arise or in cases when existing policies appear to be ineffective. Central bank policy board members often come from a variety of backgrounds (academia, industry, central banks, etc.), may adhere to different economic schools of thought (neoclassical, monetarist, new Keynesianism, etc.), and may have been appointed at different times by different executives. Ideas may matter, but perhaps not in a systematic way.

Policy ideas may also compete with other interests, including material ones. As discussed above, central bank independence is contingent; it can wax and wane depending on the context. Depending on the timing, a political executive may have influence if he or she has the chance to make appointments to the board. An executive may attempt to select nominees with shared views on macroeconomic policy, and the legislature can attempt to influence the selection of candidates by using the power of confirmation to block candidates of which they disapprove. The government can make threats—that may be more or less credible depending on the number of veto points—to limit independence.

The challenge for an ideational approach is to provide a political account of what makes ideas salient (Hall 1997; Berman 2001). For ideational explanations to be convincing, one must account for how ideas are formed, how they become shared, and, most importantly, how one particular set of ideas wins out over other competing ideas or material interests and finally translates into policy choices. As observers have noted, scholars studying ideas have not always been successful in this regard (Schmidt 2010; Berman 2013; Schonhardt-Bailey 2013; Baumgartner 2014; Campbell and Pedersen 2014; Daigneault 2014).

There have been growing efforts to address these issues. Researchers have explored a range of processes that impact ideational influence, but it has not always been apparent how to navigate between the various explanations. Such is the case with the body of work that studies ideas from two different directions: the convergence of ideas and their diffusion (typically transnationally), and the generation and reproduction of specific ideas in more local contexts (often national). Work in sociological institutionalism highlighted the diffusion in institutional forms and practices, widely defined to include norms and cognitive scripts (DiMaggio and Powell 1983; Dobbin 1994). Such institutional isomorphism occurs through processes such as mimesis and the professionalization of occupations that can extend beyond a given organization. One critique of this work, though, is that this approach tends to downplay contention and conflicts of interest (DiMaggio and Powell 1991, 12; Hall and Taylor 1996, 954).

Drawing on Haas's (1992) concept of an epistemic community, scholars in international relations have explored how transnational communities of experts have influenced the diffusion of ideas, including in monetary institutions more specifically. McNamara (1998) explains how the convergence of leaders around a common set of ideas paved the way for monetary union; others have also traced how an epistemic community of international bankers and economic officials contributed to the diffusion of CBI (Verdun 1999 King 2005); and Johnson (2016) highlights the role of the transnational central banking community in transplanting CBI, norms and other practices into the postcommunist states.

Meanwhile, others have emphasized the nationally based nature of ideas. Blyth (2007) finds that locally generated ideas explain the US's specific response to a common international challenge during the 1930s—deflation—that gave rise to the New Deal. A study of policy research organizations in industrialized democracies finds that different knowledge regimes—ideas that influence policy and policy debate—are still primarily national in nature (Campbell and Pedersen 2014). Fourcade's work (2009), while acknowledging that economics is a global profession, examines how national institutions shape the discipline of economics, noting, "Economics arose everywhere. But everywhere it is distinctive" (2009, 3). Schmidt (2007) finds that antiglobalization national discourses in France have inhibited the emergence of new ideas. Similarly, in the Japanese context, Wakatabe (2015) argues that a national discourse that emphasized the root of the Japanese economy's stagnation as structural in nature obscured the importance of macroeconomic policy, while Hamada and Noguchi (2004) contend that particular Japanese preconceptions led to macroeconomic policy mistakes. Finally, other work looks more explicitly at the intersection of the transnational and national factors to examine the translation of ideas into national contexts. In this vein, Ban (2016) looks at how the spread of neoliberalism was refracted through different local contexts in Spain and Romania and generated two distinctive types of neoliberalism.

Across this literature, many of the same processes have been identified as generating different outcomes: diffusion transnationally versus distinctive local patterns. This is in part an issue of boundaries. The diffusion and coherence of ideas across one context—an organization or nation—may in fact limit diffusion at another level of analysis, such as transnationally. For instance, learning within organizations, which has received growing attention in the ideas literature, may limit learning from other transnational sources. As Campbell and Pedersen

(2014, 14) further note, when convergence processes (such as normative learning or mimetic learning) work in different nationally specific combinations, they can produce ideational divergence. Indeed, they find that different combinations of mechanisms across Denmark, France, Germany, and the United States generated different knowledge regimes.

How do we adjudicate between these overlapping levels and competing sources of influence? The profession of economics clearly has shaped the discourse on monetary policy, and its influence has been transnational. Economic ideas flow across borders, and central bankers are part of transnational epistemic communities that intersect with the field of economics. At the same time, central bankers are also embedded in very different domestic contexts as well, not least of which includes elite hierarchical institutions—the central bank organizations themselves—but also extends to different nomination and policymaking practices.

Policy Networks and Ideas

The literature on ideas has identified a wide array of institutions and processes that determine ideational influence. Which actors matter and what processes of ideational influence are operative in a given context we regard as open empirical questions. Thus our approach seeks to establish the actual channels of influence as a starting point. We draw on the policy networks literature to understand the politics of how ideas become influential in the policy process. The policy network approach provides a framework for establishing a hierarchy of influences around the policy process, which allows us to look at the intersection of material interests, institutions, ideas, and power. This approach also provides analytic leverage by allowing us to identify which of the wide range of ideational processes that scholars have identified—such as professional training, the circulation of elites, socialization, organizational practices, adaptation, learning—are most salient and, by extension, which are less so.

A network is a "stable or recurrent pattern of behavioral interaction or exchange between individuals or organizations" (Ansell 2008, 1). A policy network specifically is the constellation of actors and their interactions with expertise and influence over a given policy domain, e.g., monetary policy. Rhodes defines them as "sets of formal institutional and informal linkages between governmental and other actors structured around shared if endlessly negotiated beliefs and interests in public policy making and implementation" (2008, 426). Policy networks serve as conduits for the flow of ideas and influence. By including informal social institutions, policy networks extend beyond formal decision-making institutions (such as a monetary policy board). As the older work in this vein has highlighted, in contrast to pluralist models, policy is often determined by a small subset of actors with specialized knowledge and access (Heclo and Wildavsky 1974; Heclo 1978). Policy networks shape the politics of policy decisions by structuring the relative influence of different actors through their degree of inclusion and exclusion. Actors can also cultivate policy networks and draw on them as resources to achieve their goals.

In the context of monetary policy, policy boards are vested with authority over monetary policy in central banks that have legal independence. Policy boards, though, are embedded within a complex network of relationships. Most directly, policy boards are part of large hierarchical organizations, namely the central banks themselves. Policy board members interact with central bank staff members, who provide data, analysis, and in some cases a clear point of view as well. Policy boards, depending on the specific context, exchange views and share information with the executive, legislators, finance ministries, business, and others. Policy boards are also embedded in a broader institutional political context that influences the selection of board members. Collectively, we refer to these connections as the *monetary policy network*.

Thus all monetary policymaking institutions are part of a larger network. Ideas, though, are likely to have a more predictable and consistent effect when they circulate through a monetary policy network that is centralized, closed, and stable. By centralization, we mean that the network has one node that exerts a high degree of influence on the discourse. In a closed network, membership in the network is more restricted and there are fewer channels for external influence. Stability refers to the extent to which the network remains consistent over time. A stable network is one where the same positions and institutions have a regularized metaphorical seat at the table. For the sake of brevity, we refer to a network with these attributes—centralized, closed, and stable—simply as a "closed" network. A closed network creates conditions for specific dominant ideas to emerge and persist since these network attributes tend to limit ideational diversity and dissent. With monetary policy networks that are more open, there is greater scope for ideas to come into conflict, thus making the connection between ideas and outcomes less predictable (although no less important).

In Japan, the monetary policy network had all the attributes of a closed network until prime minister Abe Shinzō dismantled it. The BOJ as an organization (not just the Policy Board) had a privileged role in the monetary policy network. Even within a hierarchical organization like a central bank, however, there is no reason to assume that an organization has a widely shared worldview. As Barnett and Finnemore aptly note, "Organizational coherence is an accomplishment rather than a given" (1999, 724). As we discuss in chapters 4 and 5, the BOJ developed a relatively coherent view that reflected its long institutional history, and its internal practices—recruitment, training, and promotion—reinforced this view. These practices prioritized the organizational worldview over a professionally oriented one geared toward broader disciplinary knowledge, such as macroeconomics, an observation about Japan's administration consistent with Silberman's distinction between an "organizationally-oriented" bureaucracy versus a "professionally-oriented" one (Silberman 1993).

Until the advent of Abenomics in late 2012 and early 2013, the BOJ was able to shape the discourse and limit dissenting views within the decision-making Policy Board through the influence it wielded over the monetary policy network. As covered in chapter 5, the BOJ cultivated internal candidates within the BOJ for leadership positions, and it exercised informal influence over appointments to the monetary Policy Board through informal interagency deliberations. Through informal practices, the BOJ staff also influenced monetary Policy Board deliberations more directly. In the concluding chapter, we return to this discussion of the connection between the monetary policy network, the persistence of ideas, and ultimately the coercive replacement of these policy ideas. Looking more broadly, we examine how pre-existing policy ideas and monetary policy networks have determined the receptiveness of other central banks to unconventional monetary policies.

The Impact of Ideas on Monetary Policy

Building on a growing and sophisticated literature (Chwieroth 2007, 2010; Abdelal, Blyth, and Parsons 2010; Nelson and Katzenstein 2014; Ban 2016), we use a mixed methods approach that employs a combination of text analysis and case studies of the BOJ's key monetary policy decisions. The text analysis allows us to address what Chwieroth (2007)—borrowing from Parsons (2002)—describes as the "how to" and "how much" problem in the study of norms and ideas. Research on ideas and norms, he points out, raises a dual challenge: how does one measure something intangible like an idea, and then estimate the magnitude of its effect in a rigorous way that controls for alternative explanations? Chwieroth proposes professional training as a proxy for ideas—specifically, when individuals received their degrees—that he demonstrates can be measured quantitatively and used with statistical techniques to estimate the effect of ideas. Others too, such as Nelson (2014), have employed a similar method. While this approach has its merits—not least of which is that it facilitates cross-national research—we use text analysis for two reasons. First, the BOJ core policy ideas did not vary that much, at least between 1998 and 2012. Second, we believe that using the BOJ minutes of Policy Board meetings, which we discuss in chapter 6, are a more direct means of capturing ideas. We create a quantitative indicator that measures the sentiment toward prices and inflation as expressed in minutes of the Policy Board. We then model the effects of this sentiment statistically on monetary base expansion. We acknowledge that this indicator has its limits since it captures only one dimension of the BOJ's worldview. This approach, nonetheless, allows us to test this dimension of the BOJ's policy ideas against the effects of alternative explanations while controlling for economic conditions.

We also employ case studies, which have been widely used in ideational studies, of key monetary policy decisions drawing on BOJ Policy Board transcripts, BOJ Policy Board minutes, interviews with elites, transcripts of parliamentary testimony by BOJ officials, speeches, and other sources. The case studies allow us to examine with greater nuance how the broader BOJ's policy worldview, beyond its stringent interpretation of price stability, shaped its interpretation of economic facts and the broader policy deliberation. The case studies also help disentangle the preferences within the BOJ Policy Board and those of other actors such as the government and legislators, thereby providing insight into the tension between political demands and the Policy Board's view. While the Policy Board adhered to a remarkable degree to the BOJ's core policy ideas until the start of 2013, there were key moments when the BOJ Policy Board changed policy course; these episodes were due to external pressure rather than an abandonment of the BOJ worldview.

This chapter lays out the case, indeed the necessity, for incorporating the role of ideas into the study of monetary policy, and it provides an approach for doing so. Rationalist approaches leave too much that is essential to monetary politics unexamined, including central bankers and the myriad influences on them. These influences extend far beyond the principal-agent framework that informs much of the existing work. Given the global sea change in monetary policy since 2008 that has seen central bankers deploying (and considering) policies once virtually inconceivable, it is hard to overstate the role of ideas in monetary policy. Indeed, the debates over monetary policy by politicians, central bankers, economists, and others have been largely over the policy ideas themselves. In turning to ideas, the challenge is to specify not only the ideas but also the mechanisms by which they gain influence (or don't). This is the subject of the following two chapters.

Chapter 4

THE BOJ WORLDVIEW AND ITS HISTORICAL DEVELOPMENT

> Under the current system, the quantitative control over monetary base cannot be the starting point of monetary policy.
>
> —Okina Kunio, former director general of the BOJ's Institute for Monetary and Economic Studies, Shūkan Tōyō Keizai, March 13, 1993

The BOJ's policy ideas evolved over its long history since its establishment in 1882. This chapter first describes the BOJ worldview toward monetary policy and then traces how these policy ideas were shaped by its experiences. We focus on three elements of the BOJ view: a premium on price stability, skepticism about the extent to which monetary easing can spur economic growth and concern that it can generate adverse impacts; and an expansive interpretation of central bank independence.

After laying out these elements of the BOJ worldview, the chapter traces the evolution of this view, examining how BOJ officials perceived economic conditions, the effectiveness of their policy instruments, and their relationship with other players in the government. The chapter follows this process over six periods: (1) the BOJ's formative years from 1882 through the Bank Law of 1928, (2) the 1930s through the end of World War II, (3) under the US military occupation from 1945 to 1952, (4) the era of rapid growth from the 1950s to the late 1960s, (5) from the demise of the Bretton Woods monetary system to the beginning of the bubble economy in the mid-1980s, and (6) from the bubble economy to establishment of BOJ independence in 1998. The BOJ's post–World War II monetary policy experiences have been especially influential in shaping the BOJ's perspective, particularly those since the 1970s as Japan became the world's second largest economy and came under growing pressure to help manage the global economy.

The BOJ's Worldview

The notion that there is a BOJ worldview is reflected in the observation by commentators and economists alike that the BOJ is guided by a "BOJ theory" (*nichigin riron*), a term that predates the period of post-1998 monetary policy that is the focus of this book. We have identified the following three components. The first is the premium that the BOJ places on price stability. As "guardian of the currency" (*tsūka no ban-nin*), the BOJ has long committed itself to protecting the people's trust in the Japanese currency, the yen. Stability in the value of the currency refers not only to price stability but also to a stable exchange rate. Of the two objectives, the BOJ has put greater emphasis on price stability, and it maintained a strong aversion to inflation. The BOJ has also often shown a preference for monetary tightening believing that when the discount rate is higher that it has greater monetary policy leverage and freedom.[1] In the case of contemporary Japan, memories of postwar hyperinflation in the late 1940s, the "wild inflation" (*kyōran bukka*) in the mid-1970s, and the asset-price inflation of the bubble economy in the late 1980s have haunted the BOJ.[2] This BOJ preference for price stability and low inflation is not uncommon among central bankers, particularly in Germany, which also experienced hyperinflation during the Weimar Republic (Henning 1994). The BOJ though has long maintained a hawkish and literal interpretation of price stability, reportedly insisting on zero percent inflation as its monetary policy goal.[3]

The second element of the BOJ worldview is the belief that the central bank has limited ability to shape economic outcomes through manipulation of the monetary base. The BOJ believed, at least until Abenomics, that expanding the monetary base would not necessarily have a predictable or positive impact without the appropriate market conditions. This issue was central to the famous

---

1. Yamawaki (1998) documents how the BOJ considered it a "win" when it managed to raise the discount rate but a "loss" when it had to lower it, especially in terms of its competition with the MOF, which tends to prefer a lower discount rate to stimulate the economy and generate higher tax revenue. One former Policy Board member (1998–2003) also noted that raising interest rates makes the BOJ feel more powerful, as others come begging and cajoling the BOJ to lower them (personal communication, September 15, 2015).

2. Critics of the BOJ's timid monetary policy against deflation in the late 1990s have noted that the BOJ appeared to be haunted by the "ghost of inflation," fearing that the excess liquidity in the market would trigger sudden hyperinflation ("Infure no bōrei wo osoreru nichigin" [The Bank of Japan that fears ghost of inflation], *Nihon Keizai Shimbun*, June 30, 1999).

3. Shirakawa (2008, 81–84) compares different countries' targets for increasing prices (CPI), with Japan at 1 percent and other advanced economies (New Zealand, Canada, UK, Australia, Switzerland, and the Eurozone) between 1 and 3 percent (with a mode of 2 percent). Also, a former BOJ policy board member's interview with the authors, September 15, 2015.

"Iwata-Okina debate" that played out on the pages of a Japanese economic journal, *Tōyō Keizai*, from 1992 to 1993. Okina, a BOJ economist with a PhD from the University of Chicago who later became the director general of the BOJ think tank (Institute for Monetary and Economic Studies), insisted that money supply (the money circulating in the real economy) is determined by actions and decisions in the financial sector, not by the monetary base. An increase in the monetary base that does not reflect the financial sector's credit (banknote) needs could in fact lead to volatility in interest rates and inflation. Hence, the BOJ considered the short-term interest rate to be the only effective tool of monetary policy.[4] Conversely, Iwata, an academic economist (who later became BOJ deputy governor under Kuroda), argued that an increase in the monetary base would lead to a suppression of interest rates, which would enhance demand for banknotes and an expanded money supply. He also argued that the BOJ's hesitance to manipulate the monetary base during the first few years after the bubble burst in the early 1990s led to the contraction of the money supply.[5]

The BOJ's belief regarding the limited effectiveness of monetary base expansion has led it to prioritize the health of the financial sector and to emphasize that factors outside of its control—such as demography or supply-side structural constraints—determine growth. The BOJ has insisted that unless investment and credit needs arise from the users of the banknotes, any quantitative expansion of the monetary base would either have a negligible effect or would lead to an uncontrollable swing in interest rates and possibly hyperinflation.

A third aspect of the BOJ worldview is its expansive interpretation of central bank independence (CBI), which stems from long-standing norms and its history of bristling under the control of the government, especially the Ministry of Finance (MOF). Until 1998, the BOJ had a lower level of de jure independence than central banks in other industrial countries such as the United States and Germany (Cargill and Dwyer 2015). Despite its low independence, Japan nonetheless had a fairly successful record of price stability for most of the postwar period.

One explanation of how the BOJ could maintain low inflation despite low legal independence is that the BOJ had de facto independence (Cargill, Hutchison, and Itō 1997; Kamikawa 2005, 2014). There are, however, as discussed below, many periods where the BOJ clearly capitulated to government pressure. Regardless, it is clear that from the BOJ's perspective, the meaning of independence was more expansive than merely achieving legal institutional independence through,

---

4. Until 1998, the BOJ used discount rate (*kōtei buai*) as the monetary policy target, but since 1998, it has used uncollateralized overnight call rate as the target.

5. This was a series of articles appearing in *Shūkan Tōyō Keizai* from September 12, 1992, to March 13, 1993. For a digest version of this debate, see Ueda 1992a.

for instance, protecting board members from arbitrary dismissal. The BOJ also was keen to maintain its control over its goal independence (e.g., determining the appropriate target for inflation) in addition to instrument independence, that is, the freedom to choose specific policy tools (Kujiraoka 2017, 272; Shirakawa 2008, 100–101). The BOJ's interpretation of independence prioritizes institutional reputation, credibility, and survival. Hence, even after attaining de jure independence in the New BOJ Law of 1998, the BOJ has been very concerned about becoming entrapped in certain policy decisions that might either compromise its monetary policy autonomy or discredit it in the eyes of the public or the market. Monetization of debt through central bank purchases of government debt has been viewed as one of the great dangers that the BOJ should avoid. The BOJ has been deeply wary of government pressure to absorb debt since, among other things, its asset position and reputation would be at risk if it were to absorb a large amount of public debt. From the BOJ's perspective, such dangers should be averted through a clear separation of fiscal and monetary policy. After 1998, some critics argued that the BOJ faced an "independence trap," where the BOJ leadership desired to demonstrate their policy independence by resisting political pressure and coordination with the ministries or with the government (Cargill, Hutchison, and Ito 2003).[6]

Evolution of the BOJ Worldview over the Course of Its History

The sections below describe how the BOJ's policy ideas evolved over the bank's long history, in particular the period from the 1970s through the 1990s.

From the Establishment of the BOJ to the Bank Law of 1928

The BOJ Ordinance established the BOJ in 1882 as a central bank under the direction of the MOF, thus launching the first phase of the BOJ's history. After the Sino-Japanese war (1894–95), Japan switched from the silver standard to the gold standard, converting its war reparations from China paid in sterling in 1897. Growing economic integration, stimulated by the transition to the gold standard, exposed Japan's expanding economic activities to greater volatility from the collapse of the gold standard after World War I (1914–18). Periods of economic expansion were punctuated with episodes of rapid contraction,

---

6. This does not seem to be a particularly Japanese phenomenon; for instance, the first European Central Bank president Wim Duisenberg said of the Bundesbank that "[it] is like whipped cream. The harder you beat it, the stiffer it gets" (Van Overtveldt 2011, 37).

Box 4.1: Chronology of the Bank of Japan

June 1882

The Bank of Japan Law of 1882 is promulgated; the bank is to have capital of ten million yen and is given a license to operate for thirty years from the start of business.

October 1882

Business operation begins.

May 1884

Money system is established (Convertible Bank Note Act is promulgated).

March 1887

An increase in the bank's capital is announced from ten million yen to twenty million yen.

August 1895

An increase in the bank's capital is announced from twenty million yen to thirty million yen.

April 1896

The Head Office is moved to a new building at the present location.

March 1897

The gold standard is established (Monetary Act is promulgated) with the money from China as war reparation.

February 1910

The bank is given a license to operate for thirty more years from October 10, 1912, and an increase in the bank's capital is announced from thirty million yen to sixty million yen.

June 1917

Gold export is embargoed.

November 1922

Fiscal deposit system is introduced (treasury system is abolished).

May 1927

The Bank of Japan Special Accommodation and Compensation Act is enforced (for dealing with financial crisis).

May 1930
The embargo on gold export is lifted.

December 1931
Gold export is embargoed again (and the convertibility of gold note is abandoned)

February 1942
The Bank of Japan Law of 1942 is promulgated; the bank is to have capital of one hundred million yen.

May 1942
The bank is reorganized under the Bank of Japan Law of 1942.

June 1949
The Policy Board is established.

May 1957
The Act on Reserve Deposit Requirement System is enforced (the system starts running in September 1959).

November 1962
A new monetary control method is introduced.

December 1971
Yen is revalued.

February 1973
Japan transitions to the floating system.

October 1988
The Bank of Japan monetary network system starts running.

November 1988
Short-term financial market management is revised.

June 1997
The Bank of Japan Law of 1997 is promulgated; the bank is to have capital of one hundred million yen.

April 1998
The Bank of Japan Law of 1997 comes into effect.

leading to a vigorous discussion on the role of the BOJ and how much influence the government should exert over the BOJ's monetary policy.[7]

Before any of the reform proposals materialized, however, the severe Shōwa financial crisis of 1927 shifted the debate from the BOJ's role in monetary policy to its role in stabilizing the financial sector. The crisis came in the aftermath of the Great Kantō Earthquake of 1923, when the bankruptcy of Tokyo Watanabe Bank in March 1927 triggered the collapse of other banks. These bank failures were caused by bad assets in the form of earthquake bills twice discounted by the BOJ. Desperate to avoid financial catastrophe and despite its earlier restrictive attitude toward bank bailouts, the BOJ had to lend large sums to rescue foundering banks, including the Taiwan Bank, which was central to the Japanese government's colonial policy at that time.

In the aftermath of the financial crisis, the government enacted the Bank Law in 1928 to encourage bank mergers in order to dispose of bad assets. Under the Bank Law, the number of banks decreased almost 60 percent (from 1,283 to 538) in the five years between 1927 and 1932. The new law strengthened the MOF's regulatory and supervisory functions for ensuring a sound banking system. The MOF also gave the BOJ a role in inspecting banks so that the BOJ would consider itself directly responsible for the country's financial health.[8]

From the end of World War I to the early 1930s, the price of goods declined continuously except for the period right after the Great Kantō Earthquake. Business earnings deteriorated, and agricultural rural areas suffered not only from the effects of recession but also a bad rice harvest. In response to deflation and recession, the BOJ lowered the official discount rate until 1927. Along with the BOJ's emergency financing to deal with the aftermath of the Shōwa financial crisis of 1927, this reduction increased the BOJ's concern about excessive liquidity; the BOJ feared it would complicate Japan's expected return to the gold standard. To facilitate a rapid return to the gold standard, a new government in July 1929 pursued fiscal austerity. After returning to the gold standard, in early 1930 the price of goods declined sharply due to the Great Depression and Japanese exports collapsed. In response, the BOJ lowered the official discount rate in October 1930 while maintaining fiscal austerity.[9]

---

7. There were some proposals by private research groups for decreasing the government's political influence over the BOJ by reforming the selection process of officials and introducing supervision of commercial banks, which ran counter to the purpose of the BOJ Ordinance of 1882 ("The BOJ," *Nihon Ginkō Hyakunenshi*, vol. 3, 294–341).

8. Ibid., 264–93.

9. Ibid., 364–71, 446–73. Metzler and Bytheway (2016) argue that a main reason behind the Japanese government's push toward returning to the gold standard came from the intracentral bank cooperation between the BOJ and the BOE.

From the Militarist Regime through the End of World War II

In the 1930s, the BOJ's history entered its second phase as the Japanese government increasingly directed economic policy to support military mobilization. In 1931, after the Mukden Incident, which led to the Japanese invasion of Manchuria, and the UK's departure from the gold standard, the Japanese government faced massive reserve losses and decided to leave the gold standard again (as did other industrialized countries). To stimulate the economy, Finance Minister Takahashi Korekiyo shifted from austerity to expansionary fiscal policy and lowered the discount rate. The Keynesian-style policy[10] supported the increasing budget requests demanded by the military for Manchukuo, the Japanese-controlled puppet state in Manchuria. The so-called Takahashi Fiscal Policy combined with exchange rate depreciation succeeded, and the economy expanded rapidly in 1932. Takahashi later tried to curb excessive military spending in 1934, fearing the rapid expansion of the budget and inflation, but he faced strong resistance. Having antagonized the military, he was assassinated at the time of the so-called 2.26 coup attempt.[11] After agreeing with the MOF in 1932 to underwrite the government bonds, the BOJ supported the demand for rapid expansion of liquidity in the market and facilitated massive fiscal expansion. Although it seemed that Japan was successful in stabilizing its economy until the mid-1930s, subsequently inflation rose from 1935 to 1938.

Assessments of the expansionary macroeconomic policy from this period are divided. Some argue that it caused excessive inflation and contributed to the militarization of the economy, while others contend that it ended the recession by generating a boom in domestic demand (Nakamura 1971; Cargill 2000). The BOJ, however, interpreted its decision to underwrite the government bonds as one of its biggest policy failures. Indeed, the BOJ's own historical volume published to celebrate its one-hundred-year anniversary in 1982 described this expansionary policy as the most serious failure in its one hundred years of operation.[12] For the BOJ, the decision undermined the functioning of the central bank and served as an important lesson for the BOJ in later years.

As the government's nationalistic quest and war mobilization intensified, the government moved to gain even greater control over the BOJ. In 1942, the government enacted the Bank of Japan Law (BOJ Law) to allocate the nation's

---

10. Takahashi's policies are sometimes referred to as "Keynesianism without Keynes."

11. Takahashi Korekiyo is one of the most prominent figures in the modern history of Japanese finance. He served as Japan's finance minister five separate times (1913–14, 1918–21, 1927, 1931–34, and 1934–36), as BOJ governor once (1911–13), and as prime minister once (1921–22) before being assassinated by a military youth group in 1936.

12. "The BOJ," *Nihon Ginkō Hyakunenshi*, vol. 4, 51–56.

financial resources in accordance with the spirit of the General National Mobilization Act of 1938. The 1942 BOJ Law increased government control over the BOJ in several ways. Under the new law, the BOJ was to support national policy through regulation of the currency, control of finance, and maintenance and development of the credit system (Article 1) and to achieve national goals (Article 2). The mandate, not surprisingly, did not include "price stability." The law also placed the BOJ under the supervision of the MOF (Article 42). The finance minister could direct the BOJ to implement policies it deemed necessary (Article 43). As for personnel, while BOJ governors would serve five-year terms (Article 16), the government had the power to appoint or dismiss them (Article 47).

The US Occupation (1945–1952)

The Japanese economy experienced a period of hyperinflation, where wholesale prices increased by ninety-six times from 1945 to 1951. This inflation was sparked by two key factors: (1) large government subsidies for jump-starting production of raw materials (such as coal and fertilizers) and food, and (2) the BOJ's purchase of a large volume of bonds issued by the Reconstruction Finance Bank (RFB), a government financial institution created to aid the postwar recovery effort (Park 2011, 57–58). The BOJ's experience during the occupation reinforced the perceived risk of inflation and the danger of direct monetary financing by the BOJ.

In an attempt to rein in inflation, the government enacted the Temporary Interest Rate Adjustment Act in 1947, which set a maximum interest rate, in order to stabilize the price of goods. Under the act, the finance minister, when he deemed it necessary, could compel the BOJ governor to set the maximum deposit interest rate, change it, or abolish it. As a result, the BOJ could not move the interest rate structure without the MOF's approval.[13]

Ultimately, it was austerity measures introduced under the supervision of American banker Joseph Dodge, an adviser to SCAP (Supreme Commander for the Allied Powers), that brought inflation under control. The "Dodge Line," introduced in 1949, slashed subsidies, balanced the national budget, and fixed the exchange rate at 360 yen to the dollar. The occupation authorities also abolished the RFB, which had been largely financed by the BOJ.

During the occupation, the BOJ had a degree of de facto independence from the MOF thanks to its direct support from SCAP. SCAP relied more on the BOJ than the MOF for economic policy (Mabuchi 1991). Under the strong leadership

---

13. Ibid., vol. 5, 161–62.

TABLE 4.1 Bank of Japan governors from 1945 to 1998 and their previous affiliations

NAMES	COME FROM	STARTED	STEPPED DOWN
Araki Eikichi (First)	BOJ	October 9, 1945	June 1, 1946
Ichimada Hisato	BOJ	June 1, 1946	December 10, 1954
Araki Eikichi (Second)	BOJ	December 11, 1954	November 30, 1956
Yamagiwa Masamichi	MOF	November 30, 1956	December 17, 1964
Usami Makoto	Private Bank	December 17, 1964	December 16, 1969
Sasaki Tadashi	BOJ	December 17, 1969	December 16, 1974
Morinaga Tei'ichiro	MOF	December 17, 1974	December 16, 1979
Maekawa Haruo	BOJ	December 17, 1979	December 16, 1984
Sumita Satoshi	MOF	December 17, 1984	December 16, 1989
Mieno Yasushi	BOJ	December 17, 1989	December 16, 1994
Matsushita Yasuo	MOF	December 17, 1994	March 20, 1998

Source: https://www.boj.or.jp/about/outline/history/pre_gov/index.htm/.

of the BOJ governor Ichimada Hisato (1946–54), nicknamed "the Pope" because he had direct access to General Douglas MacArthur, the BOJ played a crucial role in monetary policy. SCAP had a general preference for tighter monetary policy, but Governor Ichimada also had latitude to increase the monetary base to counter the deflationary effect of the government's fiscal austerity (Kure 1981, 56–70; Yoshino 2014, 328–62).

Under the supervision of SCAP, the BOJ Law was revised in 1949. The revision was a compromise that did not fully satisfy the BOJ's desire for greater independence. The issue of BOJ control emerged soon after the end of the war. Some strongly advocated changing the 1942 BOJ Law since it had been enacted under the control of an authoritarian government. In October 1945, the "Preparatory Committee for Revising the BOJ System" was established at the initiative of Governor Araki Eiichi, who wanted to amend the 1942 BOJ Law to improve economic policymaking. The committee, composed of members of the MOF and the BOJ, submitted a final report that suggested limiting the government's authority and establishing more independence for the BOJ, recommendations that reflected the BOJ's position. The MOF, not surprisingly, was reluctant to accept greater BOJ independence and in the end did not respond to the final report.[14] Several committees from the Japanese side and from SCAP considered numerous proposals for reforming the financial system. In the end, SCAP proposed a BOJ reform plan that introduced a policy board within the BOJ; interestingly, SCAP's original plan

---

14. Ibid., vol. 5, 268.

had proposed creating a policy board separate from the BOJ. The new policy board within the BOJ was to "formulate as well as direct, supervise, and publish monetary and credit policy for the Central Bank so as to harmonize the interests of all agencies of the Government and the entire banking system in such a way as to serve the best interest of the national economy." In the short term, it was understood that this meant coordinating tighter monetary policy with Dodge's fiscal austerity policy.[15] Under the influence of SCAP, the MOF and BOJ agreed to the policy board plan.[16]

The Policy Board consisted of seven members: the governor and representatives of the MOF, the Economic Stabilization Board, big city banks, regional banks, the commercial or industrial sector, and agriculture. The four representatives from the private sector were appointed by the cabinet subject to the consent of the Diet and were not to be dismissed during their four year terms. Yet there were some critical ambiguities, most importantly the precise relationship between the MOF and the Policy Board regarding the Policy Board's independence. Although the Policy Board assumed that it would take responsibility in making monetary policy decisions that used to be under the authority of the MOF, the MOF insisted that the BOJ Law gave the MOF supervisory authority over the BOJ, and, as discussed below, in practice the MOF continued to have strong influence over monetary policy.[17]

The Era of Rapid Growth—the 1950 to Late 1960s

During this period, two factors affected the BOJ's monetary policies: the relatively low level of BOJ independence and the Bretton Woods monetary regime, which served as an external constraint on Japan's monetary policy. During the first half of the rapid growth era from the late 1950s into the 1960s, the BOJ's principal challenge was to prevent overheating of the Japanese economy.[18] Under the Bretton Woods system, Japan maintained a fixed exchange rate of 360 yen per dollar, which gave the BOJ grounds for tightening Japan's monetary policy. The BOJ used monetary tightening to address balance of payments deficits in order to maintain the country's par value.

The global norm associated with the fixed exchange rate regime, therefore, helped the BOJ to deflect partly domestic political pressure for a more expansionary policy. Nevertheless, the choice to use macroeconomic policy tightening to

---

15. Ibid., vol. 5, 318.
16. Ibid., vol. 5, 308–12.
17. Ibid., vol. 5, 312–21.
18. Governor Araki's speech ("The BOJ," *Nihon Ginkō Chōsa Geppō*, January 1956, 1).

adjust for external payments deficit conflicted with the economic growth policy pursued by the LDP. Monetary policy measures, such as changes in the discount rate and "discount window operation" were conducted primarily by the BOJ subject to the approval of the MOF. Although political parties were not given much direct leeway in monetary policy, the LDP put pressure on the BOJ through the MOF when priorities diverged (Sakakibara and Noguchi 1977).

Due to the BOJ's low level of independence, the tug of war between elected officials and the BOJ slowed down monetary tightening.[19] Since the late 1950s, the BOJ had given priority to the wholesale price index (WPI) to judge when the discount rate should be changed.[20] Given a rising index as well as the long-standing concerns about price stability after Japan's experience with hyperinflation a decade earlier, the BOJ governor proposed raising the discount rate in 1956. But MOF officials, who opposed introducing tighter monetary policy and supported a low interest rate policy to stimulate the Japanese economy, succeeded in defeating the BOJ.[21] The BOJ did manage eventually to raise the interest rate in 1957 despite the MOF's opposition.[22] The move was a response to a balance of payments deficit resulting from an increase in imports, which had been triggered by the government's expansionary budget plan. Despite the legitimate balance of payment concerns, the BOJ governor Yamagiwa recalled that the BOJ's decision to raise the discount rate still encountered intense opposition from the cabinet and the MOF.[23]

TABLE 4.2 Comparison of price indexes: 1955–1970 (annual average of inflation rate %)

	1955–1960	1961–1965	1966–1970
Wholesale price index	0.5	0.4	2.1
Consumer price index	1.6	6.0	5.4

Source: "Oroshiuri bukkashisu Hyakunen no Ayumi" [History of 100 years of Wholesale Price Index]. The BOJ, *Nihon Ginko Chosa Geppo*, December 1987, 53.

---

19. A report from the BOJ attributed slow implementation of monetary policy partly to low de jure independence of the BOJ compared to the Bundesbank of West Germany ("The BOJ," *Nihon Ginkō Chōsa Geppō*, November 1958, 14–15).

20. According to Nakagawa (who worked at the General Affairs Division of the BOJ in 1971), during the rapid growth period, it was difficult to apply CPI as a criterion because there was concern that targeting a stable CPI could result in a fall in the WPI. At that time, WPI was relatively stable due to a rapid increase in productivity of manufacturing industrial goods, while the CPI was constantly increasing because of rising prices for food and services (Nakagawa 1981, 167).

21. "The BOJ," *Nihon Ginkō Hyakunenshi*, vol. 5, 486.

22. Ibid., vol. 5, 490.

23. The BOJ governor, Yamagiwa Masamichi, talked about the strong political pressures from the government (Yamagiwa Masamichi Denki Kankokai 1979, 585–90).

This type of conflict between the BOJ and the government intensified under the "rapid economic growth plan" during the first half of the 1960s. Under Prime Minister Ikeda Hayato (1960–64), the government promoted a policy known as the "Income Doubling Plan" that set an annual economic growth rate target of 7.2 percent. Since this policy was based on low interest rates and large fiscal expenditures, the BOJ's tight monetary policy conflicted with the government's plan. Under this expansionary policy, the balance of payments continuously showed a deficit from January 1960 onward due to a rapid increase in imports. During this period, the WPI was stable, so the BOJ used the balance of payments deficit to argue for tightening. The BOJ advocated a higher discount rate but could not secure consent from the government until July 1961.[24]

Throughout this period, the BOJ bristled at its relatively subservient position and advocated for revision to the BOJ Law. Revision was discussed twice, first in 1957–60 and then in 1965, but in both cases, the BOJ failed to secure reforms.[25] In 1955, Finance Minister Ichimada Hisato, a former BOJ governor, proposed a revision of the BOJ Law. The Financial System Research Committee, established in 1956, took up the issue of BOJ reform in 1957. Within the committee, there were clear differences between those from the MOF and those from the BOJ on the issue of the appropriate level of BOJ independence. The MOF officials claimed that the central bank should conduct policies consistent with the government's economic policies. Meanwhile, the BOJ representatives argued that BOJ independence was essential for stabilization of the currency.[26] Despite three years of intense discussion, the committee could not reach a consensus on independence and thus the plan to revise the BOJ Law initiated by Ichimada was abandoned.

BOJ governor Yamagiwa Masamichi (1956–64) initiated a second attempt to revise the BOJ Law. During questioning in the Diet, Governor Yamagiwa expressed his desire to revise the BOJ Law as soon as possible. Tanaka Kakuei, the finance minister, then gave a similar address expressing concern that the BOJ Law needed to be updated. At the time, Japan was on the verge of upgrading to IMF Article 8 country status. Governor Yamagiwa and Finance Minister Tanaka shared the view that monetary policy would be more critical in an open economy and that reforming the BOJ Law was necessary to improve monetary policymaking. The MOF and the BOJ exchanged views, but a large gap in their respective positions remained.[27] The MOF supported a proposal that allowed the

---

24. "The BOJ," *Nihon Ginkō Hyakunenshi*, vol. 6, 36–39.

25. Ibid., vol. 5, vol. 6.

26. Ibid., vol. 5.

27. Yamagiwa's reply at the Diet to the question about the relation between the MOF and the BOJ (*Shūgi'in Ōkura iinkai Kaigi roku*, March 26, 1964, 6–11).

government to "direct" the BOJ when it feared that the BOJ's monetary policy would conflict with government policy. The BOJ insisted that when their views diverged, the MOF should only have the right to request that the Policy Board postpone its policy.

The MOF was eager to submit a BOJ bill to the Diet that would improve its position relative to the BOJ. Among other things, the MOF's proposal aimed to formalize the MOF's consultative role.[28] The MOF, however, could not muster support from the LDP for its proposal, and thus no bill was submitted by the end of the Diet session in 1965. Not until more than thirty years later did the issue of reforming the BOJ Law finally emerge again with the establishment of the "Central Bank Study Group" in 1996 (Suda 2014, 38).

Not only did the BOJ fail to achieve de jure independence, after the end of the occupation, the MOF regained influence over Japan's monetary policy. The BOJ was contemptuously referred to as the "Bank of Japan Office in the Coordination Division of the Banking Bureau of MOF" (Kawakita 1995, 65).[29] While the level of MOF influence has been debated, a convention emerged after 1969 whereby former BOJ and MOF officials took turns as BOJ governor, a practice called "*tasukigake jinji*," or cross-ministry appointment. For MOF officials, the BOJ governorship was considered the most prestigious *amakudari* (literally "descent from heaven") postcareer position. Furthermore, many MOF officials were seconded to important positions within the BOJ (Amyx 2004, 103). On the budgetary front, too, the MOF maintained authority over the BOJ's annual budget allocation (Yamawaki 1998, chap. 3). Finally and most importantly, the Policy Board often had limited influence on actual policymaking (Yamawaki 1998, chap. 2). During these years, the BOJ governing body—its governors, deputy governors, and seven BOJ executive directors—decided on policy in consultation with the MOF (Kawakita 1995).

From the End of the Bretton Woods System to the Mid-1980s

Critical experiences in the early 1970s continued to shape the BOJ's ideas about price stability, monetary policy, and the dangers of excessive political influence. The BOJ's first monetary policy failure after World War II was the high inflation of 1973–74, often called "the wild inflation" (*kyōran bukka*), which hammered home for the BOJ the importance of price stability and the dangers of

---

28. "The BOJ," *Nihon Ginkō Hyakunenshi*, vol. 6, 276–80.
29. Honda Etsurō, former special adviser to the Abe cabinet who used to work at the MOF from 1978 to 2012, interview with the authors, September 18, 2015.

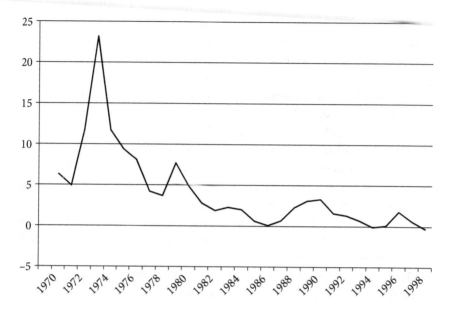

FIGURE 4.1. Rate of change in CPI: 1971–1999 (%)

political accommodation (see figure 4.1). This inflation flare-up can be traced back to several factors: (1) the shift in the exchange rate regime after 1971, (2) international pressure, especially from the United States, to reduce its balance of payment surplus, and (3) the government's preference to use accommodative macroeconomic policy rather than exchange rate policy to do so.

In 1971, President Nixon closed the gold window, suspending the convertibility of dollars into gold, the first of several measures that spelled the end of the Bretton Woods monetary system. In the wake of this so-called Nixon Shock, BOJ officials realized that Japan had to accept a further revaluation of the yen in response to the increasing balance of payment surplus that first turned positive in 1969 (Sagami 1982).[30]

After an initial revaluation of the yen, the government resisted further revaluations. Exporters, including small businesses, vigorously opposed yen revaluation for balance of payment adjustments, and both the ruling LDP and the opposition parties were highly responsive to these domestic preferences (Kojo 1996).

---

30. From the "Nixon Shock" of August 1971 until the transition to a floating exchange rate system in February 1973, the ten leading industrialized nations including Japan negotiated the so-called Smithsonian agreement. This agreement established a temporary fixed exchange rate system at a devalued dollar rate, which inevitably led to a revaluation of the yen. This agreement, however, did not last long and was followed by the collapse of the Bretton Woods fixed exchange rate system.

Accordingly, the government pledged to reject any further revaluation during this period (McKinnon and Ohno 1997). During the early phase of the post–Bretton Woods floating exchange rate system, the government had the BOJ intervene in the foreign exchange market by purchasing large amounts of US dollars to control yen appreciation. The Japanese government's intervention, however, came under international criticism as a "dirty float" intended as currency manipulation, which forced the Japanese government to shift course.

The transition to a floating exchange rate reoriented the politics of monetary policy. Under domestic political pressure to avoid yen appreciation and external pressure not to intervene in the foreign exchange rate market, the government relied heavily on expansionary macroeconomic policy for payments adjustment (Nakagawa 1981). Fiscal expansion in particular was the policy instrument of choice; in the three consecutive fiscal years from April 1971 through March 1973, the national budget grew far more than it had in the preceding period. Despite this effort to inflate the economy to bring down its balance of payments surplus, Japan's surplus continued to increase into 1972. This was partly due to the J-curve effect, where the trade balance correction lags behind the foreign exchange rate adjustment because of the temporary increase in the value, but not volume, of exports from the surplus country. The US government also tried to carry out multilateral currency adjustment by urging Japan and the European countries to readjust their foreign exchange rate, but the effort had limited impact.

Expansionary macroeconomic policy as an alternative to yen revaluation continued to be the preferred route, even when the domestic economy recovered in early 1972 and the WPI started to climb rapidly after the summer of 1972. Given the domestic preferences, the political parties all acquiesced to the government's choice of expansionary policy as a means of balance of payments adjustment even if it meant tolerating greater inflation. MITI (Ministry of International Trade and Industry) minister Nakasone Yasuhiro made this point explicitly at a meeting with business leaders, stating that if he had to choose between further revaluation and controlled inflation, he preferred controlled inflation.[31] Prime Minister Tanaka Kakuei (July 1972–September 1974), who supported a major regional development plan called "Transforming the Japanese Archipelago," also advocated an expansionary policy; he argued that fear of rising prices should not prevent the use of expansionary policy.[32] Opposition parties demanding increases in welfare spending supported expansionary policy, as did labor groups calling for higher wages.

---

31. "Nenkan 5-okudoru chikaku kuroji wo sakugen" [Nearly 500 million dollar reduction of surplus for a year], *Nihon Keizai Shimbun*, August 16, 1972.

32. "Shushō kishakaiken no naiyō" [Prime Minister press conference], *Nihon Keizai Shimbun*, October 1, 1972.

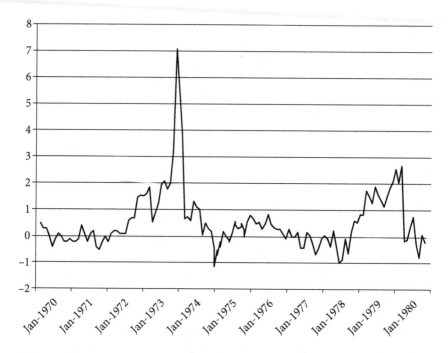

FIGURE 4.2.   Monthly percentage change in wholesale price index: 1970–1975

The BOJ came under political pressure to support this policy course and was forced to lower the discount rate.[33] The BOJ's expansionary monetary policy, along with the first oil shock, led to the "wild inflation" of 1973–74. As inflation spiraled out of control, starting in 1973 the BOJ raised the discount rate five times. The rate reached 9 percent, the highest rate in the postwar period, although in real terms the rate was negative.

The experience of "wild inflation" was a critical juncture that caused a paradigm shift in the BOJ's monetary policy thinking.[34] Some prominent economists, such as Komiya Ryūtarō, criticized BOJ's loose monetary policy prior to the oil shock as the fundamental cause of the inflation in 1974 (Komiya 1988). BOJ governor Morinaga Tei'ichirō (1974–79), a former MOF vice minister, led an effort to examine the source of the policy failure. Before the "wild inflation" episode, the BOJ did not focus on the relationship between money supply growth and inflation. Although a visit by Milton Friedman to Japan in 1963 stimulated

---

33. "The BOJ," *Nihon Ginkō Hyakunenshi*, vol. 6, 308–10.

34. When policies fail is a prime time for policy entrepreneurs to suggest alternatives (King 2005). Critical junctures like these can cause a paradigm shift (Marcussen 2005).

interest among some BOJ officials,[35] the BOJ did not apply monetarist theory. Instead, the BOJ continued to focus closely on the WPI and paid little attention to money supply growth. The study led by Morinaga noted that in the run-up to the "wild inflation" the money supply began expanding as early as 1971; by contrast, the WPI began increasing only in 1972. After the study, the BOJ shifted its monetary policy to focus on slowing money supply growth and achieving greater price stability (Suzuki 1993). To implement this new approach, the BOJ began announcing estimates of the growth rate of the money supply at the beginning of every quarter, referencing data it had collected.[36]

Morinaga's leadership played an important role in the paradigm shift to a "money-focused" monetary policy as well. But it was the bitter experience of "wild inflation" that prompted the public, including the media, to appreciate the need for price stability.[37] Public consensus provided the political support for the BOJ's paradigm shift in monetary policy.

The consensus that the policy failure was due in part to political pressure led to greater support for the BOJ and higher de facto independence. BOJ governor Sasaki Tadashi (1969–74), regarded as a "prince" of the BOJ, was criticized for not opposing pressure from Prime Minister Tanaka Kakuei, who had pushed for expansionary policy. After the 1970s, informal networks also improved relations between the BOJ and the government and provided the BOJ with a greater measure of independence. During this period, many BOJ governors were influential in policy debates with the government. During the 1950s, BOJ governor Ichimada (1946–54), with his deep relationship with politicians, was a case in point (Yoshino 2014, 346). In the late 1970s and early 1980s, Governor Morinaga Tei'ichirō (1974–79), a former vice minister of the MOF, and Governor Maekawa Haruo (1979–84), who had spent his career at the BOJ, both maintained close personal relationships with Prime Minister Ōhira Masayoshi (1978–80). These relationships helped Morinaga and Maekawa persuade the government to swiftly carry out monetary tightening (Suzuki 2014, 465–67), as discussed below.

After 1976, Japan's (as well as Germany's) increasing balance of payments surplus became a major international economic issue. In principle, with the transition to a flexible exchange rate, balance of payment adjustments should have occurred automatically via changes in exchange rates. As the exchange rate of the surplus country strengthens relative to the currency of the deficit country, trade imbalances would be reduced automatically. As early as the mid-1970s, it

---

35. "The BOJ," *Nihon Ginkō Chōsa Geppō*, October 1963, 1–18; Kure 1981.

36. "The BOJ," *Nihon Ginkō Chōsa Geppō*, 1–11.

37. Since Governor Morinaga tried to release the information of discussion within the BOJ with the slogan of "Open the BOJ," it has been easier for the BOJ to get public support for price stability (Kamikawa 2005).

became apparent, however, that this mechanism was not working. Japanese trade surpluses generated yen appreciation relative to the dollar, but despite yen appreciation, the balance of payments did not adjust. Increasingly, the uneven current account balance among industrial states began to be recognized as a global problem.[38] In particular, Japan and Germany accumulated larger balance of payment surpluses relative to the United States. In response, the United States intensified demands on Japan (and Germany) to take measures to restore balance, and in 1978 Japan agreed to stimulate its domestic economy at the G-7 Bonn Summit.

The government began to consider additional expansionary measures in order to avoid further yen appreciation, but Governor Morinaga resisted; he argued that it would be better for Japan to accept the possibility of a stronger yen than risk hyperinflation.[39] Then, in facing the second oil shock of 1979, the BOJ quickly responded by raising the discount rate three times that year. The BOJ's swift decision reflected its new conviction that even in recession, monetary tightening was necessary to avoid a repeat of "wild inflation."[40]

The next BOJ governor, Maekawa, who succeeded Morinaga, took a similar stance based on his view that the BOJ's policy failures had led to the "wild inflation." The BOJ raised the discount rate in 1980 to restrain inflation in the aftermath of the second oil shock. Governor Maekawa asked Prime Minister Ōhira to allow the BOJ to raise the discount rate in the midst of budget deliberations in the Diet. This was the first case of the BOJ attempting to change the discount rate when the Diet was debating the budget, as the government traditionally had avoided such a practice out of fear that such change would negatively influence budget bill deliberations. The MOF opposed the BOJ's request due to concern that a discount rate hike would delay passage of the budget.[41] Given the new consensus on price stability after the "wild inflation" scare, however, Governor Maekawa successfully persuaded Prime Minister Ōhira in person. In early 1980, faced with growing inflation, the BOJ tightened monetary policy, and inflation subsided by May of that year. As a result of greater de facto independence and the BOJ's record of price stability after the late 1970s, the debate over legal independence largely faded.

---

38. As discussed in chapter 2, the impossible trinity (otherwise known as "trilemma" or "unholy trinity") is a macroeconomic condition where a country can effectively attain only two of the three policy goals: capital mobility, stable foreign exchange rate, and macroeconomic policy autonomy. In increasing capital mobility from the late 1960s, it became difficult to attain both a stable foreign exchange rate and macroeconomic policy autonomy.

39. "The BOJ," *Nihon Ginkō Hyakunenshi*, vol. 6, 490.

40. This conviction was expressed in the letter that BOJ governor Morinaga wrote to Prime Minister Fukuda Takeo around April 1978 (The BOJ, *Nihon Ginkō Hyakunenshi*, vol. 6, 491, 500).

41. Ibid., vol. 6, 509–12.

The BOJ's experience with "wild inflation" played a critical role in the evolution of its policy ideas. It reinforced the belief that the BOJ should be vigilant in policing price stability and also brought home the need to look beyond price indexes, such as the WPI, and to watch the money supply more carefully. While greater political support for BOJ autonomy allowed it to reflect these ideas in its policy, economic and political changes soon created a very different policymaking context, one in which the BOJ once again came under greater pressure to cooperate with the government's goals.

The Bubble Economy and Aftermath

In the late 1980s, Japan's macroeconomic policy was constrained by three factors: current account adjustment, yen appreciation, and the government's commitment to fiscal reform; collectively these pressures pushed the Japanese government to rely more on monetary easing. With the yen strengthening against the dollar and persistent balance of payment surpluses with the United States, the Japanese government confronted growing pressure on two fronts. First, the United States continued to apply direct pressure on Japan to do more to address Japan's large imbalances: take measures to strengthen the yen and to stimulate domestic demand. Second, in the context of yen appreciation relative to the US dollar, domestic pressure for economic stimulus that would offset the effects of yen appreciation intensified. Due to the government's renewed commitment to fiscal discipline, the BOJ came under especially intense pressure to pursue monetary easing as the government sought to avoid fiscal stimulus. Ultimately, the BOJ complied.

From the perspective of the BOJ, excessively loose monetary policy fed the now famous asset bubble of the late 1980s. The bursting of the economic bubble ushered in Japan's "lost decade," a period of prolonged recession and a drawn-out financial crisis that was not resolved until the early 2000s. The experience further reinforced for the BOJ the danger of excessive money supply expansion, the need to watch prices—including asset prices—vigilantly, and once again the dangers of capitulating to political pressure.

Bubble Economy in the Late 1980s

The aggregate current account deficits of the OECD countries as a whole shrank in 1981 for a while, only to increase sharply in 1984. The uneven current account positions between the United States on the one hand and Japan and Germany on the other re-emerged as a major problem by 1985. In response to US pressure, the Plaza Accord of 1985 committed Japan and other countries to a realignment of exchange rates, specifically appreciating their currencies relative to the dollar. To counter the effect of yen appreciation on the Japanese economy, the government pursued an expansionary monetary policy, which contributed to the unprecedented asset-price inflation of the late 1980s (Ueda 1992b).

Until the Plaza Accord, the exchange rate movements among major currencies widened payment imbalances instead of eliminating them. The US dollar appreciated from 1980 through 1985, while the yen and the Deutsche mark depreciated against the dollar. Despite its current account and trade deficits, the continued appreciation of the dollar led the US to acknowledge that its policy contributed to these imbalances; high interest rates in the US contributed to a strong dollar, which in turn exacerbated its balance of payment problems (Volcker and Gyohten 1992).

After the Plaza Accord, the yen started to appreciate sharply. The MOF and the BOJ preferred realignment of exchange rates for payments adjustment, rather than expansionary macroeconomic policy.[42] The government's strong yen policy after the Plaza Accord was therefore welcomed by the MOF and the BOJ (Funabashi 1989, 95; Ito, Koike, and Shizume 2015, 96). Indeed, the BOJ had worried that the government would respond to US pressure to reduce balance of payment surpluses by leaning on the BOJ to ease monetary policy. To pre-empt this, BOJ governor Sumita Satoshi (1984–89), a former vice minister of the MOF, signaled his unwillingness to go along with any such plan by suggesting a possible future interest hike.[43]

As the yen continued to appreciate after 1986, demand from businesses and political parties to control yen appreciation intensified (Kojo 2002), and the BOJ agreed that the yen had appreciated excessively (Ito, Koike, and Shizume 2015, 99). The BOJ lowered the discount rate three times in 1986 from 5.0 percent to 3.5 percent to offset yen appreciation.

After the early 1980s, the government committed to fiscal consolidation under the banner of its self-described policy of "fiscal reconstruction without a tax hike." Under this policy, the MOF avoided expansionary fiscal policy for balance of payment adjustment. Instead, the MOF intervened in the foreign exchange market by buying dollars to stabilize the exchange rate. The US government nonetheless continued to pressure the Japanese government to implement expansionary macroeconomic policy to address bilateral trade imbalances. In response to this pressure, the government formed a committee led by former BOJ governor Maekawa to identify a new growth model. The resulting "Maekawa Report" outlined an economic strategy that would rely on spurring greater domestic consumption so as to reduce excessive dependence on external demand.

---

42. "The BOJ," *Nihon Ginkō Chosa Geppo*, May 1985, 25.

43. This statement was regarded as an unusual comment by the BOJ governor ("Shimbun no mōten" [Blind spot of newspapers], *Kin'yu zaisei jijō*, October 14, 1985: 12–13).

The Japanese government agreed with the US to stimulate domestic demand, and the BOJ lowered the discount rate again to 3.0 percent. In January 1987, however, the yen started to appreciate sharply once again. The yen appreciation sparked domestic criticism that the government seemed unable to stabilize the exchange rate. The political debate led to a stronger government commitment to stop yen appreciation (Kojo 1996). The BOJ lowered the discount rate again to 2.5 percent, a historic low at the time (February 1987), largely as a measure to stabilize the exchange rate. Trying to draw a line in the sand, Governor Sumita declared that it would be difficult for the BOJ to lower the discount rate further.[44]

The G-5 Louvre Accord in February 1987 acknowledged the desirability of stabilizing the exchange rates at current levels. Surplus countries would commit to stimulating their domestic economies, and the deficit countries would address the domestic policies that contributed to their imbalances. The Japanese government was initially reluctant to apply expansionary fiscal measures even after the Louvre Accord. As pressure for greater fiscal stimulus from political parties and exporters intensified, the government shelved its fiscal consolidation plan and shifted to fiscal stimulus.

Financial turmoil after Black Monday in October 1987 led to further yen appreciation. After the spring of 1988, however, the yen began to depreciate relative to the dollar. As its trade deficit eased, the United States also moderated demands for exchange rate realignment and expansionary macroeconomic policy, but it continued to apply pressure on Japan to decrease its trade surplus by passing a new trade law in 1988. Japan's current account surplus finally decreased from 1988 to 1991, and the yen depreciated. In May 1989, after an interval of two years and three months, the BOJ raised the discount rate to 3.25 percent.

The BOJ's Perspective Facing the Bubble in the Late 1980s

The BOJ was uncomfortably aware of the excessive money supply and rising asset prices as early as 1986.[45] But not only was it unable to decide on a discount rate hike, it was also pressured to lower the discount rate three times in 1986 to avoid further yen appreciation following the 1985 Plaza Accord. The MOF focused on fiscal austerity policy to restore budget balance, while the BOJ remained cautious about further monetary easing. The BOJ hoped that yen appreciation would improve the terms of trade, enhance private consumption, phase out inefficient industries, and expand domestic investment (Itō, Koike, and Shizume 2015, 117–18). Stable

---

44. This statement by Governor Sumita was regarded as an unusual comment for the BOJ governor (*Kin'yū zaisei jijō*, October 14, 1985: 12–13).

45. The BOJ officially expressed its concern over rising price of land and increasing money supply in 1987 and stated that monetary policy should be applied for price stability ("The BOJ," *Nihon Ginkō Chōsa Geppō*, October 1987, 14–26).

wholesale prices after 1986 and concern that yen appreciation might lead to a recession made it difficult for the BOJ to raise the discount rate.[46] After Black Monday in October 1987, the BOJ could not raise the discount rate because of the government's priority on international policy coordination; it maintained its low interest rate throughout 1988 despite its original plan to raise the discount rate (Ohta 1991).[47] Despite the BOJ's concern over excessive money supply and rising asset prices, a MOF official stated that there was no problem with Japan's macroeconomic conditions since the CPI remained stable. The MOF at the time was still committed to fiscal consolidation and thus worried that monetary tightening might increase government pressure for expansionary fiscal policy (Karube 2015).[48]

Deputy Governor Mieno Yasushi resisted lowering the discount rate further because he thought it would prioritize international concerns at the expense of domestic considerations, especially price stability. By contrast, officials in the BOJ's international division showed greater sensitivity to requests for international cooperation (Ohta 1991; Ogata 1996; Karube and Nishino 1999; Kosai, Shirakawa, and Okina 2001; Karube 2015). In the media, the so-called Japan anchor theory (*nihon ankā ron*), which called for Japan to play a global role in maintaining low interest rates in order to stabilize international financial markets, grew in influence.[49]

In early 1989, the BOJ started to warn of signs of inflation and stressed the importance of price stability for the financial system, implying the necessity of tighter monetary policy.[50] As land prices increased, the MOF, in particular the Banking Bureau, began to recognize signs of inflation and allowed the BOJ to raise the discount rate, although the BOJ deemed the move to be too late.[51]

After the Bubble

The BOJ continued its monetary tightening until July 1991, raising the discount rate five times, from 2.5 percent to 6.0 percent, and at times generating conflict with the government. From 1989 to 1991, the stock market contracted

---

46. Aoki Akira, former executive director of the BOJ, interview (Economic and Social Research Institution 2011, 582–83).

47. Former BOJ director Aoki stated that Miyazawa, the finance minister, had firm policy orientation to comply with the agreement of G5 and G7 and resisted raising the discount rate (Economic and Social Research Institution 2011, 564); Governor Sumita, former governor, interview, *AERA*, March 13, 1990, 6.

48. Gyōhten Toyoo, former MOF vice minister of finance for international affairs, pointed out the firm commitment of the government to fiscal reform and stated that the government relied heavily on monetary policy in the late 1980s (Economic and Social Research Institution 2011, 512–13).

49. Former BOJ officials pointed out that the domestic thinking was going against the BOJ (Economic and Social Research Institution 2011, 513, 616–17).

50. "The BOJ," *Nihon Ginkō Chōsa Geppō* February 1989, 1–29.

51. Aoki Akira, former director of the BOJ, interview (Economic and Social Research Institution 2011, 589–90).

by 60 percent and land prices declined sharply. The BOJ's firm policy stance was supported initially by the public, which was concerned about rising land prices. But as the economy fell into recession in 1993 and 1994, people's concerns shifted quickly to the economic slump and the question of whether the BOJ's monetary policy could sufficiently stimulate it. Although the BOJ cut the discount rate nine times from 1991 to 1995 to stimulate the economy, it was criticized for being slow to reflate the economy as the recession dragged on. In 1993, the LDP lost political power for the first time since 1955, ushering in a period of relatively rapid turnover of prime ministers. Faced with a non-performing loan problem and recession, prime ministers during early 1990s focused on structural reform such as deregulation to revive the economy rather than macroeconomic policy (Wakatabe 2015).

The BOJ's Perspective in the 1990s

In April 1990, the BOJ officially admitted that expansionary monetary policy contributed to the spike in land prices.[52] Governor Mieno Yasushi (1989–94) emphasized the BOJ's responsibility for price stability, which he argued contributed to international economic growth. Although he acknowledged the importance of adjusting current account imbalances for the sake of international cooperation, he viewed price stability as essential for the health of the domestic economy.[53] From the BOJ's perspective, interest rate cuts and monetary base growth over the 1990s showed that the BOJ was doing as much as possible but that ultimately these measures also demonstrated the limits of monetary easing in reviving the economy (Bernanke 1999). Reflecting the evolving "BOJ Theory," the BOJ believed that the problem of the slow expansion of the money supply (despite monetary base growth) was due to two factors: (a) the banks were reluctant to lend, and (b) there was a shortage of demand for capital (Kawakita 1995, 154).

The failure of two financial institutions—Yamaichi Securities and Hokkaidō Takushoku Bank—created a credit crunch that led to weakening demand from 1997 to 2000. Despite calls by politicians for more monetary easing to stimulate the economy,[54] the BOJ insisted that the effectiveness of monetary policy was limited. Rather than viewing Japan's economic problem as one of an output gap, the BOJ believed it was Japan's economic fundamentals such as the demography,

---

52. "The BOJ," *Nihon Ginkō Chōsa Geppō*, April 1990, 34–85.

53. Governor Mieno, speech, February 1, 1990 ("The BOJ," *Nihon Ginkō Chōsa Geppō*, February 1990, 30–41).

54. Kanamaru Shin, vice president of the LDP, stated that if the BOJ governor did not obey the prime minister's policy, the government should fire him to lower the discount rate and boost the economy (*AERA*, March 10, 1992, 67).

capital stock, and growth in total factor productivity that predominantly determined an economy's growth potential (Shirakawa 2008, 194). The negative effect
of asset-price deflation on Japan's financial system during this period raised serious concerns about the stability of Japan's financial institutions. Japanese banks,
once regarded as the most secure in the world under the MOF-led "convoy system," were quickly downgraded by credit rating agencies, and a spreading non-
performing loan problem paralyzed the economy.

Many now regard the period from the emergence of the bubble through the
aftermath of its collapse as the BOJ's biggest monetary policy failure (Nishimura
1999; Suzuki 1993). This experience reinforced for the BOJ the importance of
price stability, including asset prices. This fear of asset inflation in particular has
led the BOJ to embrace a view that is quite similar to the so-called BIS view
(Okina 2009; Umeda 2011, 242). The BIS view tends to be skeptical of central
banks' ability to use monetary policy to balance full employment and inflation.
The BIS view instead underscores the risks to excessive monetary easing, namely
the creation of financial imbalances that can lead to bubbles and financial crises. From this perspective, central banks should act pre-emptively to avoid the
buildup of such bubbles.

The experience of the "bubble economy" and its collapse also rekindled
the debate over central bank independence. The BOJ's slowness in raising the
discount rate in the face of the "bubble economy" was attributed to its political dependence. When requests for international coordination conflicted with
domestic economic goals in the 1980s, the government and the MOF prioritized
international policy coordination, while the BOJ attempted to forestall monetary
easing. Governor Mieno believed that BOJ independence was essential to sound
monetary policy, and he regarded securing independence as the most important
priority for the succeeding governor (Mieno 1999).

This chapter has traced the evolution of the BOJ's policy ideas: its strong prioriti-
zation of price stability, its skeptical view of the efficaciousness of monetary policy, abiding concern that monetary easing could unleash negative side effects, and
a deep belief that independence should be maintained at all cost. It is not a much
of a leap to understand how these policy ideas colored the BOJ's attitude toward
quantitative easing. QE represented an assault on virtually its entire worldview.
By blurring the line between the BOJ and the government's fiscal affairs, QE
threatened the BOJ's independence. Indeed, this is what happened under Japan's
military regime, which forced the BOJ to underwrite its spending, an episode
that the BOJ's own historical account describes as one its biggest failures. QE
also harked back to policies that sparked inflation, not just during wartime, but

also immediately after the war, when the BOJ's purchase of bonds issued by the government's Reconstruction Finance Bank contributed to hyperinflation. The 1970s' "wild inflation" reinforced for the BOJ the need to focus on the money supply and not just on price levels, as did the experience of the bubble, when asset prices inflated even as the price of goods and services remained moderate. Lastly, QE represented to the BOJ the kind of activist monetary policy it had come to believe was not effective in stimulating the economy but that might have adverse effects such as sparking runaway inflation, an idea that became encapsulated in the so-called BOJ Theory. As we discuss in the later chapters, this notion was further reinforced by the BOJ's own dubious conclusion that its first experiment with QE was largely ineffective.

While many of these events occurred long ago, they very much informed the view of the BOJ until Kuroda took over as governor. Adam Posen—an economist from the Peterson Institute for International Economics with extensive contact with the BOJ over the years—made the following observation about why the BOJ was reluctant to accept QE:

> The other big historical memory of the Bank of Japan was of course the pre-war monetary financing of the government deficit forced under the military regime. And, again we can debate intellectually how much that really should have been relevant to the Japan of 1990 or right up to 2000 as a democracy of sixty plus years standing. Nonetheless, that was very totemic for the Bank of Japan leadership and many mid-level Bank of Japan staff and other people associated with the Bank of Japan that I encountered through the years. And so, akin to some of the people from the Bundesbank and other places in Europe. . . . they saw the risk of monetary financing on every corner and viewed it as in almost Christian terms, you know, Christian damnation terms.[55]

The analytic question that must be addressed, then, is how these ideas were reproduced, institutionalized, and ultimately reflected in a formally independent Policy Board's decisions. This is the subject of the next chapter.

---

55. Adam Posen, former member of the Monetary Policy Committee, Bank of England, and president of the Peterson Institute for International Economics, in discussion with the author, October 7, 2017.

Chapter 5

THE MONETARY POLICY NETWORK

> As the BOJ's monetary policy attracts increasing attention and as
> I see exchanges between the BOJ and the economists around the
> world, I become intensely concerned that it is not Japan that is alien
> (*nihon ishitsu ron*), but it is the BOJ (*nichigin ishitsu ron*)
>
> —Nakahara Nobuyuki, August 11, 2000

The New BOJ Law, which came into effect in April 1998, transformed the institutional structure of policymaking. The BOJ occupied a central position in a closed monetary policy network, which allowed the BOJ worldview described in the previous chapter to prevail for the next fifteen years, despite ongoing bouts of deflation, financial crises, domestic political pressure, and the wider diffusion of unconventional monetary policies among the advanced economies. In this chapter, we explain the institutional basis for how the BOJ's worldview continued to influence monetary policy. The first section explains the origin and key reforms of the New BOJ Law that created a new institutional context for monetary policymaking. The next sections elaborate how, despite the formal powers granted to the Policy Board, the policy network and informal practices created an institutional bias that privileged the BOJ orthodox view. In the last section of the chapter, we contrast the monetary policy network in Japan with those in other contexts (United States, United Kingdom, Eurozone, and Sweden) to highlight the specific aspects that made Japan's network closed.

Epigraph: Nakahara's comment as the BOJ decided to lift the ZIRP. BOJ transcript from the August 11, 2000 Board meeting, p. 112 (translation by the author).

The New Bank of Japan Law of 1997:
A New Beginning for the Bank of Japan

The Japanese government established a new policymaking structure and de jure central bank independence with the New BOJ Law, which passed the legislature in June 1997 and came into effect in April 1998. Although one of the rationales for legal independence, at least according to the theory of central bank independence (CBI) discussed in chapter 3, is inflation control, the BOJ's transition to independence in the late 1990s was not attributable to high inflation, nor to monetary policy failures, nor to a push by the BOJ for policy autonomy. At the time of the deliberation and passage of the New BOJ Law, Japan was in fact experiencing very low inflation, which then turned to deflation by the latter half of 1998. The BOJ's monetary policy track record did come under criticism during the 1990s, with some experts arguing that the BOJ's extremely loose monetary policy during the latter half of the 1980s after the Plaza Accord fed the asset bubble, and that the BOJ was too slow to lower rates as the bursting of the bubble gave way to recession (Posen 1998b; Ueda 2000; Grimes 2002). These critiques, however, were not a driving force behind the reform process; as Cargill, Hutchison, and Ito (2000, 112) note, "The 1998 revision had little to do with dissatisfaction over past monetary policy."

The catalyst for reform of the BOJ Law was rather the attack by Diet politicians against the MOF, which had been embroiled in several scandals and had become viewed as responsible for the country's financial malaise (Grimes 2002; van Rixtel 2002; Amyx 2004).[1] As a consequence, the government moved to strip the MOF of authority over financial policy, thereby separating monetary and fiscal authority (*zaikin bun'ri*). The financial supervisory function, embodied in the Financial Supervisory Agency (later FSA), was separated from the MOF in the same year that the New BOJ Law came into effect, though the MOF reform stopped short of taking budgeting functions away from the ministry (Park 2011; Nakakita 2001).[2] It did not help the MOF that leaders in the LDP viewed the

---

1. Kamikawa (2014, 37–46) called this a "windfall" revision for the BOJ, as the MOF scandals and political backlash against the handling of the housing loan corporation *Jūsen*'s bankruptcy in 1995 all fueled the push for MOF reform. One former BOJ official also noted that there was no push from the BOJ and that independence was in fact a "windfall." Former executive director of the BOJ, interview, Tokyo, January 29, 2016.

2. Cargill and Dwyer (2013) argue that the MOF accepted BOJ reform in an effort to avoid even worse damage to the ministry, as politicians were trying to divide its fiscal and financial responsibilities. Nakakita (2001, 68) notes that the MOF saw the loss of MOF authority over the BOJ "as a sacrificial lamb to the reform." The same point was noted by Dwyer (2004, 255).

MOF as having been too cooperative with the previous coalition government (1993–94), which had excluded the LDP (Mabuchi 1997; Cargill, Hutchison, and Ito 2000).

Following the moves to reform the MOF, a study group consisting of scholars and business executives was assembled as the prime minister's advisory body in July 1996 to deliberate the BOJ Law revision. After ten intensive sessions, the group submitted its report to Prime Minister Hashimoto in November of the same year.[3] Electoral calculations as well as the ongoing central bank reform in Europe explain the timing and the speed of the New BOJ Law's passage in the late 1990s, as the government set out to demonstrate its commitment to economic reforms that it claimed would revive the economy (Dwyer 2004, 246).

The BOJ under the New BOJ Law

The New BOJ Law laid a new institutional foundation for monetary policymaking. As discussed in chapter 4, under the 1949 revision to the BOJ Law, a Policy Board was established, but in reality the board had little power. Under the New BOJ Law, an independent Policy Board makes the final decision over Japan's monetary policy (Article 15). At the same time, the law stipulates that the BOJ "always maintain close contact with the government and exchange views sufficiently" (Article 4).

The BOJ Policy Board consists of nine members including the BOJ governor, two deputy governors, and six other members (Article 16). The first three are the "executive members" of the Policy Board heading the BOJ Secretariat (figure 5.2 below). The other six Policy Board members are considered nonexecutive members. All Policy Board members serve renewable five-year terms (Article 24.1). Candidates are nominated by the Prime Minister's Office through his cabinet and must be approved by both chambers of the Diet (Article 23. 1 and 23. 2).[4] Once appointed, the status of these board members is protected for the duration of their tenure against arbitrary dismissal (Article 25).[5]

---

3. For a detailed discussion of this study group, see Yamawaki 1998, esp. chap. 3. The final report is available at the Cabinet Office website, http://www.kantei.go.jp/jp/singi/cyugin/hokokusyo.html.

4. Unlike other legislation where a rejection by the upper house can be overturned by a two-thirds majority of the lower house, this personnel approval process will be final at the upper house.

5. Article 25 (2) specifies that the cabinet or the finance minister can remove Policy Board members if a Policy Board member (i) enters into bankruptcy, (ii) receives punishment under the BOJ Law, (iii) is sentenced to prison, or (iv) is deemed incapable by the board itself to carry out his or her duties due to mental or physical disorder.

The size of the BOJ's Policy Board is within the international norm.[6] The FRB has twelve members in its Federal Open Market Committee, while the BOE has nine and the ECB has twenty-four. The practice of deciding monetary policy by committee has become a visible global trend among the central banks in recent years (Shirakawa 2008); seventy-nine out of eighty-eight central banks surveyed by Pollard (2004) rely on committees for their monetary policymaking.[7]

The Policy Board meets twice a week on operational matters (*tsūjō kaigō*; ordinary sessions) and twice a month on important monetary matters.[8] The latter are called Monetary Policy Meetings (*kin'yū kettei kaigō*; hereafter "Policy Board meeting"). At the Policy Board meetings, the board decides on monetary policy under a majority vote system (Article 18.2), with each individual vote counted, a method similar the one taken by the BOE. Policy proposals can be submitted by the governor or any other members of the Policy Board.

With the New BOJ Law, the BOJ has acquired an explicit price stability mandate (Article 2). One ongoing debate has been over how central banks should balance this mandate with maximization of employment. In comparative terms, the FRB has the most explicit dual mandate (Federal Reserve Act section 2a), while the ECB does not have any mandate to support employment. The BOJ and the BOE sit between these two extremes, with price stability set as the immediate goal behind these central banks' contributions to employment and economic growth.[9] Although some analysts say that the BOJ is closer to having a dual mandate (Umeda 2011), critics of the BOJ insist that it only focuses on price stability and ignores the overall health of the Japanese economy.[10]

The BOJ maintains its function as a lender of last resort (Article 38) as well as the entity in charge of settlement of funds (Article 1) and handling the national government's affairs concerning currency and finance (Article 36). With the New BOJ Law, however, the BOJ's financial supervisory function was limited to "on-site" examination (*kōsa*) of financial institutions (Article 44), while other financial

---

6. In the survey conducted by Pollard (2004), out of eighty-two central banks surveyed, fifty-five banks had between five and ten board members making monetary policy decision, while nineteen had fewer and eight had more.

7. Blinder (2007, 110) argues that committee decisions are superior at least on three grounds: (a) group decision is insurance against possible extreme preferences of an individual central banker, (b) pooling knowledge should lead to better analysis, forecast, and decisions; and (c) a group of people processing information and reaching decisions differently may outperform the most intelligent individual when it comes to the execution of complex tasks.

8. The frequency of the Policy Board meetings was reduced to eight per year effective January 2016.

9. Article 2 of the New BOJ Law reads, "Currency and monetary control by the Bank of Japan shall be aimed at achieving price stability, thereby contributing to the sound development of the national economy."

10. LDP Diet member (lower house, August 1993 to present), interview, Tokyo, September 14, 2015.

TABLE 5.1   Roles and functions of the central banks

	BANK OF JAPAN	FRB	BANK OF ENGLAND	ECB
Price stability	Yes	Yes	Yes	Yes
Maximum employment	Indirectly	Yes	Indirectly	No
Settlement of funds	Yes	Yes	Yes	Yes
Lender of last resort	Yes	Yes	Yes	No
Financial supervision	No (FSA)	Yes	Yes since 2011	Yes since 2011
FX market intervention	No (MOF)	Yes (with Treasury)	Yes (with Treasury)	Yes

Source: Shirakawa (2008, 21) and Umeda (2011, 4).

supervisory work belongs to the FSA. Finally, decisions on foreign exchange market intervention are the purview of the Ministry of Finance (Article 40). Table 5.1 compares the roles and the functions of the BOJ to other central banks.

The Monetary Policy Network in Japan from 1998 to 2012

As the central actor of Japan's monetary policymaking, the Policy Board has acquired policy autonomy through the New BOJ Law. The Policy Board is nevertheless embedded in a system of formal democratic and political control as well as an informal network. The former has the potential power to channel government wishes and demands on the Policy Board, but it is the latter that has allowed the BOJ worldview to influence monetary policy from 1998 to 2012.

As shown in figure 5.1, the key groups in the policy network are the Prime Minister's Office, the Diet, the BOJ Policy Board, the Ministry of Finance (MOF), and the BOJ itself. The New BOJ Law provides four *formal ways* through which the government can influence the Policy Board. First, in accordance with the spirit of Article 4 mentioned above, the heads of ministries (or their representatives) have the right to attend the Policy Board meetings, make policy proposals at these meetings, and request postponement of votes (Article 19). This is a weak instrument of control, however. The Policy Board can overturn requests for postponement by leveraging its majority vote. This happened once when the Policy Board rejected the government's request for a postponement before its decision to end ZIRP in August 2000 (discussed further in chapter 7).

Second, the government can hold the BOJ accountable for the Policy Board's monetary policy decisions. The new law requires the BOJ and its Policy Board to explain its monetary policy directly to lawmakers (Article 54.3), and this is where the BOJ Executive Board members are directly exposed to political pressure

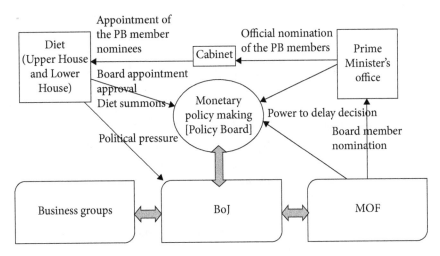

FIGURE 5.1. Monetary policymaking network

(Kamikawa 2014, 270).[11] The executive members of the board are often called upon to attend committee meetings and sessions at the two houses of the Diet.[12] Meanwhile, board members are obligated to give public speeches explaining BOJ policies. They also receive phone calls from politicians and many other types of pressure.[13] In this new context, the BOJ's relationship with the Diet and legislatures has become increasingly vital. The BOJ established a Diet Liaison Division and an office within the Diet building to keep contacts, gather information, and communicate with Diet members.[14]

---

11. Article 54 of the New BOJ Law specifies the direct reporting obligation to and attendance at the Diet on the part of the BOJ governor.

12. Hayami noted in his speech in February of 2003 that he appeared in the Diet to answer questions during his term in office (until January 2003) 382 times (http://www.boj.or.jp/en/announcements/press/koen_2003/ko0302a.htm/). Since 2002, the BOJ publicizes a list of attendance of the BOJ leadership and board members to the Diet and the Diet committees (https://www.boj.or.jp/announcements/kokkai/index.htm/). Also see Shirakawa (2008). The average number of appearances of BOJ governors at Diet sessions is between twenty and thirty per year, which far exceeds the numbers for the FRB chair or the BOE president (fewer than ten times each). "Shuyō chūgin sōsai de mottomo isogashī Kuroda shi (Mr. Kuroda is the Busiest Governor among the Major Central Bank Governors)" *Bloomberg*, June 25, 2015, http://www.bloomberg.co.jp/news/123-NQFQBZ6JIJV801.html.

13. Former BOJ Policy Board member, multiple interviews from September 2015 through April 2016.

14. This has been a new challenge for the BOJ, as it historically lacks allies among the legislators. Under the long-ruling LDP, there has never been any such thing as a *Nichigin zoku* (policy tribe in support of the Bank of Japan) that can look after its monetary policy interests and that can protect the BOJ politically (Kawakita 1995). In addition, due to lack of experience in engaging with politics, the BOJ professionals tend to be "politically tone-deaf (*seiji on'chi*)" (Kawakita 1995, 67). This is corroborated by a former executive director of the BOJ in an interview with the authors in Tokyo on January 29, 2016.

Third, the power of appointment belongs to the government (Article 23). As analyzed below, the nomination and appointment of governors and deputy governors are particularly important due to the influence of these members on the Policy Board. It is the Prime Minister's Office that decides on the nominations of these executive members, and the appointment is made by the cabinet. The role of the Diet in the appointment process depends on the composition of both chambers. Since the House of Representatives (lower house) chooses the prime minister, the prime minister typically has no problem in securing support for nominees in that chamber. In cases where the upper chamber of the Diet—the House of Councillors—is controlled by the opposition, however, it can play a decisive role in the selection process, as happened in 2008, an episode discussed in more detail below.

Finally, as a "nuclear option" beyond the controls illustrated in figure 5.1, legislatures can threaten to take away some of the BOJ's independence through legal changes to the BOJ Law. A government, for instance, might threaten to reduce the BOJ's independence by making it possible to remove the governor or other members of the Policy Board. This option has, of course, never been taken under the new law, but the idea was repeatedly floated throughout the fifteen years since 1998 as legislators expressed frustration at the BOJ's monetary policy decisions (chapter 7).

In short, the government has at least four channels of influence on the BOJ Policy Board. These formal channels of influence are only part of the picture, however. A number of informal linkages have given the BOJ organization influence over the Policy Board, and hence over monetary policy decisions. The BOJ's informal linkages are indicated by three broad arrows connecting the three principal actors in the policy network in figure 5.1: the MOF, business groups in general and the financial sector in particular, and most critically the BOJ, which formally serves under the executive leadership of the Policy Board.

The Bank of Japan

The BOJ is the central organization in the monetary policy network. Although the Policy Board formally sits atop the BOJ, it is the larger organization that is locus of the BOJ worldview discussed in the previous chapter. In practice, influence has often flowed from the organization to the Policy Board. The coherence of the BOJ's worldview in the organization is a product of practices that socialize career staff. Johnson (2016, 35) argues that expert staff who design and implement central bank training and technical assistance programs are the most important ingredient in guiding central banks' day-to-day decisions and operations.

The BOJ is a relatively small central bank with about five thousand staff members; by contrast, the Federal Reserve System altogether employs more than twenty thousand (Okina 2013).[15] The BOJ hires about forty career bankers per year, mostly from a relatively small number of elite schools.[16] In accordance with Japan's elite hiring practice, the BOJ hires recruits with bachelor's degrees in economics or law, typically without advanced degrees. The new recruits are then immersed in the BOJ's macroeconomic models through on-the-job training. The career-class recruits are trained to be generalists, and they rotate positions every two to three years (never exceeding three years in one position). The elite career path at the BOJ includes a rotation at one of the thirty-three local branch offices as well as an international position, such as at the New York office or the BIS. Some have criticized this promotion system, arguing that the frequent rotation prevents central bankers from developing into stronger economists (Yamawaki 1998, 203–4). A former BOJ staff member, Shirakawa (not the same individual as the former BOJ governor), summarized the standard rotation of a "BOJ man."

> After joining the BOJ, he works at the main office in Tokyo for one year as a trainee, then he will be sent to one of the branch offices away from Tokyo for two years. Then after taking a one-month brush-up course on economics, he comes back to the main office. After a few years, some would pass the selection to go study abroad. . . . In his seventh to eight year, he will be seen as a full-fledged '*Nichigin-man* (BOJ man)' and start working at different positions as a group head . . . [if he is successful as the head of these groups], in about 20 years, he becomes division chief, and in 25 to 30 years, he gets sent to be a Branch Manager. . . . Some of the rotations include the OECD or the BIS, or attending to the Governors (Shirakawa 2014, 32–33).[17]

The BOJ's promotion system has been faulted for fostering "yes men" and creating an atmosphere of deference and ingratiation rather than an environment of open discussion and constructive criticism (Yamawaki 1998, 216).

In the process of socialization and training, the BOJ tends to favor the worldview and practices it has developed during its own institutional history over

---

15. When one standardizes this per one million population, setting Japan as 1, the FRB in the United States has 1.79 times as many staff members, and Europe (adding all the European central banks including the ECB) has 3.8 (Okina 2013).

16. The four universities where most of the new recruits come from are the University of Tokyo, Hitotsubashi University, Keio University, and Kyoto University (van Rixtel 2002, 127).

17. Translation by the author.

economic theory; there is a prevailing sense that general economic theories are overly simplistic, too rigid and unchanging to apply to an ever-moving monetary reality.[18] Furthermore, as a former BOJ official notes, there is a strong sense of distinction between "insiders" and "outsiders" in the BOJ.[19] It is this prevailing worldview regarding the key priorities and appropriate instruments of monetary policy that characterizes the elite BOJ "insiders." Among the "insiders," there is a tendency toward groupthink that increases as group cohesiveness intensifies (Janis 1982).[20] The BOJ structures and practices enhance such cohesiveness and ensure the reproduction and continuity of its worldview.

The "insider" mentality is nurtured in various ways. As described above, the BOJ promotes generalists over those with more specialized training and research backgrounds, and most of the BOJ officials are trained on the job. Some BOJ officials are sent to graduate programs, often abroad, typically for master's degrees in economics or MBA degrees but occasionally for PhDs, although the number is relatively low, about ten to fifteen people per year (Shirakawa 2014). The influence of those who return with doctorates tends to be confined since those with PhDs are concentrated in the BOJ-affiliated think tank—the IMES—that is kept separate from the policymaking apparatus. There have been some exceptions, notably Okina Kunio, who received a PhD in economics from University of Chicago. He became quite influential within the BOJ and articulated the "BOJ Theory" discussed in the previous chapter that suggested that monetary base expansion would not be effective in stimulating the economy.[21]

Furthermore, as one former BOJ official noted, BOJ researchers typically do not necessarily aspire to rise within the ranks of the BOJ[22] but instead often aim

---

18. Fujii (2004) notes that Governor Hayami commented during the board member study group that formal models might work for the ivory tower, but they are useless in understanding real-world monetary policy. A prominent Japanese economist, Komiya (1988), also argues that the BOJ has a tendency to disregard abstract economic theories. He summarizes that the BOJ's decisions have been based on its local logic, arising from members' accumulated knowledge and experiences as well as their understanding of patterns. A former executive director of the BOJ, interview with the authors, Tokyo, January 28, 2016.

19. A former BOJ official, interview, Tokyo, January 27, 2016.

20. Janis (1982, 9) defines groupthink as "a mode of thinking that people engage in when they are deeply involved in a cohesive in-group when the members' striving for unanimity overrides their motivation to realistically appraise alternative courses of action."

21. The BOJ economists who earn PhDs in economics have an "exit option" advantage (an option of becoming a scholar in academia), which reduces their incentive to follow the tight institutional control over research by the BOJ. A former BOJ official and a prominent economist, interview, Tokyo, January 27, 2016.

22. One of the former BOJ economists who moved to the academia noted that there was heavy control over what he could publish and that only about 20 percent of his original work could be made public. A former BOJ official, interview, September 9, 2016.

to become university professors. Hence, rather than drawing from the ranks of professors, the BOJ tends to spin off its own researchers into these positions.[23] The BOJ has extensive in-house data-gathering, data-analysis, and research functions. These functions were enhanced between 2002 and 2004 to strengthen control over information and therefore its ability to shape the debate and engage with the government (Bank of Japan 2004, 173–75; Lukauskas and Shimabukuro 2006, 150).

Moreover, the BOJ also has power to control who becomes "extended insiders" in the BOJ among Japanese economists. The BOJ determines whom to involve in prestigious BOJ research collaboration projects by providing research funding and lecture/conference invitations to those academics who have supportive views on monetary policy.[24] The BOJ also hosts a large annual conference on monetary policy—the Kin'yū Gakkai—and reportedly those who are seen as hostile to the BOJ view might not be invited to speak.[25] Those who take positions outside the BOJ mainstream may also no longer be invited to luncheons or lectures or receive invitations to other international seminars.[26] The IMES, the BOJ's think tank, invites outside scholars as affiliated researchers, and through these invitations it can promote scholars aligned with its worldview. Even foreign scholars who voice critical opinions on BOJ policy may become *personae non grata* for research collaboration.[27] It should be noted that there is some suspicion of foreign scholars, particularly Americans. There is a view within the BOJ that if Japan had not heeded US calls for monetary easing after the Plaza Accord of 1985 that the bubble and its consequences might have been avoided. Some believe this is a major part of why the BOJ has been so reluctant to take advice from Americans.[28]

---

23. House of Councillors member from the DPJ, who had previously been a BOJ official, interview, September 16, 2015.

24. Honda Etsurō, former MOF official and former adviser to Prime Minister Abe, in discussion with the authors, Tokyo, September 18, 2015.

25. A Yale Economist, a vocal critique of the BOJ, and one of the most important monetary policy advisers to the Abe administration, Hamada Kōichi (2012), notes that many Japanese economists are reluctant to criticize the BOJ and its monetary policies. He suspects that these economists worry that if they are too critical they might not be selected as a Policy Board member someday, might not be invited as one of the lecturers at the BOJ training sessions, might lose the opportunities to be invited to the BOJ conferences, or their students might not gain employment at the BOJ.

26. Honda Etsurō, former MOF official and former adviser to Prime Minister Abe, in discussion with author, Tokyo, September 18, 2015. Nakahara Nobuyuki, former BOJ Policy Board member, in discussion with author, September 14, 2016.

27. But apparently it is not only the BOJ that implements such exclusion. Conti-Brown (2016, 92) reports a high-profile American case where the Nobel Laureate Paul Krugman was shunned from the FRB's Jackson Hole conferences for a decade because of his criticism of Alan Greenspan.

28. Adam Posen, former member of the Monetary Policy Committee, Bank of England, and president of the Peterson Institute for International Economics, in discussion with the author, October 7, 2017.

The BOJ and the MOF

The link between the BOJ and the MOF constitutes a critical component of the monetary policy network. As discussed in chapter 4, the relationship between the MOF and the BOJ has been a long and fraught one in which the MOF and the BOJ battled for institutional control over monetary policy. They also have come into conflict over the specific direction of policy including after the establishment of de jure independence. Furthermore, the BOJ and the MOF, along with the FSA, over which the MOF has influence, have had differences at times over the appropriate policy course for stabilizing the financial sector.

There have been, however, informal practices that have fostered coordination. The BOJ and the MOF rotate personnel between the two institutions. At the top level, prior to the New BOJ Law, high-ranking MOF officials rotated into some of the BOJ's most prestigious positions, through *amakudari* from the rotating governorship to executive director positions (van Rixtel 2002, 129). At a more junior level, those BOJ officials who are the cream of the crop may be seconded to work at the MOF and to the FSA, and vice versa. This practice, which has continued after 1998,[29] has been considered a way to nurture the connection between the two institutions (Yamawaki 1998, 113). While the New BOJ Law ended the MOF's official control over the BOJ's monetary policymaking,[30] the MOF still maintains certain powers of approval over the BOJ in areas such as operations (Articles 7 and 11), budget (Article 52), and private financial business other than what is defined in the New BOJ Law (Article 43).[31]

Despite the rivalry and differences in policy priorities, the views of the BOJ and the MOF toward the potential use of large-scale unconventional monetary policy such as QE (and inflation targeting) were largely aligned prior to Governor Kuroda. From the MOF's perspective, there are several reasons why it agreed with the BOJ's resistance to unconventional policy. This convergence of views had the effect of amplifying the influence of the BOJ worldview, at least until Abenomics.

First, the MOF has worried about the loss of fiscal discipline through the monetization of government debt (i.e., the purchase of debt by a central bank) that would result from the BOJ aggressively using QE.[32] Given Japan's chronic budget deficits and high level of government debt during this period, from the

---

29. A former BOJ staff member, interview, Tokyo, January 19, 2016.

30. Heckel (2014, 199) argues that there was a "single principal-agent relationship between the MOF and BOJ before the revision, where the MOF had power to approve the budget, over BOJ operation as well as appointment of governor."

31. We thank the staff of the Committee Department of the Secretariat of the House of Representative, Shōji Keishi, for detailed explanation of the legal foundation of the MOF jurisdiction over the BOJ.

32. Yosano Kaoru, former minister of finance and minister of state, in discussion with the author, January 20, 2016.

view of the MOF, monetization would undermine any attempt to achieve fiscal discipline.

Second, the MOF has also been concerned about the inflationary consequences of excessive easing, which might push up the interest rate of JGBs and raise the servicing costs of Japan's huge debt, the largest in the industrialized world. This fear of rising interest payments on JGBs was the major reason why the MOF also opposed using an inflation target and supported the stance of the BOJ governors from 1998 through 2012. As discussed in chapter 2, however, others point out that inflation and economic growth should improve a country's fiscal position by generating greater revenue.[33]

Third, the BOJ and the MOF also viewed large-scale QE with caution due to concerns about financial losses that might accrue to the BOJ's balance sheet. Under the New BOJ Law, profits from the BOJ's monetary policy operations are transferred to the MOF (Article 53). On the one hand, the BOJ's power of seigniorage (i.e., the right to mint money), along with the disbursement of profits accrued through BOJ loans and the purchase of JGBs, can potentially increase transfers. After subtracting BOJ expenditures from these profits, the BOJ "returns" the balance to the MOF in the form of payment to the national treasury (*kokko nōfukin*), which adds to the government revenue.[34] On the other hand, however, if the BOJ's large-scale purchases of risky assets or long-term JGBs through QE lead to losses, these transfers would dry up, and the MOF might possibly be on the hook to cover losses. On the latter point, though, there is some ambiguity. Under the old BOJ Law prior to the 1997 revision, the BOJ was legally indemnified against losses; the MOF was legally obligated to step in. This provision was abolished under the New BOJ Law.[35]

From the perspective of the BOJ, there was reason for caution as well, especially since the BOJ is no longer explicitly indemnified against losses. One former Policy Board member has noted this as a reason that the BOJ was careful in terms of its policy choices (Suda 2014).[36] Reflecting the BOJ's concern over maintaining

---

33. One of Abe's key economic advisers, Honda Etsurō, a former MOF official, has been highly critical of this view of the MOF, arguing that the logic is backwards since greater inflation will lead to higher revenue, improving Japan's fiscal balance.

34. According to Yamawaki (1998, 106–7), these funds have often been used as a "hidden pocket" (aka "piggy bank" or "shadow budget") by the MOF, usually at the end of the fiscal year. Oguri (2000, 108) argues that Japan's system is unique compared to the FRB, BOE, and Bundesbank in that there is little distinction between the government's general revenue and the BOJ's seigniorage payment to the MOF.

35. At the same time, the BOJ's obligation to hedge its bank note issuance by owing self-capital consisting of prime assets was also abolished.

36. For comparative information on the financial reporting and accounting procedures of seven central banks (Japan, FRB, BOE, ECB, Bundesbank, Reserve Bank of New Zealand, and Bank of Canada), see Mori and Furuichi 2005.

independence, the BOJ had sought to avoid financial risk also out of concern that losses might lead to a loss of policy autonomy (Okina 2015). In order to create a buffer against losses, the BOJ has since 1998 set its goal to maintain the ratio of its net worth to its bank note issuance within plus or minus two of 10%.[37] While the concern about balance sheet losses was the prevailing view within the BOJ and the MOF, as discussed in chapter 2, many economists believe that these losses would be exceeded by the fiscal gains from greater inflation and economic growth that QE could stimulate.

The Policy Network and Politics of Board Member Nominations and Appointments

In practice, because members for all intents and purposes cannot be removed, the prime minister's opportunity to make appointments and influence the board has depended on the timing of when positions on the Policy Board become vacant. As Chang (2003, 2) notes, appointments are one of the key means by which politicians can influence monetary policy within the institutional constraint of central bank independence. Given the rapid turnover of prime ministers in Japan, however, most of their tenures were too short to have any influence on the board. During the three-year period from 1998 through 2001, there were three prime ministers, and during the seven-year period from 2006 through 2012, there were seven prime ministers (counting Abe twice).

During the fifteen years between 1998 and 2012, the nomination process for Policy Board members involved the Prime Minister's Office, the BOJ, the MOF, and, at key points, business.[38] In accordance with the convention, the Prime Minister's Office selected nominees primarily through consultation with the BOJ (as well as with former high-ranking BOJ officials) and the MOF. Board member nominations go through the Minister's Secretariat, which officially suggests candidates and also participates in consultations with the Prime Minister's Office.[39]

---

37. Since the beginning of the QE in 2001, the BOJ's net worth ratio has steadily declined and hovers around 7 percent, a zone that is considered problematic (Suda 2014; Ueda 2003). If the BOJ applies the standard capital-to-asset ratio used by other financial institutions, that ratio had hovered between 3 and 6 percent since 1998 (Kumakura 2015) and has dipped to between 2 and 3 percent under Governor Kuroda's QQE in 2015 ("Nichigin jiko shihon tsumimashi: Kanwa 'deguchi' no risuku ni sonae 13 nen buri ni 8 pāsento dai ni" [Bank of Japan increases its capital base: The capital ratio reaches 8 percent for the first time in 13 years in preparation for the risk of "exit" from easing], *Nihon Keizai Shimbun*, May 28, 2015).

38. As we discuss in chapter 8, Prime Minister Abe's advisers deliberately chose to limit the BOJ's influence in the process.

39. Academic economist and former BOJ Policy Board member, interview, Tokyo, September 15, 2015.

Nominations and appointments had been a key informal channel of BOJ influence on the Policy Board. The BOJ sought to have like-minded members appointed. As discussed below, the BOJ campaigned for former BOJ officials, e.g., *haenuki*, as candidates for appointments at the highest level: the governor of the BOJ. The BOJ also drew on former high-level BOJ officials, allied business leaders, and members of the Diet at key moments to influence the appointment process. Former top BOJ officials often take posts in the private sector and can develop connections by joining business groups, such as the Keizai Dōyūkai.[40]

Appointments of Governors

The appointment processes of the first three governors (Hayami, Fukui, and Shirakawa) illustrate how BOJ preferences have prevailed. From 1998 until early 2013, all three BOJ governors were career *haenuki* BOJ officials. Only with the fourth governor, appointed by Prime Minister Abe, was this pattern disrupted with the appointment of Kuroda Haruhiko, a former MOF official. Some deputy governors were also *haenuki* BOJ officials, while others had backgrounds as academics, journalists, or officials from the MOF (Mutō Toshirō, for example). BOJ officials must first resign from the BOJ to become members of the Policy Board. Unlike the relatively low-profile and less politicized appointments of the non-executive policy board members (discussed below), the appointments of the BOJ governors (and to a lesser extent the deputy governors) have received intense scrutiny and attention.

The first governor, Hayami Masaru, served from 1998 until 2003; he was appointed just before the New BOJ Law took effect in April 1998. In some ways, Hayami was an accidental selection. As discussed more below, the governorship opened up after former governor Matsushita had to step down to take responsibility for a BOJ corruption scandal, and the heir apparent, Fukui Toshihiko—then the deputy governor—resigned as well. Nevertheless, with Hayami, the BOJ managed to have another *haenuki* appointed. As is common, retired BOJ officials—referred to as "OB" for "old boys"—played a critical role in the appointment.[41] The BOJ governor who preceded Matsushita, Mieno Yasushi—another *haenuki*—lobbied behind the scenes in support of Hayami (Fujii 2004) and

---

40. Keidanren is the biggest business group, but only corporate entities can be members. Individuals can join Keizai Dōyūkai. For instance, former BOJ governors Hayami and Fukui have been active members.

41. A former BOJ Policy Board member from September 2015 through April 2016, multiple interviews.

formed an alliance with Miyazawa Kiichi, an LDP heavyweight who had previously served once as prime minister (1991–93) and twice as finance minister (1986–88, 1998–2001).[42] Then president of Keidanren (Japan Business Federation), Toyoda Shō'ichirō, also expressed support for Hayami (Heckel 2014, 207).

Because of the continuing economic turmoil and the political wrangling associated with monetary policy decisions such as the premature phasing out of ZIRP in 2000 (chapter 7), the appointment of the next BOJ governor, Fukui Toshihiko (2003–8), was much more contentious. After resigning from the BOJ deputy governor's position in 1998 due to the BOJ scandal, Fukui at the time of appointment was a retired BOJ official who had moved to the private sector, serving as the deputy chairman and president of the Keizai Dōyūkai and a board member of Kikkōman, a company with a long tradition of making soy sauce and condiments. Fukui, the BOJ's inside candidate for governor who had moved up the ranks quickly and was regarded as a "prince," was strongly supported by Hayami, the outgoing governor.

Prime Minister Koizumi's final selection of Fukui was surprising in several respects. Japan had already experienced deflation at the end of the decade, and in the early part of Prime Minister Koizumi's tenure, the threat of deflation again reared its head, with continuing negative growth in the CPI.[43] Koizumi supported a reflationary monetary policy, as did some of his key economic advisers. Takenaka Heizō, head of the Council on Economic and Fiscal Policy, the prime minister's key advisory council, had publicly criticized the BOJ's monetary policy and called for a more reflationary policy. The general secretary of the LDP, Yamasaki Taku, also called for more proactive measures, including setting an inflation target.

Koizumi, who had expressed enthusiasm about the idea of selecting appointees from the private sector in general, also indicated a preference for finding a private-sector appointee to the BOJ governorship, a sentiment shared by Takenaka. Koizumi reportedly wanted to appoint Imai Takashi, chairman of Nippon Steel. His chief cabinet secretary discussed this with Governor Hayami, who still backed Fukui but could not openly oppose Koizumi.[44] Imai, however, made it clear in public comments that he would not take the job. As the search progressed, another private-sector candidate strongly committed to reflation emerged: Nakahara Nobuyuki, a former Policy Board member (1998–2002) from the private sector (his detailed profile is discussed below). Nakahara was known

---

42. Former governor Mieno was known for his monetary tightening after the collapse of Japan's asset bubble.

43. Both the domestic wholesale price index and CPI contracted by 0.5 percent (year-on-year) from 2000 to 2001.

44. "Nichigin ni Fukui: Keizai kai no ato oshi ketteida" [Fukui to Bank of Japan: Support from the business world a determining factor], *Nihon Keizai Shimbun*, February 25, 2003.

for his outspoken calls for the BOJ to pursue a more active reflationary policy, including setting an inflation target, a policy viewed skeptically within the BOJ. The consideration of Nakahara, with strong reflationary preferences, was a cause for concern within the BOJ, which lobbied actively for Fukui. Governor Hayami appealed directly to Koizumi's chief cabinet secretary, Fukuda Yasuo, to remove Nakahara from consideration (Fujii 2004). The BOJ also drew on its connections with the private sector to secure endorsements from the business community. Deputy Governor Yamaguchi Yutaka, a former career BOJ official, and other BOJ officials lined up support for Fukui from the chairman of the Nippon Keidanren and the Japan Chamber of Commerce and Industry.[45]

How much effect this pressure had is difficult to know precisely, but news reports suggest that voices from the business community effectively ended the consideration of Nakahara. Ultimately Koizumi chose Fukui, a BOJ insider who was well known to be moderate and cautious, over Nakahara. Koizumi did balance the influence of the BOJ by nominating as the two deputy governors Mutō Toshirō, a former deputy minister of finance, and Iwata Kazumasa, a Tokyo University economics professor and a member of the Cabinet Office. Both had reputations for being more supportive of reflationary policies than Fukui,[46] and their presence likely pushed policy in a more reflationary direction. Interestingly, however, Mutō, a former MOF official, did stop short of embracing inflation targeting, echoing the MOF view that high inflation would cause interest rates to rise, thereby imperiling Japan's public finances. Mutō also supported ending Japan's first QE program in 2006, a move that Abe Shinzō criticized sharply at the time (see chapter 7).

The appointment of the next governor, Shirakawa Masaaki, was also somewhat accidental in that it emerged from a contested political process. Shirakawa is another BOJ *haenuki* official who served as the executive director in charge of monetary policy. He was known as a scholarly type whose "hobby is monetary policy" (Kamikawa 2014, 158). As Fukui's five-year term came to a close, Prime Minister Fukuda Yasuo (September 2007–September 2008), Koizumi's former chief cabinet secretary, faced a difficult confirmation process because the LDP lost seats in the 2004 upper house elections and no longer controlled the House of Councillors. The key roadblock was that the DPJ (Democratic Party of Japan), which controlled the House of Councillors, insisted that the next governor not be a former MOF official. Reflecting its strong support of separation of the monetary function from the fiscal one, the DPJ insisted that the appointment of an MOF official would

---

45. Ibid.
46. Fukui had published an article during his time at the Fujitsu Research (late 1990s) that revealed his strong opposition to inflationary measures (Heckel 2014, 214).

undermine the independence of the BOJ. Nonetheless, Prime Minister Fukuda tried to force the hand of the DPJ, nominating an ex-MOF official, Mutō Toshirō, who was then serving as the deputy governor.[47] With the onset of the GFC, Fukuda supported Mutō because of his experience as deputy governor. Ultimately, the DPJ rejected Mutō in the House of Councillors on the grounds of separation of fiscal and monetary policies and the protection of BOJ independence, especially in light of the possible revival of the practice of "*tasukigake-jin'ji*," having former BOJ and MOF bureaucrats take turns serving as BOJ governor (Kamikawa 2014, 160). The process then repeated itself as Fukuda nominated another ex-MOF official, Tanami Kōji, and again the DPJ rejected him. This time, however, the DPJ confirmed one of Fukuda's nominees for the deputy governor position, Shirakawa Masaaki. As the stalemate progressed and the governorship remained unfilled even in the midst of economic crisis, the LDP and DPJ ultimately settled on Shirakawa as a compromise candidate for the top position at the BOJ.

During discussions for this round of nominations, several deputy governor nominees were also rejected by the DPJ, which at that time supported the BOJ's stance against inflation targeting (a position the DPJ later changed) and supported the BOJ's expansive view of independence. The candidates rejected by the DPJ included Itō Takatoshi, a University of Tokyo professor and a known proponent of inflation targeting, and Watanabe Hiroshi, former vice minister of finance for international affairs.[48] In the end, the economist Nishimura Kiyohiko from the University of Tokyo was appointed as one of the deputy governors on March 18. The second position remained vacant until October of the same year, when former BOJ executive director Yamaguchi Hirohide was finally appointed.

The Policy Board and Its Monetary Policy Decisions

The selection of three former BOJ *haenuki* officials as governors between 1998 and 2012 was a key channel through which the conventional BOJ worldview was reflected in the Policy Board's deliberations and decisions. Institutional power places the BOJ governor at the center of influence, as he presides over the BOJ

---

47. Deputy BOJ governor Toshirō Mutō (March 20, 2003–March 19, 2008), a former vice minister of finance, acted as a facilitator between the BOJ and the MOF, enabling monetary policy under Governor Fukui, who held his position during the same period, to respond more smoothly to political demands (Kamikawa 2014, 126).

48. The DPJ was adamant about the separation of fiscal and monetary policy and hence opposed Watanabe because of his previous post at the MOF, while the DPJ's opposition to Itō came largely from the fact that he was a member of the Council on Economic and Fiscal Policy from 2006 to 2008.

staff and also serves as the chairman of the Policy Board meeting (Okina 2009).[49] The BOJ administration formally provides support to the executive members— the governor and two deputy governors—and the other six members of the Policy Board. In practice, the BOJ executive director (*riji*) in charge of monetary policy and supporting departments can exert great influence on the monetary policymaking process. While executive directors officially no longer work for the BOJ,[50] they often retain institutional biases that align them with the BOJ world-view. Of the six executive director positions, five are designated by convention for ex-BOJ officials (see figure 5.2). The one remaining executive director post is designated for an ex-MOF official.[51]

BOJ executive directors and their main support offices (*kikaku-shitsu*) have several channels of influence in BOJ Policy Board decisions. The executive director in charge of monetary policy, with help from the relevant departments

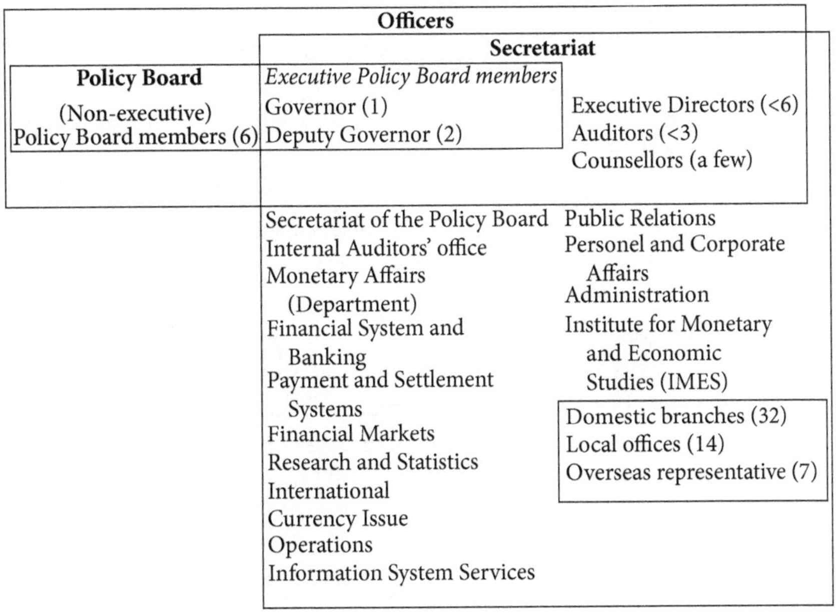

Officers		
	Secretariat	
Policy Board	*Executive Policy Board members*	
(Non-executive)	Governor (1)	Executive Directors (<6)
Policy Board members (6)	Deputy Governor (2)	Auditors (<3)
		Counsellors (a few)
	Secretariat of the Policy Board	Public Relations
	Internal Auditors' office	Personel and Corporate
	Monetary Affairs	Affairs
	(Department)	Administration
	Financial System and	Institute for Monetary
	Banking	and Economic
	Payment and Settlement	Studies (IMES)
	Systems	Domestic branches (32)
	Financial Markets	Local offices (14)
	Research and Statistics	Overseas representative (7)
	International	
	Currency Issue	
	Operations	
	Information System Services	

FIGURE 5.2.   BOJ and Policy Board organizational chart

Source: BOJ (http://www.boj.or.jp/about/organization/index.htm) and Shimizu 2004, 24.

---

49. A chairperson of the board is elected among the board members (Article 16.3), and it has become the convention since September 2000 that the BOJ governor serves as the chairperson.

50. Current BOJ officials formally must also resign from their BOJ posts in order to become executive directors.

51. A former executive director of the BOJ, interview, Tokyo, January 29, 2016.

(Monetary Affairs, Research and Statistics, etc.), plays an influential role in deliberations, including agenda setting. The organizations provide data and analyses on macroeconomic conditions, markets, foreign exchange, and the financial system prior to the Policy Board meeting (Umeda 2011). Beyond helping frame the narrative and analysis surrounding deliberations, the executive directors and the heads of key bureaus also lay the groundwork for the members of the Policy Board to persuade them of the "right" policy course. Before the meetings, the BOJ directors and staff work behind the scenes to establish a consensus by lining up support among individual members (a process known as *nemawashi*).[52] BOJ directors and staff members also often have held informal "study groups" (*benkyōkai*) with the six nonexecutive members to provide briefings and lead discussions prior to formal Policy Board meetings.[53] There is a convention to limit collusion among nonexecutive board members by requiring any meetings among these members to be fully documented and reported to the Secretariat.[54] As the chairperson of the Policy Board meetings, the BOJ governor can exert tremendous leverage, representing the majority view at board meetings and also wielding tie-breaking power (Article 18.2).[55] Moreover, in the past it was conventional for the Secretariat to take an informal vote on each item prior to the meetings; if an item could not secure at least six votes, it would be quietly removed from the meeting agenda (Kamikawa 2014, 167).[56]

The resources available to the six nonexecutive members to conduct independent macroeconomic analyses are limited. Each is assigned one BOJ staff member, usually at the level of deputy division chief, as well as one secretary and a driver. The staff member's putative purpose is to support the board member with analysis, but his real duty is to "guide" his assigned member to follow the norms and policy preferences of the BOJ. During this staff member's performance evaluation (conducted by the BOJ Secretariat and not by the Policy Board), he or she may receive demerits if the assigned board member made irregular or opposing comments during the Policy Board meetings (Shimizu 2004).[57] Even though all

---

52. A former deputy governor of the BOJ, interview, Tokyo, January 29, 2016.

53. A former BOJ staff member, interview, Tokyo, January 19, 2016.

54. A former BOJ official and a prominent economist, interview, Tokyo, January 27, 2016.

55. This power has been used only once in the new BOJ history, during the Shirakawa governorship at the Policy Board meeting in October 2008 (chapter 7).

56. Okina (2009) theorizes that the board members worry about the market reaction when the board is split, and hence some of them refrain from opposing the governor's view.

57. In pursuit of more independent data and information free of BOJ influence, many members use their professional networks to gather information. One former board member, Miki Toshio (April 1, 1998–March 31, 2002), utilized economists on staff at his former institution, Nippon Steel, to acquire data and analyses. Wakatabe (2015, 33) notes that Nakahara Nobuyuki also used his vast network of academic and business economists to present his own diagnosis and policy remedies. A political scientist who specializes in BOJ analysis, interview, Osaka, January 22, 2016.

Policy Board members technically have authority to weigh in on the promotion of career BOJ officials to executive director status as per Article 23.4 (Shimizu 2004), the lion's share of personnel issues are handled by the executive members of the Policy Board rather than the six nonexecutive members.[58] Thus, in practice the nonexecutive members have little influence over the staff.

Nonexecutive Policy Board Members

There was a tradition since 1949 of appointing members with diverse backgrounds to a "sleeping board" (the title given to the old Policy Board that did not have any policymaking power). The membership included one representative from the various city banks and regional banks as well as specific sectoral interests such as commerce and agriculture (chapter 4). This preference for diverse background comes partly from the fact that the BOJ Policy Board not only decides on monetary policy but also oversees other BOJ business and day-to-day operations. Unlike the FRB's Federal Open Market Committee (FOMC), where the members only participate in monetary policymaking and not the daily operations of the central bank (Shirakawa 2008), the BOJ Policy Board is expected to oversee a wide variety of areas beyond monetary policy.[59]

The cabinet, in theory, appoints Policy Board members, with the approval of the Diet (Article 23.1). In practice, the BOJ and its governors have helped ensure the selection of the members who support the BOJ's priority of creating a "collegial policy board."[60] In order to maintain continuity, nonexecutive board members are appointed in a staggered manner. The nomination of nonexecutive policy board members has always been done (at least until Abe's second term) in consultation with the BOJ and the MOF, and until 2008 nominations were rarely overturned.[61] Since these positions were viewed as less important than governors and deputy governors, their selections had been handled by the office

---

58. A former executive director of the BOJ, interview, Tokyo, January 29, 2016.

59. The FRB president and executive officers, however, do take part in decisions other than monetary policy. Meanwhile, the BOE is a hybrid where the governor and deputy governor and two members appointed by the governor (hence four in all) make up the internal committee, while the other five (called the external committee) only participate in monetary policymaking.

60. For example, during the first round of board member selection, the BOJ (and more specifically then–deputy governor Fukui) had significant influence in choosing the candidates (Fujii 2004).

61. It was the hope of the BOJ secretariat to have a regularized system in which two independent lists are submitted, one by the BOJ and the other by the MOF, before narrowing down the Policy Board member candidates, as was done for the first round in 1998. But that system did not become routinized, and the nomination of the candidates became case-by-case (a former executive director of the BOJ, interview, Tokyo, January 28, 2016).

of the deputy chief cabinet secretary, rather than the prime minister and his chief cabinet secretary.[62]

With a few exceptions discussed below, the general lack of monetary policy expertise had made the nonexecutive Policy Board members more susceptible to capture by the BOJ staff and also less likely to introduce their own policy proposals that might contradict the predominant BOJ worldview. As listed below (table 5.2), the six nonexecutive board members have come from various backgrounds ranging from academia, the private sector (banks, trade companies, energy, and steel), research institutions, and the media.[63]

That said, there have been a number of highly regarded monetary economists on the board, and in some cases these experts have been able to exert influence on the board's deliberations. For instance, Ueda Kazuo (April 1, 1998–April 7, 2005), a highly regarded monetary economist, contributed to introducing forward guidance, the policy of signaling a central bank's future intentions by setting

TABLE 5.2 Occupational histories of executive and nonexecutive board members: 1998–2015

	JOB EXPERIENCE (%)		JOB IMMEDIATELY PRIOR TO BOARD (%)	
	NON-EXE. SIX	EXEC. MEMBERS	NON-EXEC. SIX	EXEC. MEMBERS
BOJ	0.0	50.0	0.0	33.3
Academia	26.1	33.3	26.1	33.3
Private finance	43.5	0.0	30.4	0.0
Non fin. private sector	39.1	8.3	39.1	8.3
Government (MOF)	4.3	16.7	0.0	8.3
Government other than MOF	8.7	8.3	0.0	8.3
Other (a)	8.7	8.3	4.3	16.7
TOTAL (b)	130.4	125.0	100.0	108.3

Source: List of BOJ board members from 1998 through 2015 from the BOJ website, and other Who's-Who databases.[1]

(a) Other includes journalists and international civil service workers (from the IMF and Asian Development Bank)

(b) Total exceeds 100 percent due to several members with multiple job experiences and affiliations.

1. Who Plus, Jinji kōshin roku, Nihon Shinshi roku, Kokka kōmuin shokuin roku, newspaper databases including Nikkei Telecon, Kikuzo II, Yomidas, and Maisaku.

---

62. A former BOJ Policy Board member, multiple interviews, September 2015 through April 2016.

63. Meanwhile, the FOMC tends to enlist academics, economists, and bankers, while a large percentage of FRB governors have worked at the FRB, although the number of prominent academic economists taking up the FRB governorship is on the increase (Shirakawa 2008).

criteria under which monetary easing will be wound down.[64] Another particularly prominent Policy Board member, Nobuyuki Nakahara, came from a business background as the former CEO of Tōa Nenryō Kōgyō Co. Ltd. With his education from University of Tokyo and Harvard University, he had extensive connections to economists around the world with whom he consulted often to formulate his monetary policy proposals (Nakahara 2006). More than any other board member, Nakahara cast dissenting votes to the BOJ worldview and supported greater monetary easing. Given the BOJ's influence in selecting nonexecutive members, his selection is puzzling. According to Nakahara himself, his selection was due to a personal friendship with former BOJ governor Fukui, and the BOJ had little idea of his policy views before his selection.[65] In an interview, Nakahara also concurred that the lack of monetary expertise among the six nonexecutive board members has had the effect of keeping the BOJ policy network relatively closed to new ideas.

The Voting Record at Monetary Policy Board Meeting

The voting record from the Policy Board meetings during the first fifteen years of the New BOJ Law has reflected the governors' policy views, and the voting behavior of the Policy Board members has shown increasing and striking unanimity in support of the governors' proposals (table 5.3). Under the first three

TABLE 5.3 Monetary policy meetings voting data summary: April 1998–April 2016

GOVERNOR (TIME FRAME)	TOTAL NUMBER OF PROPOSALS AT MONETARY POLICY MEETINGS	PROPOSALS WITHOUT OPPOSITION	PROPORTION OF FULL SUPPORT TO PROPOSALS (%)	AVERAGE OPPOSING VOTES WHEN NOT UNANIMOUS
Hayami (April 1, 1998–March 19, 2003)	92	24	26.1	1.57
Fukui (March 20, 2003–March 19, 2008)	77	47	62.7	1.70
Shirakawa (April 9, 2008–March 19, 2013)	80	76	97.4	2.50
Total (under first three governors)	249	147	59.0	—
cf. Kuroda (March 20 2013– as of April 28, 2016)	45	22	48.9	1.39

Source: BOJ summary minutes of the BOJ Policy Board meetings from 1998 through 2016. See appendix for the entire list of proposals with vote counts.

---

64. A former BOJ staff member, interview, Tokyo, January 19, 2016.
65. Nakahara Nobuyuki, former BOJ Policy Board member, in discussion with the author, September 14, 2015.

governors, 249 proposals were made regarding monetary policy. None of these were rejected, and 147 proposals, or 59 percent, passed without any opposing votes. These voting statistics put the BOJ's monetary Policy Board meetings somewhere between the more individualistic BOE (where an average of 35 percent of monetary policy meetings saw no opposition votes in 1997–2007) and the quite collegial FRB (which had 68 percent).[66]

Immediately following the New BOJ Law, the Policy Board did not appear particularly supportive of its governor. Under the first Hayami governorship (1998–2003), only 26.1 percent of the governor's proposals enjoyed unanimous support (table 5.3). But recalcitrance mostly came from two particular board members, Nakahara and Shinotsuka, who came from opposite sides of monetary policy spectrum. Nakahara was an inflation dove who demanded a more expansionary monetary policy, while Shinotsuka was an inflation hawk who opposed any loosening monetary policy out of concern that inflationary pressure would harm ordinary people. Nakahara in particular believed that the governor's policy proposals were not aggressive enough at tackling deflation; he cast sixty dissenting votes out of seventy-seven proposals brought forward during his tenure (April 1, 1998–March 31, 2002).[67] If the opposition votes by these two members are discarded as idiosyncratic, the proportion of support for Hayami's proposals with no other dissenting votes rises to 59.8 percent. During the Shirakawa governorship (2008–13), only two of the eighty proposals (97.4 percent) put forward by the governor had any opposing votes by Policy Board members. This trend has seen a reversal under Governor Kuroda (2013 to April 2016) with 48.9 percent of full support (between March 20, 2013, through April 28, 2016), as he has implemented an aggressive QQE policy under Abenomics, as discussed in chapter 8.

As shown in the appendix, the largest number of dissenting votes against any governor's proposals was four, which happened three times during the fifteen years; there were also three occasions when the opposition received three votes. Under Governor Hayami, as discussed above, the opposing votes were split between those pushing for greater easing (Nakahara) and those pushing for greater tightening (Shinotsuka). Governor Fukui's monetary expansion through QE was often opposed by more hawkish Policy Board members concerned about the speed of expansion. The two times when Governor Shirakawa's proposals

---

66. Data collected by King (2007), cited in Okina 2009.

67. Shinotsuka voted against expansionary policy proposals because that would have negative impacts on pensioners and housewives, as the return on savings could go down and prices might increase. She cast forty-two no votes out of fifty-nine proposals during her tenure (April 1, 1998 to March 31, 2001).

encountered opposing votes, the opposition views were again mixed between hawks and doves. Notably, as discussed more extensively in chapter 8, the opposition to Governor Kuroda was consistently against his aggressive monetary easing. Despite Article 16 (2) of the New BOJ Law that specifies that "the Governor and the Deputy Governors shall perform their duties as Board member independently of each other," it is an unwritten norm that the executive members (the governor and the two deputy governors) vote in a bloc; consequently, there was only one occasion in the fifteen-year history under the first three BOJ governors where one of the deputy governors opposed a proposal.[68] The practice of executive members voting as a bloc at the Policy Board meetings strengthened the power of the governor and the BOJ Secretariat.

Monetary Policy Networks: A Comparative Perspective

As demonstrated above, one key difference in the case of the BOJ has been the ability of the organization to exert, at least until Abenomics, greater influence over monetary policy decision making. This influence was due not only to the BOJ's central position in the network, but also to the stability of the network itself: the key institutions largely remained the same, even with changes in government between the LDP and DPJ. In selecting Policy Board members, the BOJ had a consultative role with the Prime Minister's Office. The MOF did as well, although it seldom acted as a counterweight and largely supported the BOJ's position regarding unconventional monetary policy and inflation targeting. Until the appointment of Kuroda Haruhiko in 2013, the selection of governors, all three of whom had spent the majority of their careers at the BOJ, further contributed to the centralization of the BOJ's influence. The BOJ arguably had even more say in the appointment of nonexecutive Policy Board members, who tended to support members with a similar worldview, although there have been a few notable exceptions. Lastly, career BOJ officials also influenced the policy deliberations through informal practices, such as the advance discussion of Policy Board decisions with individual members. All in all, the BOJ's policy network represents a closed network as discussed in chapter 3. By contrast, the monetary policy networks in other countries have features that have made them more open

---

68. This occurred when Deputy Governor Iwata Kazumasa voted against a call rate increase to 0.5 percent at the Policy Board meeting on February 21, 2007, citing his concern about the robustness of the price increase.

and porous. First, the policy networks in other countries are less *centralized*, that is, less dominated by one actor. Second, the policy networks have been less *stable*, that is, they have fluctuated more over time depending on the executive or composition of the legislature.

The Federal Reserve Bank

Compared to the BOJ, several aspects of the policymaking network make the FRB relatively open. The FRB as a larger organization does have an important relationship with its policy board. FRB economists can exert influence on policy deliberations (Conti-Brown 2016, 86).[69] Formally, the FRB also has direct representation on the FOMC. The decentralized structure of the FRB with its regional banks, however, creates greater institutional and ideational diversity. Indeed, the regional branches are known to cultivate their own perspectives. For instance, the St. Louis branch reportedly subscribed to a more strongly monetarist view (Woolley 1985, 9).[70] The head of the Federal Reserve Bank of New York is automatically a member of the FOMC, and four seats are reserved for heads of other regional reserve bank presidents on a rotating basis. Other reserve bank presidents can also attend the Policy Board meetings and participate in discussions, although they do not have the right to vote. The rotation of seats reserved for four of the regional central bank presidents creates a mechanism that increases diversity of views on the policy board.

Another key difference from the BOJ is in recruitment; the FRB on balance favors professional disciplinary expertise in economics over internal socialization. Former FRB chairman Ben Bernanke observes that the environment within the FRB is highly academic.[71] The FRB hires many staff members that join the organization with advanced degrees. The FRB hires twenty to thirty PhDs per year at the Washington, DC, office alone, and there are hundreds of PhDs working at the regional branches of the FRB. There are about two hundred in Washington, DC, fifty at the New York office, and twenty across the other ten branches. The top posts at these branches are largely held by those with PhDs who actively

---

69. Ben Bernanke, former chairman of the Board of Governors of the Federal Reserve system and distinguished fellow in residence, Brookings Institution, in discussion with the author, August 31, 2017.

70. A former vice chairman of the Board of Governors of the Federal Reserve system, interview, Washington DC, December 8, 2015.

71. Ben Bernanke, former chairman of the Board of Governors of the Federal Reserve system and distinguished fellow in residence, Brookings Institution, in discussion with the author, August 31, 2017.

exchange views with policymakers outside the FRB and in academia. The FRB is well-connected to the US economist community and has paid close attention to the shifting consensus of mainstream economists (Woolley 1985, 101–2). In fact, FRB economists are given time to conduct research, and they regularly submit their work to academic journals.[72] Establishing a reputation in the field by publishing work in top journals can boost one's career prospects within the FRB.[73]

Unlike with the BOJ, economists within the FRB are deployed across the organization to leadership positions related to policymaking. While these economists rotate positions, they do so less frequently than the BOJ and into positions that are related to their economic expertise.[74]

As the foregoing discussion suggests, the FRB is embedded deeply within the field of economics. That does not mean that the FRB, like other organizations, is immune to developing an organizationally mediated worldview. Conti-Brown (2016, 131) notes that the values and worldviews of the FRB economists shape their judgments about the best data and models of the economy, and the FRB economists serve as "a gatekeeper for the production of economic ideas, both inside and outside the Fed," as they balance between producing knowledge and justifying policy action (Conti-Brown 2016, 92). That said, compared to the BOJ, these views have been mediated much more by the broader influences and trends in economics.[75]

Looking outside the FRB, the broader monetary policy network is also relatively open because it is less stable. The monetary policy network centers around the White House. Presidents, their advisers, and their own networks of experts play the central role in the selection of FOMC members. For the selection of members, economists in the White House can suggest or advocate for specific candidates, although candidates for chairperson undergo much closer scrutiny from the White House.[76] The larger network involved in nominations is particular to a given administration, and thus the network shifts with changes in the executive; in other words, it is less stable. Typically, a president selects

---

72. Ibid.

73. A former economist from the FRB, interview, December 2, 2015.

74. Ibid.

75. One could of course make a broader point that the field of economics itself is a closed network that has produced a kind of groupthink, and indeed some have argued that one consequence of this was the failure to predict the largest financial crisis since the Great Depression.

76. In Ben Bernanke's meeting with President George W. Bush and his advisers, there were in fact no economists present. Ben Bernanke, former chairman of the Board of Governors of the Federal Reserve system and distinguished fellow in residence, Brookings Institution, in discussion with the author, August 31, 2017.

someone from his or her own party, although there have been many cases for instance, Paul Volcker, Alan Greenspan, and Ben Bernanke—where a president has renominated a chairperson for a second term even though the chairperson had been nominated by a president from a different party.

The FRB as an organization does not play a consultative role in the selection of the FOMC members.[77] Furthermore, there appears to be an informal norm of not drawing on former FRB officials for positions on the FOMC (other than those designated for the regional bank presidents); indeed, there has only been one FOMC member, Donald Cohn, who worked his way up the ranks.

The Bank of England

Comparatively, the monetary policy network in the UK is more open than the BOJ and less open than the FRB. The BOE, like the BOJ, is an elite and relatively hierarchical organization. The BOE also has a more direct line of influence on its policy board than the BOJ since the BOE's chief economist is automatically one of the nine members of the Monetary Policy Committee (MPC). For the other four "internal" MPC positions—the governor and three deputy governors—a comparatively high number have been drawn from the ranks of the BOE career officials.

There are, however, a number of critical countervailing institutions and practices that have pushed toward openness. First, the remaining four MPC members are designated "external" members appointed by the chancellor of the exchequer. The prime minister has used these positions in some cases to serve as a deliberate counterweight on the MPC.[78] A number of prominent members have been drawn from overseas, such as Danny Blanchflower, a UK citizen based at Dartmouth, Adam Posen, an American macroeconomist, and the current governor, Mark Carney from Canada. As we discuss later, the first two played central roles in pushing the policy board to use QE. During these deliberations, the external members were much more likely to openly challenge the governor's proposals.[79] Furthermore, the practice of majority rather than consensus voting creates an environment that can amplify the voice of individual members and lessen the influence of the governor. Former BOE governor Mervyn King, for instance, lost multiple votes on the MPC.

---

77. A former economist from the FRB, interview, December 2, 2015.

78. According one former MPC member, Danny Blanchflower, Prime Minister Gordon Brown nominated him to the MPC so that he would counter the then-governor, Mervyn King, a BOE insider.

79. Ibid.

The Riksbank

In Sweden, the Riksbank is kept at arm's length from the policy board. Informally, there is a norm of selecting members who have not spent their careers at the Riksbank, although there have been rare exceptions. Interestingly, this norm about keeping distance between the Riksbank as an organization and the board appears to extend to within the Riksbank itself.[80] Within the policy board as well, influence is also decentralized. As with the FRB, staff members from the Monetary Policy Department prepare analyses and participate in the discussion without trying to lobby for a specific policy course. The Riksbank governor and deputy governor are relatively weak, and there is no norm of consensus voting.[81]

The policy network involved in the selection of the policy members also fluctuates. The parliament appoints eleven members to the General Council of the Riksbank after elections every four years. The General Council selects members of the Executive Board, which sets monetary policy, on a rolling basis of about one every year or so depending on when terms expire; the General Council also serves as an auditor of the Riksbank. The network is less stable since the General Council reflects the partisan competition of the parliament, which changes after every general election.

The New BOJ Law has placed the Policy Board at the center of the BOJ's monetary policymaking since 1998. Formally, the Policy Board is not only independent, but it sits atop the entire BOJ organization. In practice, however, as we demonstrate in this chapter, the larger BOJ organization has exercised influence in key ways over the composition of the Policy Board and monetary deliberations. Central to this influence is the ability of the BOJ to maintain a relatively closed monetary policy network that limited dissenting views. The next two chapters explore how the BOJ's worldview influenced actual policy outcomes.

---

80. Anders Vredin, head of the General Secretariat, Sveriges Riksbank, in discussion with the author, June 9, 2016.
81. Ibid.

Chapter 6

IDEAS AND MONETARY POLICY

A Quantitative Test

> In such a situation, I don't think we could jump-start the economy
> or improve the GDP, no matter how much we increase monetary
> base or M2+CD. One hears about the so-called "liquidity trap" a lot.
> Supplying liquidity continuously is like dumping water on a plant.
> If the plant does not grow despite abundant water, it means that
> there are some other issues there. Maybe the soil is bad or fertilizer
> is needed. Or it needs more sun. Unless we improve these other
> conditions, continuous water supply only causes saturation of the
> ground and won't help the plant grow.
>
> —Hayami Masaru, 2001

This chapter presents a statistical test to demonstrate whether, and to what extent, the ideas held by the central bankers at the BOJ influenced Japan's monetary policy. The results show a systematic effect of central bankers' ideas on how they determine what should be Japan's monetary base, while controlling for the status of the economy and the political environment. Concerns about inflation are a better predictor of policy than objective economic indicators. We also find an Abe effect, a systematic impact of the policy ideas championed by Prime Minister Abe Shinzō after he came to power in 2012. There is little evidence that the political business cycle or political partisanship influenced the BOJ policy choices.

There is a major challenge in seeking a connection between the ideas held by Japan's central bankers and Japan's monetary policy: how to measure the ideas of Japan's central bankers. The question of measurement has been one of the major stumbling blocks in the research agenda on ideas and foreign policy. Schonhardt-Bailey (2005, 701) puts it best: "If political scientists are to take ideas seriously, then we should explore more effective tools with which to measure ideas, and, ideally, subject them to rigorous empirical analysis." Ideas are likely to be influential but elusive because they are impervious to measurement.

To make our case, this study relies upon recent advances in a field that is far removed from our discipline of international studies: digital humanities, the study of literary texts using computers (Jockers 2013). Scholars in literature have been using computational methods to measure and test hypotheses about the leading content of a literary corpus. When it is simply beyond the ability of any single scholar to read, parse, and distill the content of the texts that define a period or a subject matter, computational methods come to the aid by allowing scholars to analyze a corpus in its entirety rather than selectively sample from it. The application of computerized methods to the analysis of literary texts has created new insights about how literary themes emerged, evolved, and transformed themselves over time. Sometimes, well-established conclusions about specific novels or literary movements found additional confirmation. Other times, well-established conclusions found themselves under attack.

A particular feature of the application of computational methods to the analysis of text allows us to portray the ideas held by Policy Board members at the BOJ in a comprehensive manner. Given the history of the BOJ's experiences managing monetary policy discussed in chapter 4 and the institutions that made such a view salient in the policymaking process reviewed in chapter 5, we expect that Japan's central bankers should express a strong preference for price stability, a hawkish stance toward inflation, and dovishness toward very low inflation.

Measuring Ideas at the Bank of Japan

On April 9, 1998, the members of the board of the Bank of Japan met for the first time since it had gained legal independence. With BOJ governor Hayami Masaru presiding the meeting, they discussed the domestic economic and financial situation. They assessed the conditions of the foreign exchange market and the global economic outlook. The issue of deflation was at the center of the discussion.[1] For some members, it was a matter of concern; for some others, it was a fleeting issue brought about by specific conditions, such as falling crude oil prices. For the more optimistic members of the BOJ board, "there was no imminent risk of a deflationary spiral occurring." In the end, they agreed that deflation was a problem that would require further attention. The board meeting minutes summarize the overall BOJ position as follows: "the majority of the members, including those who remarked that there was no impending risk of a deflationary spiral, agreed that they should be aware of the possibility that such a risk might increase in the future."

At the end of the meeting, the BOJ members took a vote that would direct Japan's monetary policy until the following Monetary Policy Board meeting

---

1. The full text of the minutes of the BOJ board meeting held on April 9, 1998 is available at https://www.boj.or.jp/en/mopo/mpmsche_minu/minu_1998/g980409.htm. The quotes below are taken from the minutes of the April 9, 1998, meeting.

of the BOJ Policy Board. With a unanimous vote, they decided that "the Bank should maintain the current easy stance of monetary policy and promote the continued permeation of its effects on interest rates on term instruments and on the stability of the market sentiment." In concrete terms, that decision translated into an average increase of the monetary base by ¥99.5 million per day.

From that first meeting in April 1998, the members of the BOJ board would meet regularly once or twice a month to determine monetary policy. The law granting the BOJ de jure independence mandates that the discussion would be recorded and made public shortly after the meeting as meeting minutes, a summary of the discussion that did not identify the speakers.[2] The entire transcript with verbatim notes of each speaker's comments with the names attached would be made public after ten years. We use the minutes instead of the entire transcripts for our quantitative content analysis since they are available for all meetings since 1998. Due to the ten-year embargo on the transcripts, they were not available at the time of this writing for some of the most critical periods, such as the global financial crisis (GFC) in 2008 and the "3–11" triple disaster of 2011. The minutes, which run between ten and twenty pages in length in Japanese, are accurate records of what was said at each meeting and are officially approved by the Policy Board. They reflect how the board members viewed the financial and economic situation in Japan and in the world at each meeting, without identifying the source of each opinion.

The summaries of the board deliberations are the texts we use to measure the policy ideas prevalent at the BOJ. As they assess the facts of the economic and financial conditions in Japan and in the world, the BOJ members also express their beliefs and their concerns about inflation, deflation, and the price level (*bukka*). Those beliefs and concerns reflect not only their expertise regarding how the global economy *works* but also their *policy ideas* about how the global economy *should work* and about their responsibilities as central bankers. In so doing, the BOJ board members convey, to themselves and to the public, the ideas that guide their decisions.

Any speech act performed in front of an audience is a performance act (Goffman 1959). There are many reasons why people might dissimulate or withhold their views: they might be concerned about embarrassing themselves or their interlocutors; they might have ulterior motives; they might be unwilling to challenge the predominant view out of fear or simple laziness. For these reasons and more, one can fairly ask if what people say is what they truly think.

---

2. The schedule of publication of the BOJ board meetings changed over the years. Initially, right after being granted de jure independence, the BOJ published the summary minutes three days after having the Board Members sign off on it during the meeting after next. In September 2000, this was revised to have the minutes published within one month after the meeting, and by July 2008, it was agreed that the BOJ would publish the minutes right after the next meeting.

The answer, some suggest, may be no. Timur Kuran (1995) drew a fundamental distinction between private preferences and public preferences: the former are the ideas and beliefs that people hold in their minds and, as a consequence, are known only to themselves; the latter are the ideas and beliefs they decide to reveal. The two need not be the same. When private and public preferences differ, people engage in preference falsification, with dramatic consequences for social interactions and historical development. Institutions that seem to be supported by a large consensus might be the proverbial colossus with feet of clay. Behind the veneer of superficial support there might be only hidden disdain or contempt. One can't know for sure because we only have access to the people's public preferences; that is, the ideas they decide to reveal.

Kuran's (1995) distinction between private and public preferences has profound implications. It explains why revolutionary movements seem to come out of nowhere. It explains why it is easy to overstate the support political institutions might have. It is a reminder of how creative people can be in carving up and preserving autonomous spaces in perilous situations. It also shows how difficult it is to obtain valid measures of people's ideas. Social scientists, thus, should be careful not to take what people say at face value.

But while challenging, the task of measuring ideas is not impossible. In our framework of analysis, some of the most consequential implications from Kuran's (1995) theory do not apply. We are not concerned about whether the BOJ Policy Board members engaged in deception by misrepresenting their beliefs and concerns about inflation and deflation. As discussed further below, we have reason to believe this is not the case. Even if they did, it would be irrelevant for this study since the theoretical interest is to demonstrate that the choices made by Japan's central bankers cannot be explained by looking only at economic and political parameters. While those factors may be relevant in some cases, this study seeks to find out if central bankers act upon their specific policy ideas about their role and how the economy works. If each BOJ board member held ideas that differed from the ones publicly stated at the meetings, it would not alter our conclusions. It would simply illustrate how embedded those ideas were in the institutional fabric of the BOJ.

Our approach follows Schonhardt-Bailey's (2013) path-breaking book *Deliberating American Monetary Policy*. As with her book on debates in the FOMC at the FRB, we view the transcripts of the BOJ board meetings as a reflection of authentic debates. Throughout a board meeting, the BOJ officials would express their views, emphasizing their concerns and providing their input in the decision-making process. In the process, their disagreements would also emerge. Within the constraints of institutional rules, personalities, and the prevailing policy understandings, those debates could potentially persuade bank officials to change their minds.

During the meeting of November 12, 1999, for example, the board members discussed the outlook for prices amid considerations about the impact of the Y2K problem and a return to a growing economy. The transcript of the minutes report that "One member expressed the view that, with the economy turning and starting to improve amid relatively stable prices, it could no longer be said that deflationary concern had not been dispelled."[3] That is to say, from the perspective of one board member, the deflationary concern had been dispelled. Implicitly, that board member was conveying the idea that inflation should again be seen as the problem to guard against. Others disagreed and pointed out that "there was still a risk of the inflation rate remaining negative."[4]

The discussion was hardly academic: an assessment of deflationary concerns underpinned the perspectives on the zero interest rate policy (ZIRP) the BOJ had adopted a few months earlier in February 1999. The BOJ members voted to continue the policy, with two objections.[5]

The reasons for the dissent are also revealing. For one of the two dissenters, "prices were stable, and the economy was definitely not experiencing deflation."[6] For the other dissenter, the ZIRP would not only create distortions in the economy but also a spiral of expectations of further monetary easing. As the minutes report, the dissenter provided the following reasons:

> First, the longer the extremely accommodative policy was maintained, the more serious the distortion of income distribution became. Second, market participants were taking risks based on the assumption that the policy would be extended for a considerable period, and if this situation continued any longer, the repercussions of the termination of the policy would become greater. And third, the policy was reducing firms' incentive to implement structural reform. Furthermore, the member noted that the emergence of extreme views requesting a further monetary easing or intentional creation of inflation despite the fact that the economy was improving seemed to indicate the public's ignorance of future costs of macroeconomic policies, and the emergence of such arguments was attributable in part to the continuation of the zero interest rate policy.[7]

---

3. The English translation of the BOJ board meeting of November 12, 1999, are available at https://www.boj.or.jp/en/mopo/mpmsche_minu/minu_1999/g991112.htm/.

4. Ibid.

5. Ibid.

6. Ibid.

7. Ibid.

The dissenter argued that failure to combat inflation would create pernicious expectations that would hurt the economy in the long run. On that basis, the board member advocated terminating the zero interest policy by articulating a view consistent with the baseline BOJ worldview we described in chapter 4.

Obviously, there is plenty to learn from a close reading of the BOJ documents. Their nuance and insights bear witness to the thinking of the BOJ board members. The wide-ranging and in-depth discussions suggest that they spoke their minds as they decided upon Japan's monetary policy. While skeptical views about the role of ideas in decision making will not—and probably cannot—be fully assuaged, the reason-based argumentation reflects the deliberative nature of the meetings and suggests that the BOJ documents have analytical value.

In sum, while dissimulation or silence might take place during the debates at the BOJ board meetings, we can discount the concerns that dissimulation or silence would be so pervasive and pernicious to invalidate any attempt to measure the policy ideas of the BOJ central bankers from the summaries of those meetings. We can, therefore, gauge from what was said during the debates to what extent taming and controlling inflation was portrayed as the primary goal of the BOJ.

But how do we turn the text summarizing the debates into a measure of policy ideas?

Coding Protocols

Our corpus—the collection of texts for our analysis—consists of 255 summaries from April 1998 until April 2014. While inflation was turning into deflation and Japan's economy stagnated, what did the Policy Board members in charge of deciding the country's monetary policy have to say? We focus on a specific set of words, the sentences they are embedded into, and the meaning they convey. In so doing, we use a hybrid approach in which automation joins forces with human judgment.

The starting point is simple: each sentence is a self-contained unit of meaning. For a comprehensive assessment of the texts, therefore, we retrieve all the sentences that contain the specific words that would characterize the policy ideas of the BOJ central bankers, using a machine-based procedure. We use humans, however, to code the sentences. Given the absence of dictionaries that have been extensively tested and validated, there is no substitute for human judgment.

Our key words are "inflation," "deflation," "and price," which in turn can be found in the context of rising (inflationary) or declining (deflationary) trends. These are the words that most closely capture the expertise and responsibilities of central bankers. Those are the parameters around which monetary policy turns. If the debate at the BOJ board meeting is an expression of the central bankers' worldviews, those words are the most direct and accessible sources for those worldviews.

This approach is an example of what in the literature on text analysis is called sentiment analysis, that is, the study not just of the content and topics of a text but also of the affective meanings that are conveyed by a text (Pang and Lee 2008; Krippendorff 2013, 245). The methodologies for sentiment analysis range from the simple to the mathematically sophisticated. At one end of the spectrum, there are the approaches that measure the frequency of words against predefined dictionaries (Pennebaker 2011; Elson et al. 2012; González-Bailón and Paltoglou 2015). At the other end of the spectrum, there are the approaches that exploit advances in statistical theory to classify documents according to the sentiments they convey (Taddy 2013).

We strike a middle ground between these two poles. We opt for simplicity and human judgment in the coding protocols. Entirely automated procedures that rely on predefined dictionaries have great appeal. They help insulate the coding process from the vagaries of human attention and hidden bias. At the same time, the coding based on predefined dictionaries is only as good as the input dictionaries themselves. In some research areas, well-established dictionaries exist (Pennebaker 2011). But in other areas, they do not. As a consequence, the findings based on inaccurate dictionaries might be even less reliable than the ones human coders would attain (González-Bailón and Paltoglou 2015).

Coding Sentiments about Inflation and Deflation

Operationally, we proceeded as follows. After removing from the texts the sections where the government representatives at the meeting expressed their views, we selected all the sentences where the words "inflation," "deflation," and "price" appeared. Two native speakers of Japanese then coded the meaning attached to our key words in each of the sentences on the basis of a simple template.[8] Was the word used in an optimistic manner, to denote a trend or a scenario to be welcomed? If that was the case, the coders were instructed to code the sentence as "positive." Was the word used to denote a concern, a trend or a scenario to guard against? If that was the case, the coders were instructed to code the sentence as

---

8. These codings were then reviewed by the Japanese-speaking members of our research team: Saori Katada, Yoshiko Kojo, and Gene Park.

"negative." Or was the word used in a neutral manner to describe a situation or a fact? In this case, the sentence was coded as "neutral."

Tables 6.1 through 6.3 illustrate our approach by presenting a selection of sentences from the texts in our corpus, along with the classification they were given by the coders. The systematic coding of the sentences containing the words "inflation," "deflation," and "price," therefore, opens up an avenue to track the relationship between the BOJ Policy Board members' views and their decisions.

Table 6.1 presents three sentences with the word "inflation." The first sentence, which comes from a meeting in February of 1999, refers to policies taken by a country (incidentally, Brazil) and the IMF. The key point in that sentence is the reference to the "economy picking-up" after the announcement of a policy aimed at the reduction of inflation and fiscal consolidation. That sentence is coded as "positive":

TABLE 6.1   Coding the sentences: Inflation

DATE	ORIGINAL	TRANSLATION	CODING
1999-02-12	しかし、2月初に、同国政府とIMFスタッフが、インフレ抑制と一段の財政健全化方針を盛り込んだ共同声明を発表したあとは、幾分持ち直している	However, the economy of the country has picked up somewhat after the joint announcement by the IMF and its government regarding the policy of further inflation reduction and fiscal consolidation.	Positive
2005-04-28	米国経済について、何人かの委員は、インフレ懸念が強まる際には、より強い金融政策面での対応もあり得るが、その場合、住宅投資の減速等を通じた経済面への影響、金融市場を通じたエマージング諸国などの世界経済への影響が懸念される、との認識を示した	Some members commented on the US economy that if inflationary pressures were to build in the economy, there would be concern that the subsequent changes in monetary policy might have negative effects on economic activity via, for example, a slowdown in housing investment as well as on the global economy, particularly emerging economies, via developments in financial markets.	Negative
2006-02-09	この間、既往のエネルギー高から物価は一時的に高い上昇率を示しているが、基調的なインフレ率は緩やかな上昇となっている	During this time, the basic inflation rate has shown only slight uptick, although the rate of price increase (inflation rate) has been temporarily high due to past high energy prices.	Neutral

this is a scenario to be welcomed. The second sentence in the same table, from April 2005, illustrates the perspective of a board member regarding the negative effects that might be triggered by inflationary pressures in the US economy. Accordingly, the sentence is coded as "negative": it conveys a concern about inflation.

Not all sentences in which the BOJ officials talk about the economic prospects of Japan and the world reflect a judgment. As experts, the BOJ officials make arguments based on facts. Thus there are sentences in which the references to inflation are neutral. The third sentence in table 6.1, from February 2006, is a clear example. It illustrates a factual statement about the inflation rate and the reasons that explain its level.

A similar assessment about the prevailing ideas at the BOJ can be made by looking at the use of the word "deflation." These sentences in table 6.2 serve as examples of the nuances that are embedded in the texts. Both the first sentence, from a meeting held in October of 2013, and the second sentence, from a meeting held in November of 2012, address the issue of "overcoming deflation," in (romanized) Japanese *defure dakkyaku*. The two sentences, however, portray a subtle but important difference. The first sentence conveys a more optimistic

TABLE 6.2   Coding the sentences: Deflation

DATE	ORIGINAL	TRANSLATION	CODING
2013-10-04	政府としては、これらの施策を通じて、デフレ脱却・経済再生と財政健全化の両立に向けた道筋を確かなものとしていく	Through these measures, the government will make sure that it constructs a path to achieve simultaneously early economic regeneration through overcoming deflation and fiscal soundness.	Positive
2012-11-20	日本銀行は、日本経済がデフレから早期に脱却し、物価安定のもとでの持続的成長経路に復帰することがきわめて重要な課題であると認識している	The Bank of Japan recognizes that it is imperative for the Japanese economy to overcome deflation swiftly and return to a sustainable growth path under price stability.	Negative
2003-10-31	今回の展望レポートでは、需給ギャップが小幅縮小に止まり、依然デフレ傾向が継続すると展望されている	According to the report on Outlook for Economic Activity and Prices, the supply-and-demand gap has shrunk only little, and deflation is expected to continue.	Neutral

scenario of addressing deflation in conjunction with fiscal soundness. The second sentence indicates that the challenge of overcoming deflation is insurmountable. Therefore, the first sentence in table 6.2 is coded as "positive," while the second sentence is coded as "negative."

Both sentences are very different from the third one in table 6.2, where the text from a meeting in October of 2003 is factual and neutral. The kind of nuance illustrated by the three sentences about deflation is one of the benefits of our mixed approach that combines human coding with machine-selection of sentences. At this point in time, an automatic, machine-based procedure would be unlikely to capture the layers of meaning embedded in the examples in table 6.2.

The third word we assess is "price." In this case, we need to distinguish between different contexts. The BOJ members can talk about prices in terms of rising prices or in terms of declining prices. When it comes to the word "price," therefore, we have five alternative frames in which rising or declining prices are viewed in a "positive," "negative," or "neutral" manner. Table 6.3 presents a sentence for each of the five frames.

For example, the minutes from a board meeting held in July 2000 report that in a discussion of price trends, "judging from developments in wholesale prices, downward pressure stemming from weak demand had almost disappeared." That sentence is coded as a "positive" statement about prices. The depiction of rising prices in the first sentence of table 6.3 contrasts with the one in the second sentence. There the word "price" is used to warn against the negative consequences of rising oil prices, not only for economic growth but for further inflation. Rising prices are seen in a negative light. The second sentence also differs from the third one, where the minutes report a causal explanation of a fact about rising prices in August of 2005.

The final two sentences in table 6.3 turn to declining prices, or deflation. In one case, from a meeting held in May 2010, the BOJ board members minimize the concerns about the decline of consumer prices thanks to improving macroeconomic conditions. Thus that sentence is an instance in which deflation is portrayed in a "positive" manner. The sentence from the April 2006 meeting, however, conveys a concern about declining prices. In that case, "mildly deflationary" prices are seen as a problem "despite some signs of gradual improvement," which in this context implies that rising prices should be welcomed. That counts as an instance in which deflation is portrayed as a concern.

All in all, this approach allows us to capture nuance while being comprehensive, systematic, and transparent at the same time. The next section explains how we generate a summary measure of the policy ideas at the BOJ based on these coded sentences.

TABLE 6.3 Coding the sentences: Price

DATE	ORIGINAL	TRANSLATION	CODING
2000-07-17	さらに別の委員は、国内卸売物価を見る限り、需要不足による下落圧力はほとんどみられないとの見方を示した	Another member expressed the view that judging from developments in wholesale prices, downward pressure stemming from weak demand had almost disappeared.	Inflation positive
2000-10-30	別のひとりの委員は、原油価格の上昇が世界経済の減速をもたらすリスクのみならず、物価上昇圧力に繋がらないかという視点も重要である、と述べた	Another committee member mentioned that it is important to take note of the fact that not only the risk of the crude oil prices leading to a slowdown of the global economy, but it might also lead to upward pressure on prices.	Inflation negative
2005-08-09	国内企業物価は原油価格の影響などから上昇している	Domestic corporate goods prices have risen due to the effects like increases in the crude oil prices.	Neutral
2010-05-21	物価面では、中長期的な予想物価上昇率が安定的に推移するとの想定のもと、マクロ的な需給バランスが徐々に改善することなどから、消費者物価(除く生鮮食品)の前年比は下落幅が縮小していくと考えられる	On the price front, under the assumption that the medium to long term expected inflation rate remains stable, the year-to-year rate of decline in consumer prices (excluding fresh food) is likely to reduce gradually owing to the slowly improving macro supply and demand balance.	Deflation positive
2006-04-28	しかしながら物価の動向を総合してみると、改善がみられるものの緩やかなデフレ状況にある	However, the overall trends in the prices remain mildly deflationary despite some signs of gradual improvement.	Deflation negative

An Empirical Measure of the BOJ Policy Ideas

Many central bankers, especially those from countries that have suffered from bouts of hyperinflation (Henning 1994), view combating inflation as one of the primary missions of a central bank. Economic theory and historical experience have coalesced to create a common vision in which low inflation is a condition that promotes economic growth and prosperity regardless of the weak empirical support for this vision (as discussed in chapter 3). Policies that reduce inflation are therefore to be pursued because of their overall benefit to the economy, even if they might cause short-term costs. At the risk of oversimplification, we call this type of orientation the standard, hawkish, view in monetary policy. Conversely, whenever lowering prices are seen as a problem and taking steps to countering deflation is a goal to pursue, we have a manifestation of a different perspective that challenges the standard view. For lack of a better term, we call this orientation the dovish, or alternative, view.

Obviously, the perspectives of central bank officials, at the BOJ or at any other central bank, are going to be more sophisticated and nuanced. For example, central bank officials will have different opinions about the effectiveness of different policy tools, or the transmission channels of quantitative easing, or the ability of the BOJ to influence demand or market confidence. Those opinions will not only support different decisions but also frame the context of their discussions. In stark terms, however, by coding whether inflation and deflation were portrayed through positive or negative sentiments, we can track to what extent an important aspect of bank officials' policy worldviews permeated the debates at each meeting.

As covered in chapter 4, the BOJ institutional orientation emphasizes price stability and prizes its own independence. Thus we might expect that hawkish views would be predominant. The BOJ board deliberations, however, reflect the problems at hand as much as they reflect the underlying policy ideas of the BOJ. Therefore, we expect fluctuations—sometimes even large fluctuations—in the ways either the standard view or the dovish view of monetary policy emerges throughout the deliberations.

Our measure is intuitive and simple: a "negative" sentiment for inflation belongs in the same worldview as a "positive" sentiment for deflation. Conversely, a "positive" sentiment for inflation belongs in the same worldview as a "negative" sentiment for deflation. For each use of the words "inflation" and "deflation," we can track the two sides of the same coin: the larger the number of instances in which inflation is seen in a negative light, or deflation is viewed as benign, the more the policy board members articulated their positions in the board discussions in line with a hawkish worldview about monetary policy; conversely, the larger the number of instances in which deflation is seen in a negative light, or inflation is viewed as benign, the more the policy board members articulated their positions in the board discussions in line with a dovish worldview about monetary policy. Table 6.4 summarizes the coding protocol that connects the sentiments coded from the sentences to the hawkish or dovish worldviews.

TABLE 6.4 From sentiments to monetary worldviews

WORD SENTIMENT	INFLATION/RISING PRICES	DEFLATION/DECLINING PRICES
Positive	Dovish	Hawkish
Negative	Hawkish	Dovish

TABLE 6.5 Measuring ideas at the BOJ: Four indexes

LABEL	SENTENCES WITH THE WORDS	FORMULA
Index_1	Inflation, deflation	$\dfrac{Hawkish}{(Hawkish + Dovish)}$
Index_2	Inflation, deflation	$\dfrac{Hawkish}{(Hawkish + Dovish + Neutral)}$
Index_3	Inflation, deflation, and price	$\dfrac{Hawkish}{(Hawkish + Dovish)}$
Index_4	Inflation, deflation, and price	$\dfrac{Hawkish}{(Hawkish + Dovish + Neutral)}$

Using this approach, we measure the policy ideas prevailing in each meeting of the BOJ board. We compute a number of indexes that, while sharing the same approach, differ in how they are normalized. The most basic index takes the proportion of negative references to inflation and positive references to deflation in a document over the total number of references to inflation and deflation, regardless of whether the inflation and deflation words were used in a positive or negative manner. For example, in the minutes of the meeting held on August 11, 2000, our coding protocol measured ten references to inflation and deflation. Five were hawkish references to deflation, two were dovish references to inflation, and three were dovish references to deflation. The index, thus, measures 0.5.

This index is then "augmented" in two manners: first by including neutral references to inflation and deflation, and second by including the references to rising or declining prices, as illustrated in table 6.5.

What do those four indexes convey? For each document, for each meeting of the policy board, the indexes compute the extent to which inflation and deflation were discussed in a hawkish manner over the total number of references to inflation and deflation. All four indexes can potentially vary from 0 to 1. The larger the number, the more the hawkish view permeated the debates; zero means that no hawkish references were made, 1 means that only hawkish references were made. As an illustration, see the plot of how the indexes fluctuated over time in figure 6.1.

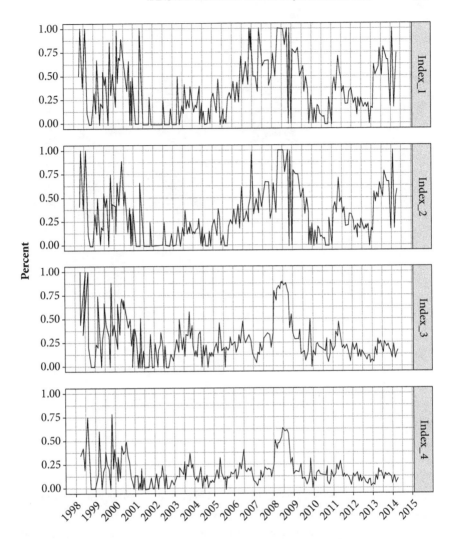

FIGURE 6.1. Policy ideas at the BOJ: The four indexes over time

The four indexes are, as should be expected, highly correlated: as shown graphically in figure 6.2, the correlations range from a minimum of 0.65 between index_1 and index_4 and a maximum of 0.97 between index_1 and index_2. Thus we can conclude that the indexes capture the same phenomenon, that is, the extent to which orthodox ideas about prices permeated the debates at the BOJ board meeting. At the same time, however, the indexes portray slightly different nuances in the debates. It is "easier" for index_1 and index_2 to reach the top level of 100 percent. That means that in the course of specific debate at the BOJ board

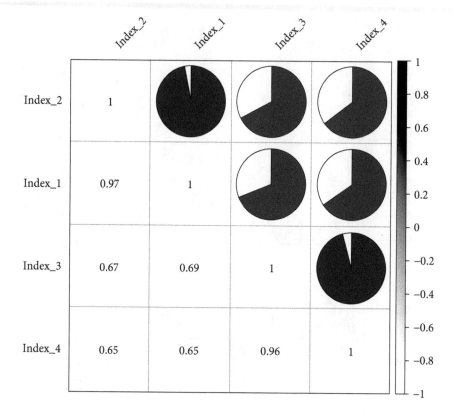

FIGURE 6.2. Correlation plot of the four indexes

meeting, inflation was exclusively portrayed in negative terms. By broadening the relevant vocabulary by assessing the ways in which the word "price" was used, we measure lower percentages given that factual and neutral statements also came into the conversation.

All in all, these measures capture the revealed preferences about inflation and deflation among the BOJ board members.

Testing the Theory

In our analysis, we seek to assess whether the discussions at the BOJ board meetings were systematically associated with the decisions about monetary policy. Our approach mirrors the one advocated by Chwieroth (2007): we ask "how much" of the variation in monetary policy decisions can be attributed to the ideas expressed by the BOJ members compared to factual economic and political conditions. The expectation, based on our theory, is that the revealed preferences expressed in the BOJ board debates will account for the monetary policy decisions above and beyond the objective conditions of the economy.

The dependent variable measures the change in the monetary base, one of the most consequential instruments of monetary policy. This includes all currency in circulation and reserve balances held at the central bank. Under conventional monetary policy, central banks alter the monetary base to target short-term interest rates, and, as discussed in chapter 2, under QE, central banks specifically set numerical targets for monetary base expansion. We do not use short-term interest rates in our analysis because interest rates have often been close to zero, and we are most interested in the BOJ's use of "unconventional" monetary policy. Since the time unit between our observations is irregular—the time between two BOJ board meetings—we calculated the average change in monetary base per day.

Table 6.6 reports our baseline models. We start with models that exclude a lagged dependent variable, that is, exclude the change in the monetary base enacted in the previous time unit. In so doing, we follow the now classic advice from Achen (2001), who warns against the pitfalls of lagged dependent variables. To assuage potential concerns, however, we also test models with a lagged dependent variable in our battery of robustness tests (see the appendix at the end of the book).

Given our theory, we expect a negative coefficient on the index variables measuring the prevailing ideas about inflation at each BOJ board meeting. In other words, a negative coefficient on the BOJ ideas index means that the more the BOJ board members talked about inflation and deflation in a hawkish manner, the less they expanded the monetary base. We use a square root transformation for the indexes to capture the idea of declining effects, the idea that each additional reference to inflation or deflation is likely to have a smaller impact on the decisions about the monetary base.[9]

The models also include a battery of additional factors that might shape the political and economic context within which the monetary base decisions were made. In so doing, we not only assess our key theoretical variable in a broader framework, but we also ensure that a battery of political and economic factors that might have induced a spurious relation between the BOJ ideas and the monetary base is explicitly modeled beforehand (King 1991).

---

9. The square root transformation also makes the distribution of the index variables more symmetric, as illustrated in figure 6A-1 in the appendix.

TABLE 6.6 Regression models: Change in the monetary base

	INDEX 1	INDEX 2	INDEX 3	INDEX 4
Intercept	1427.07(***)	1457.72(***)	1381.11(***)	1300.59(***)
	(469.78)	(476.14)	(477.86)	(470.05)
BOJ ideas	−329.36(***)	−364.10(***)	−310.20(**)	−342.79(*)
	(122.76)	(133.96)	(143.01)	(190.25)
Monetary base	0.48	0.51	0.62	0.62
	(0.60)	(0.58)	(0.60)	(0.60)
Economic growth	−69.74	−71.03	−66.98	−65.95
	(50.30)	(50.44)	(50.52)	(50.64)
Change in CPI	−5855.23	−5634.90	−5429.55	−5594.72
	(4226.44)	(4171.32)	(4148.66)	(4156.22)
Debt	−1.35	−1.44	−1.32	−1.23
	(0.97)	(0.97)	(0.96)	(0.96)
Political business cycle	5.46	1.30	47.17	46.86
	(66.54)	(68.87)	(95.76)	(96.13)
Legislative veto points	492.78(**)	510.30(**)	500.74(**)	487.29(**)
	(228.09)	(228.62)	(227.97)	(226.96)
Abe 1 dummy	372.64(*)	381.62(*)	268.11	260.32
	(222.07)	(223.36)	(217.32)	(216.21)
Abe 2 dummy	1505.95(***)	1491.01(***)	1389.28(***)	1392.52(***)
	(480.88)	(478.87)	(464.52)	(464.64)
Partisan control of government	−669.92(**)	−672.69(**)	−733.84(***)	−728.71(***)
	(282.03)	(276.83)	(271.73)	(270.61)
Fukushima dummy	−517.12(*)	−512.86(*)	−606.51(**)	−616.35(**)
	(308.19)	(309.17)	(302.74)	(303.71)
GFC dummy	−230.17(***)	−233.28(***)	−222.75(**)	−221.25(**)
	(88.71)	(88.31)	(98.00)	(97.90)
Fukui dummy	−182.84	−177.30	−240.67	−251.02
	(165.36)	(163.29)	(171.08)	(171.95)
Shirakawa dummy	−101.35	−72.55	−211.60	−227.29
	(250.21)	(252.19)	(250.93)	(251.32)

	INDEX 1	INDEX 2	INDEX 3	INDEX 4
Kuroda dummy	93.34	128.29	−89.41	−123.80
	(602.48)	(599.11)	(593.70)	(591.36)
Num. obs.	242	243	247	248
R2	0.39	0.39	0.38	0.38
Adj. R2	0.35	0.35	0.34	0.34
L.R.	120.11	120.96	119.75	119.60

Robust standard errors; ***$p < 0.01$, **$p < 0.05$, *$p < 0.1$

In more detail, we include measures for the overall level of the monetary base, economic growth, inflation, and debt. Economic growth is measured using the changes in GDP from the previous quarter (at chained 2005 prices, seasonally adjusted series), while inflation is measured as the change in the CPI between policy meetings. To calculate the debt position, we use quarterly statistics on outstanding debt. To establish a more accurate estimate of the total debt on the date of a given meeting, we assume a linear relationship between the quarterly figures and interpolate the data on a daily basis.[10]

On the political side, we include a measure of partisanship: a dummy variable measuring whether the LDP (coded 1) or DPJ (coded 0) were in power; a dummy variable measuring whether elections for the lower house were to be held within two weeks of a BOJ board meeting; and a measure for each of Abe Shinzō's two tenures as prime minister. We also include a variable that measures whether different parties controlled the upper and lower houses of Japan's legislature, which occurred twice between 1998 and 2014. Referred to as a "twisted Diet" in Japan, this situation should make it more difficult for the government to influence the decision making of a central bank. With a divided chamber, there are more veto points, which in turn dampens the credibility of any threat by the government to take action against the central bank (Lohmann 1998; Keefer and Stasavage 2003).

Two period dummy variables, one for the GFC and one for the "3–11" triple disaster, are also included. The final set of controls takes into account the

---

10. Outstanding debt includes long- and short-term government bonds, fiscal and investment loan bonds (FILP bonds), and government borrowing.

leadership of the BOJ itself by including dummies for different BOJ governors for the period under investigation.

The results from the models are strongly consistent with our theory. The coefficients for the four indexes measuring ideas at the BOJ board meetings are negative and statistically significant, as expected from our theory. The smallest coefficient (in absolute terms) is the one for index_3 ($\beta=-310.2$); the largest is the one for index_2 ($\beta=-364.1$). A unit increase, from 0 to 1, in the BOJ index is associated with an average contraction in the monetary base of ¥310.1 million per day, at a minimum, or ¥364.1 million per day, at maximum.

One can get a better sense of how concern about inflation impacted the monetary base from figure 6.3. We plot the predicted change in the monetary base for a hypothetical situation where all the variables in our models are set at their median value, while the index measuring the ideas expressed at the BOJ board meeting vary from their minimum to their maximum. When the index is equal to zero, it means that throughout a meeting there were no hawkish references to either inflation or deflation. In that case, our model predicts a positive change in the monetary base of about ¥75 million per day. As the index grows, that is, as the number of instances in which inflation is addressed in negative terms and deflation is addressed in positive terms increases, the change in the monetary base gets smaller and smaller until a point when the anti-inflation discourse becomes so predominant that our model predicts a negative change, that is, a contraction of the monetary base.

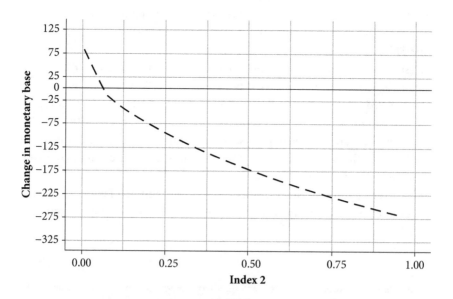

FIGURE 6.3. Predicted change in the monetary base

Of the other variables in the models, four emerge as systematic predictors. Periods in which the upper and lower houses in Japan's Diet were held by different parties were, on average, more likely to experience positive changes in the monetary bases than periods in which the two houses were controlled by the same party. This scenario occurred twice in the time period under investigation: between July 2007 and August 2009 and again between December 2012 and July 2013, when the DPJ controlled the upper house while the LDP controlled the lower house. If we take a divided chamber as an indicator of veto points, it might appear that in the Japanese case, an institutional hurdle was associated with slightly more expansionary monetary policies. The effect of the legislative veto point variable, however, is offset by the partisan control of government dummy variable, which measures the periods in which the LDP was the majority party in the lower house. Overall, political and institutional factors played a limited role in the changes in the monetary base. In particular, we did not find any systematic difference in the decision-making processes at the BOJ in the two weeks preceding an election for the lower house. We did not find an election effect even using a longer time window (four and six weeks before an election) to account for the possibility that the election date was already announced and therefore known by then.

Finally, we find two additional period effects: on average, the monetary base experienced contraction after the Fukushima disaster and after the GFC. The specific leadership at the BOJ, on the other hand, did not appear to make a difference in the overall changes in the monetary base. More specifically, once we control for the impact of the policy ideas and the political and economic conditions, we did not detect any additional differences on the monetary base across the BOJ governors.

The Abe Effect

The effect of the prevailing concern about inflation at the BOJ board meeting does not match the break associated with the rise to the premiership of Abe Shinzō. By itself, the Abe effect was at least five times as large, in the opposite direction, as the effect associated with the prevailing ideas at the BOJ meetings. The Abe effect, though, is a period effect associated with his second premiership. During his first stint as prime minister, between September 2006 and September 2007, the models estimate a positive coefficient (i.e., on average, monetary policy was more expansionist); the effect, however, is statistically significant in only two out of four models.

The results associated with Abe Shinzō's terms in power suggest that it was the introduction of "Abenomics," the policy platform advocated in the 2012 general election, rather than the prime minister per se, that made a difference. These results also help us understand why there are no significant effects for the different governors of the BOJ, in particular Governor Kuroda, who was appointed by Prime Minister Abe. As an advocate of looser monetary policy, Governor Kuroda undoubtedly had his say on Japan's monetary policy. The regression models simply do not detect any additional effect above and beyond the political and economic conditions and the status of the debates at the BOJ.

Looking at the fluctuations for our indicators of hawkish discourse at the BOJ meetings in figure 6.1, we can detect an interesting pattern: From 2013 onwards, index_1 and index_2 are systematically larger than index_3 and index_4. If we recall that index_1 and index_2 measured the sentiments associated with the words "inflation" and "deflation" only, while index_3 and index_4 also included the word "price," the BOJ members systematically expressed more hawkish views about inflation and deflation after the start of Abe's second term. The indexes that include the word "price" (index_3 and index_4), however, remained— metaphorically—more subdued, which indicates that the word "price" was used more often than not in a dovish manner.

More specifically, starting from 2013, index_1 and index_2 were, on average, between about 0.5 and 0.6. In other words, the words "inflation" and "deflation" were used in a hawkish context more than half the time. The comparison with the average scores before Abe's second term is revealing: index_1 and index_2 were, on average, about 0.3. In a statistical test, such a difference is highly significant.

But if bank officials systematically worried more about inflation after Abe's electoral victory in 2012, did it make a difference on how the BOJ worldviews related to the changes in the monetary base? To check for this possibility, we interacted the indicator for Abe's second spell as prime minister and the measures for the hawkishness of the BOJ discussions about inflation, deflation, and prices. In all instances, the interaction terms have a positive sign but do not reach statistical significance.[11]

At this point, therefore, the models do not provide sufficient evidence to discern a conditional effect of the BOJ worldviews. Substantively, however, the opposite signs for the baseline and the interaction term coefficients associated with the BOJ worldview suggest a thought-provoking interpretation. Despite a turn to a more hawkish discourse around inflation and deflation during Abe's second spell, the discourse at the BOJ board meetings had less influence on the decisions. This is because the two effects cancel each other out. While more data are needed to confirm this interpretation, it appears that the change in policy followed from Abe's political influence and the implementation of his economic agenda.

---

11. The results for the models with interaction terms are reported in table A-1 in the appendix.

Robustness Checks

Given the theoretical and policy relevance of our findings, it is important to check how robust they are. To this end, we estimated a variety of alternative specifications, reported in full in the appendix to this chapter at the end of the book. The bottom line of these tests is straightforward: the finding holds remarkably well. We lagged the economic control variables by one period; we added a lagged dependent variable; we estimated the models using an alternative formula to compute the indexes for the BOJ ideas, that is, rather than the proportions we illustrated in table 6.5, we used ratios. In the case of ratios, then, the index is equal to 1 for balanced documents, where statements of concern about inflation are as common as statements of concerns about deflation, while it is greater than 1 when the statements of concern about inflation prevail and it must be between 0 and 1 when the statements of concern about deflation prevail.

In all the models we estimated, the key variable measuring the BOJ ideas has a negative sign, as we expect from our theory, and it is statistically significant in fourteen of twenty model specifications, providing a high level of confidence in our findings.

In this chapter, we tracked the ways in which ideas about deflation and inflation emerged in the policy debates at the BOJ board meetings. We then sought to isolate the impact of those ideas over the decisions to change the monetary base. We have found that the more the central bankers worry about inflation and price stability relative to the problem of deflation, regardless of actual economic and financial conditions, the less willing they are to expand the monetary base to overcome low inflation and low growth.

Our quantitative methodology can only go so far; it can only scratch the surface of the nuance and the context in the board discussions. But in the larger mosaic of Japan's monetary policy decision making, this chapter adds yet another tile: we have shown that the more central bankers are tied to the idea of price stability and fighting inflation, the less they are willing to use unconventional monetary policy to address the challenges of deflation.

We also acknowledge that our measure of sentiment only captures one dimension of the BOJ's broader worldview—its strict and tenacious view of price stability—described in previous chapters. The next chapter leverages case studies in order to explore how a wider range of elements of the BOJ's policy ideas—its view of independence, its skepticism of the efficaciousness of monetary base expansion, etc.—shaped the Policy Board's deliberation of monetary policy and ultimately its decisions.

Chapter 7

MONETARY POLICYMAKING, 1998–2012

> Using a golf metaphor, the BOJ's current monetary policy, which does not target the ball to the hole of employment and economic recovery, is like a golfer who does not hit the ball to the hole or only uses a putter to do so by claiming that there is a (non-existent) cliff on the other side of the hole.
>
> —Hamada Kōichi, Yale economist, in his communication with Abe Shinzō, November 2012

The Japanese economy began to experience serious deflation from the late 1990s after a series of financial institutions failed. At roughly the same time, the New BOJ Law came into effect. The law established an independent Policy Board, and to increase transparency it requires the disclosure of minutes and the release of full transcripts after an embargo period. Drawing on these and other materials including elite interviews, this chapter analyzes how the BOJ's policy ideas guided Japan's monetary policy in the context of this new institutional environment. These policy ideas, sustained by the formal and informal institutions of Japan's policy network discussed in chapter 5, included a hawkish view on price stability, a belief in the ineffectiveness of monetary policy in overcoming deflation or promoting economic recovery, and an expansive view of the BOJ's independence. Amid difficult economic conditions and under growing political pressure, the BOJ Policy Board made policy choices largely informed by these ideas.

This chapter complements chapter 6 by using three case studies of the BOJ's monetary policy to illustrate how these policy ideas influenced BOJ decision making. The three cases, spread over the period from 1998 to 2012, are (1) the decision to implement and then lift the ZIRP (1998–2000), (2) the first QE policy

---

Epigraph: A fax message sent from Hamada to Abe quoted in Kujiraoka (2017, 267); translated by the authors.

(2001–6), and (3) the policies implemented in response to the GFC and then Japan's "3–11" triple disaster (the massive earthquake, tsunami, and nuclear meltdown that occurred on March 11, 2011). These case studies allow us to examine how policy ideas were translated into policies and how they survived despite major challenges: both deflation and political demands for monetary stimulus. During these fifteen years under three *haenuki* governors, the BOJ's worldview made it slow to tackle deflation head-on and cautious in its reflationary measures. The BOJ Policy Board at various times did concede to outside pressure to use unorthodox monetary measures such as forward guidance or QE. It did so reluctantly, however, and it continued to resist unconventional monetary policy and to view the problem of deflation with complacency; at times the Policy Board even cited "good deflation" resulting from increased productivity, the IT revolution, or market liberalization. When afforded room to maneuver, the Policy Board was ready to retreat quickly from monetary easing, in some cases even before the economy was fully out of deflation.

Case 1: Zero Interest Rate Policy (ZIRP) (February 1999 to August 2000)

The BOJ Policy Board decided to implement a zero interest rate policy (ZIRP) at the Monetary Policy Board meeting on February 12, 1999. At the time, ZIRP was considered to be the ultimate *conventional* monetary policy as the nominal interest rate fell to zero. From the view of the Policy Board, it was an extreme measure, one step short of turning to unconventional policies such as QE or adopting an inflation target.[1] The Japanese economy was in dire straits in late 1998 following the collapse and nationalization of two large long-term credit banks, and the Nikkei stock index had dropped dramatically. Over the objection of one Policy Board member (Shinotsuka), the remaining eight members voted in favor of the ZIRP (chapter 5; appendix). Yet only a little more than a year later, on August 11, 2000, the Policy Board lifted ZIRP with two members opposing the proposal. In short, the policy was adopted, implemented haphazardly, and then abruptly discontinued despite strong opposition from the government. What was the motivation behind the BOJ's introduction and lifting of ZIRP?

The eighteen-month history of ZIRP reveals several ways in which the BOJ's policy ideas influenced its monetary policy decisions. During this time,

---

1. Of course, later in January 2016, the BOJ lowered its call rate to below zero (chapter 8).

Governor Hayami Masaru, an inflation hawk, who believed in a strong yen, presided over the Policy Board (Wakatabe 2015, 31). First, the Policy Board resorted to ZIRP as a way to avoid a sharp rise in the interest rates on Japanese government bonds (JGBs) in support of the government's efforts to stabilize the financial industry *without* having to use QE. Second, in the BOJ's eyes, the major concerns over continuing ZIRP were the policy's possible inflationary consequences, including the emergence of an asset bubble. Such concerns are also why the BOJ Policy Board refused to accept inflation targeting. Third, Governor Hayami and his Policy Board members strongly adhered to a belief it needed to assert the policy of BOJ independence, which inhibited the BOJ's cooperation with the government, especially at the time of the ZIRP phaseout. Instead, the BOJ Policy Board sought to lift ZIRP to create the space that would allow it to use its favored policy instrument: the call rate.

Introducing ZIRP

At the time of the February 1999 Policy Board meeting where ZIRP was introduced, the Japanese economy was facing a deflationary spiral in the wake of the financial crisis of the late 1990s. The motivation behind ZIRP, however, was not to address deflation; rather, the Policy Board resorted to ZIRP to stabilize the financial sector and to *avoid* unconventional measures, specifically purchases of JGBs (Umeda 2011). The BOJ implemented ZIRP to support the government's financial recovery plan. Although the government had taken measures (such as the Emergency Measures for Early Strengthening of Financial Functions in October 1998) to stabilize the banks, the financial sector was still extremely weak, and the government and BOJ agreed to use ZIRP to help out the banks. The ZIRP's implementation was timed to amplify the effect of a ¥7.5 trillion injection of public funds to stabilize the financial system that followed soon after in March 1999 (Umeda 2011).

From the perspective of the BOJ, deploying ZIRP also critically served as a more palatable policy alternative to purchasing government bonds. In reaction to Prime Minister Obuchi's plans for another round of fiscal stimulus measures, the fiscally conservative MOF announced in December 1998 that it would suspend its JGB purchases through the Fiscal Investment Loan Program (FILP) starting in January 1999.[2] The move triggered a spike in the long-term JGB interest rate from below 1 percent to 2.512 percent by February 5, 1999. Under these circumstances, the Policy Board had three choices: (1) take no action, (2) purchase

---

2. This was widely known as the "Unyōbu shokku (Trust Fund Bureau Shock)."

JGBs, or (3) pursue the last step of conventional monetary policy (Umeda 2011).[3] From the view of the Policy Board, the purchase of JGBs was deemed the most problematic choice.

In the months leading up to the ZIRP's initiation, politicians continually pressured the BOJ to buy JGBs in order to keep the interest rates low. In response, Governor Hayami cautioned that purchasing long-term JGBs "[will] squander fiscal discipline and it could cause an inflationary spiral . . . in the future."[4] The BOJ feared that purchasing JGBs would lead to a loss of fiscal discipline and start the BOJ down the slippery slope of coming under pressure to monetize public debt (Kamikawa 2014, 59–60).[5] The Policy Board sought to maintain independence by avoiding measures that would blur what it viewed as the critical line between monetary (*kin'yū*) and fiscal (*zaisei*) affairs; consequently, the BOJ settled on its last conventional tool: ZIRP.[6]

Once ZIRP was initiated, the Policy Board worked to manage market expectations by introducing a forward guidance strategy in April 1999. The BOJ explicitly committed to maintaining ZIRP "until deflationary concerns were dispelled" (Ueda 2012, 4). Throughout 1999, political demands intensified to further ease monetary policy and address the appreciating yen, but the Policy Board resisted.[7] On September 21, 1999, for instance, the BOJ published a report, "On the Current Monetary Policy," that laid out its position. The report maintained that there was adequate liquidity in the market and indicated that the BOJ would not take additional measures to stimulate the economy.[8] Furthermore, amid pressure to use unsterilized intervention in the foreign exchange market to drive down the yen, the BOJ explicitly stated that it would be firm

---

3. BOJ transcript from the February 11, 1999, Board Meeting, esp. 83–96.

4. Ibid., 80.

5. In addition, the rising "term premium" on the JGBs was an additional concern. Fujiki, Okina, and Shiratsuka (2001, 111) note that "term premium" means the risk premium due to uncertainties in the future development of interest rates and inflation rates. And that "[h]igher uncertainty regarding future inflation would increase long-term interest rates, reflecting the increased risk premium."

6. Umeda (2011) reports that the BOJ Policy Board engaged in the study group session prior to the February 11 Board Meeting to establish a consensus that the BOJ would not engage in the purchase of the long-term JGBs. The board members were clearly feeling immense pressure from the government to take this reflationary action. Although there was no explicit discussion about the government meddling in the Policy Board's monetary decisions, many board members implicitly criticized such political pressure. Four days after ZIRP was adopted, the MOF reversed its policy against the use of FILP for JGB purchases, and the price of the JGBs went up driving down the interest rate.

7. "Seiji kara no Chūmon, Nichigin Konwaku," *Nihon Keizai Shimbun*, October 8, 1999.

8. Tōmen no Kin'yu Seisaku Un'ei ni Kansuru Kangae Kata (On the Currency Monetary Policy), available at the BOJ website, https://www.boj.or.jp/announcements/release_1999/k990921a.htm/. There was clear evidence in the BOJ transcript of the September 21, 1999, Policy Board meeting of the Policy Board reacting to the political pressure on the BOJ to further ease its monetary policy.

in rejecting "erroneous" monetary policy decisions, indicating that it opposed foreign exchange rate intervention.[9]

Lifting ZIRP

The BOJ Policy Board members began to support lifting ZIRP from the spring of 2000. Following Governor Hayami's press interview on April 12, 2000, the media reported that the BOJ would lift ZIRP in the near future (Shimizu 2004),[10] citing concerns that ZIRP might trigger inflation and an economic bubble. At the time, the CPI still hovered at just above zero percent.[11] The eagerness to exit ZIRP stemmed from two factors: the desire to restore the call rate as a policy instrument and a complacent attitude toward deflation. This view led to a premature lifting of the ZIRP by the Policy Board in August 2000.[12] On the first point, the BOJ viewed ZIRP as an anomalous monetary policy position from which it should exit as soon as possible. Governor Hayami expressed concern that ZIRP gave the BOJ no room to maneuver its monetary policy via interest rates; he described ZIRP as a "half dead (*hanbun shin'deiru*) monetary policy" since it rendered the call rate useless as a monetary policy.[13]

Governor Hayami and most of the other Policy Board members also had a relatively optimistic view of the deflation problem. In fact, the discussions during this time make reference to "good deflation" or "benign price decline." As early as January 17, 2000, three different Policy Board members (Yamaguchi, Miki, and Shinotsuka) supported the idea of "good deflation" with statements like "if the prices fall due to supply conditions resulting from technological innovation, if there is positive momentum in the economy, we do not see a strong concern for

---

9. On this point, it is useful to cite a paragraph from the note "On the Current Monetary Policy" that appeared in translation in Ito and Mishkin 2006, note 15. "The foreign exchange rate in itself is not a direct objective of monetary policy. One of the precious lessons we learned from the experience of policy operations during the bubble period is that monetary policy operation linked with control of the foreign exchange rate runs a risk of leading to erroneous policy decisions." Nonetheless, the link between a country's monetary policy and foreign exchange rate was underscored at the G7 finance ministers' meeting, when the BOJ succumbed to pressure and agreed to coordinate with the MOF to manage the foreign exchange rate (Kamikawa 2014, 68).

10. Governor Hayami's press interview conducted on April 12, 2000 ("Nichigin Sōsai zero-kin'ri kaijo ni iyoku," *Nihon Keizai Shimbun*, April 13, 2000), also see Kamikawa 2014, 71–75.

11. A former BOJ Policy Board member who was present at the August 2000 Board Meeting, interview, Tokyo, September 15, 2015.

12. Other reasons given were that no good price indicator exists, no optimal inflation rate can be identified, inflation targeting in deflation is unprecedented, the announcement alone will not be credible, the long-term interest rate will go up, and no additional instruments are available at a zero interest rate (Ito 2004, 247–51).

13. BOJ transcript from the Board Meeting on June 28, 2000, 55.

deflation."[14] Governor Hayami continued to make the case that the factors generating "good deflation" helped explain declining prices throughout 2001 after the BOJ lifted the ZIRP.[15]

With a one-month delay (due mainly to the bankruptcy of a major department store, Sogo, in July), on August 11, 2000, the Policy Board voted 7 to 2 in favor of ending ZIRP by raising the call rate to 0.25 percent. Board members Ueda and Nakahara cast the two opposing votes. Ueda Kazuo, a renowned economist from the University of Tokyo who was the only monetary economist with a PhD on the board at the time, argued that lifting ZIRP was premature and that there was no cost to waiting longer for a solid economic recovery. Nakahara, the most rebellious board member discussed in earlier chapters, cited the potential negative impact on the economy (Umeda 2011).[16]

The other members, particularly Governor Hayami, argued that lifting ZIRP was necessary to demonstrate the BOJ's policy independence from the Japanese government. During this period, the media, too, framed the decision as a showdown between the ruling LDP, which vehemently opposed lifting ZIRP, and the BOJ's resolve to assert its newly won independence (Kamikawa 2014, 74).

During the August meeting, the government expressed its concern that lifting ZIRP was premature and took the unusual step of requesting a postponement of the board's decision by invoking Article 19 (2) of the New BOJ Law.[17] The board members, including Governor Hayami, flatly rejected this motion with a vote of 8 to 1. Discussion on this issue revealed how strongly the Policy Board members objected to any government challenge to BOJ policy independence or even the appearance of succumbing to government pressure.[18] The media covered this

---

14. BOJ transcript from the Board Meeting on January 17, 2000, 35, 41 and 64. There were many speeches made during the course of 2000 where the BOJ Policy Board members, including Governor Hayami, made references to "good deflation." For example, Hayami (March 21, 2000; http://www.boj. or.jp/announcements/press/koen_2000/ko0003c.htm/), Miki (April 20, 2000; http://www.boj.or.jp/announcements/press/koen_2000/ko0004c.htm/), Fujiwara (July 22, 2000; http://www.boj.or.jp/announcements/press/koen_2000/ko0006b.htm/). Also discussed in Fujii 2004, 147–48.

15. See Hayami's speech on December 22, 2000. http://www.boj.or.jp/announcements/press/koen_2000/ko0012c.htm/. He also maintained the tone during the Policy Board meetings in the late 2001 (BOJ transcripts from October 12 and 29 board meetings).

16. BOJ transcript from the board meeting on August 22, 2000.

17. Article 19 (2) states, "The Minister of Finance, or a delegate designated by him/her, and the Minister of State for Economic and Fiscal Policy, or a designated by him/her, may, when attending the Board meetings for monetary control matters, submit proposals concerning monetary control matters, or request that the Board postpone a vote on proposal on monetary control matters submitted at the meeting until the next Board meeting for monetary control matters."

18. BOJ transcript from Board Meeting on August 11, 2000, esp. 102–4. Corroborated by the former member of the Council on Economic and Fiscal Policy (June 28, 2016) and senior vice minister of the MOF (September 14, 2015) in interviews.

story extensively and framed the story in terms of the BOJ successfully facing down the government.[19] This narrative of needing to assert independence even contributed to convincing some BOJ staff members to shift from opposing ZIRP termination to supporting it (Kamikawa 2014, 71–75).

Throughout this period, some influential economists began to advocate for inflation targeting to tackle deflation (Kamikawa 2014, 52–56).[20] Learning from the experiences of Sweden and New Zealand, countries like Canada, the UK, and Germany adopted inflation targeting policies as an effective tool for maintaining price stability (Mishkin and Posen 1998). Krugman et al. (1998) proposed that Japan adopt a forceful 4 percent inflation target over the next fifteen years to tackle deflation.[21] This was followed by continuous debate among prominent economists in Japan over the BOJ's use of inflation targeting (Iwata 2003).[22] Supporters of inflation targeting policy suggested that by committing to a certain level of "good inflation," Japan's monetary authority could establish positive expectations that would encourage investment and consumption, thereby stimulating the economy.[23] As it considered its policy options and how to deal with growing political pressure,[24] the BOJ Policy Board discussed this measure extensively from 1998 through 2003. Most members were skeptical about the policy (Umeda 2011). The Board ultimately rejected adopting one on the following grounds: (1) the policy was irrelevant to Japan because most of the foreign examples were targeted to containing inflation, not deflation, (2) difficult both on technical grounds and in managing inflationary expectations, and (3) dangerous since once set in motion, inflation would be difficult to control (Wakatabe 2015, 33). Governor Hayami, in particular, repeated his concern about inflation targeting, claiming that "inflation is most likely uncontrollable once triggered."[25] One exception was Nakahara Nobuyuki, who continuously proposed some form of

---

19. "Atomi no warusa o nokoshita zero kin'ri kaijo geki" [Leaving bad taste in the mouth; the drama over the lifting of the zero interest rate policy], *Nihon Keizai Shimbun*, August 12, 2000.

20. Inflation targeting is defined (Ito 2004) as a policy "which involves the public announcement of medium-term numerical targets for inflation with a commitment by the monetary authorities to achieve these targets."

21. "Infure mokuhyō-ron sai fujō: Nichigin no setsumei sekinin shōten" [Inflation target policy reemerges: Accountability of the BOJ in focus], *Nihon Keizai Shimbun*, November 8, 1999.

22. Ito (2004, 242–43) argued that adopting inflation targeting would be highly beneficial for the BOJ because it would (a) increase accountability and transparency, (b) provide instrument independence to the BOJ, and (c) impact inflation expectations.

23. In addition, Iwata (2011) argues that inflation targeting would be an effective way to counter the effects of the continuingly strong yen in the aftermath of the GFC.

24. Ito (2004, 244) documented the frequency of this debate from the monetary policy meeting minutes.

25. Governor Hayami's speech "Price Stability and Monetary Policy" on March 21, 2000 (http://www.boj.or.jp/announcements/press/koen_2000/ko0003c.htm/).

inflation targeting policy at every Monetary Policy Board meeting from November 1998 until he stepped down in March 2002.

It is also revealing that the IMES, the BOJ's research wing, published a report outlining the detrimental political consequences of inflation targeting. The report highlighted that the BOJ would face intense pressure to achieve an inflation target, which might require the BOJ to do whatever it takes to reach the target rate, including taking measures to purchase JGBs (Okina et. al. 2000, 13).[26] The BOJ was not alone in opposing inflation targeting. The MOF and others concerned about Japan's ballooning public debt also worried that it would potentially raise long-term interest rates on JGBs and jeopardize fiscal sustainability (Kamikawa 2014, 95–98).[27]

In sum, in the first few years under the new BOJ and Governor Hayami, the Policy Board launched the ZIRP as the last weapon in its *conventional* monetary policy arsenal. Although the BOJ was clearly reluctant to exhaust its conventional monetary policy options with ZIRP, the Policy Board considered it a better option than QE. The BOJ adopted the policy due to concerns about financial stability and also to avert political pressure to buy more JGBs. Anxious to wind down its experiment and to demonstrate its independence, the BOJ Policy Board directly defied the government by lifting ZIRP and overruling the government's request to postpone the decision. While the move received some praise in the media, the victory proved to be Pyrrhic.

Case 2: Evolution of First QE (March 2001 to March 2006)

In March 2001, the BOJ became the first central bank to implement quantitative easing (QE) in the post–World War II era. Over the next five years, the BOJ gradually increased the size and diversity of its asset purchases. The BOJ's current account balance target grew from ¥5 trillion to ¥35 trillion, and its JGB purchase target tripled from ¥0.4 trillion per month to ¥1.2 trillion per month (table 7.1). Furthermore, the BOJ Policy Board voted to support a purchasing scheme of

---

26. Besides inviting lax fiscal discipline, the BOJ worried that a large purchase of the JGBs could lead to uncertainty in inflationary prospects in the future as well as possible degrading of the JGB's credit rating due to credit risk premium (Okina 2000, 29).

27. In addition, domestic support for the policy of inflation targeting was thin. LDP backbenchers were much more interested in a fiscal stimulus that would lead directly to district votes than they were in a monetary stimulus, and Japanese businesses were not keen on an interest rate hike (Kamikawa 2014, 152–54).

TABLE 7.1   Japan's quantitative easing: 2001–2006

ANNOUNCEMENT DATE	BOJ ACCOUNT BALANCE TARGET (TRILLION ¥)	JGB PURCHASE TARGET (100 BILLION ¥/MONTH)	MAIN COMPONENTS
March 19, 2001	5	4	Introduction of QE
August 14, 2001	6	6	In support of the government's initiative on structural reform
September 18, 2001	Above 6	6	In response to 9/11 terrorist attack. Call rate at 0.10%
December 19, 2001	10–15	8	Amplify measures for monetary expansion
February 28, 2002	Ample supply	10	Secure liquidity at the end of fiscal year
September 18, 2002	Ample supply	10	Purchase of stocks held by private financial institutions
October 30, 2002	15–20	12	Term extension of purchase of bills
March 25, 2003	17–22	12	Establishment of Japan Post. Iraq War starts
April 30, 2003	22–27	12	SARS impact Asian economies
May 20, 2003	27–30	12	Nationalization of Risona Bank. Appreciation of the yen
June 11, 2003	27–30	12	Start BOJ purchase of asset-backed securities
October 10, 2003	27–32	12	Three conditions for lifting QE announced
January 20, 2004	30–35	12	Monetary loosening under acknowledgment of economic recovery
May 20, 2005	30–35	12	Acknowledged that the economy underperformed from the expectation
March 9, 2006	Lifted	Maintain the same level	Moved to the ZIRP (the ZIRP lifted in July 2006)

Source: Koike 2006, 4, from Bank of Japan Home page

equities owed by banks in September 2002, and then approved additional purchases of asset-backed securities (ABS) in March and April 2003. During these five years before the BOJ finally exited from QE in March 2006, the BOJ governorship changed from Hayami (March 1998–March 2003) to Fukui (March 2003–March 2008). This was a period when, under the strong political leadership of Prime Minister Koizumi Jun'ichiro (April 2001–September 2006) and the reformist minister of state for financial services, Takenaka Heizō (September 2002–October 2005), the Japanese government implemented aggressive financial reconstruction plans.

As signs of economic recovery became visible in 2004 and 2005, the BOJ began the process of exiting its QE policy. After the core CPI (year-on-year) rose from between 0.0 to 0.1 percent in the last quarter of 2005 to 0.5 percent in

January 2006, the BOJ Policy Board voted to discontinue QE on March 9, 2006. Four months after lifting QE (Board Meeting on July 14, 2006), the Policy Board increased the overnight call rate from zero percent to 0.25 percent.

Introduction of QE

The introduction and expansion of QE in 2001 seems to suggest a new openness within the BOJ toward unconventional monetary policies that ran counter to the bank's traditional worldview. A closer examination, however, suggests a complex picture in which the BOJ's conservative outlook largely persisted. First, the QE policy grew out of an intense backlash against the BOJ's monetary tightening—the lifting of ZIRP in August 2000—which was widely believed to have pushed the Japanese economy back into recession and deflation. Second, the BOJ saw QE as one way to support the government's moves in 2002 through 2004 to restructure and revive financial institutions by providing an accommodative macroeconomic environment. The BOJ, however, continued to express skepticism about the effectiveness of QE in defeating deflation. Finally, concerns about the negative effects of QE—the creation of an asset bubble, collapse of interest rate signals, monetization of public debt, and fear of risking BOJ independence—motivated the BOJ to lift QE, which it ultimately did despite the government's concern that the economy had not yet exited its deflationary spiral.

Ueda Kazuo, a Policy Board member and macroeconomist from the University of Tokyo, officially introduced the idea of a quantitative target as a BOJ monetary policy instrument in the first postindependence Policy Board meeting in April 1998.[28] Fellow board member Nakahara continuously proposed a similar idea after this meeting. Governor Hayami and the deputy governors were skeptical and cautious (Umeda 2011), and not a single one of Nakahara's proposals received any votes of support other than his own. The BOJ Secretariat was not convinced of QE's effectiveness, either. As late as February 2001, a month before the Policy Board's decision to adopt QE, notable BOJ researchers published a discussion paper through IMES, which concluded, "QE by conducting short-term government securities operations is not effective" (Fujiki, Okina, and Shiratsuka 2001). In short, the reasons for introducing QE did not stem from BOJ's belief in the policy's effectiveness.

The BOJ's decision came first as a result of the BOJ's desire to avoid blame for its past policy mistakes, in particular prematurely ending ZIRP. Less than half a year after the ZIRP ended and as the US tech bubble burst, the Japanese economy

---

28. BOJ Monetary Policy Board minutes from April 9, 1998.

contracted and another round of deflation threatened to emerge as the Japanese stock market fell.[29] The political backlash against the BOJ's premature tightening grew to such an extent that in November 2000 the LDP's Research Commission on the Finance and Banking Systems advocated firing Governor Hayami (Shimizu 2004, 162), and in February 2001, the same LDP commission began to seriously discuss the possibility of revising the New BOJ Law.[30]

Since simply returning to the ZIRP would be a clear admission of error, BOJ staff members preferred an alternative policy option (Arita 2007; Karube 2004, 222–31; Kamikawa 2014, 81–82). The BOJ Policy Board had to make some move to deflect the pressure, and a new and unconventional monetary policy initiative seemed important to recovering the bank's reputation.[31] The BOJ introduced a supplemental stand-by lending facility (called the Lombard Lending Facility) during the February 9, 2001, Policy Board meeting to give banks access to automatic lending in the event of a spike in interest rates. Then, during the March 19, 2001, Policy Board meeting, the members voted in favor of QE by establishing a numerical ceiling for how much the BOJ could raise its current account balance target (¥5 trillion at the initial QE) mainly through the purchase of short-term JGBs. In addition, they declared that the BOJ would continue QE until "the CPI rises stably above zero percent." The latter was quite a low bar given the Japanese economy's pattern of falling back into deflation and considering the economic consensus that inflation measures tend to overstate inflation. Along with monetary easing, "virtual" ZIRP[32] was introduced, as monetary policy focus shifted to the quantitative ceiling of the reserve target and away from the call rate.

Secondly, the BOJ was motivated to adopt the QE policy, despite its doubts about the policy's effectiveness, in order to support the government's efforts toward stabilizing the financial sector. In fact, the introduction of QE was explicitly made contingent on the government's efforts in this regard.[33]

---

29. "Bei keiki ni gensokukan Henchō kenen no koemo: Kabu tsūka kotoshi ha itten geraku" [Slowdown in the US economy and some concerns over changes in the economic mood; stock market, currency slow down this year], *Asahi Shimbun*, December 23, 2000.

30. "'Nichigin Kin'yū seisaku wa mekuramashi': Jimin kin'yū chōsakai de hihan ga zokuzoku" ['BOJ's monetary policy is witchcraft': Vocal criticisms at LDP Commission on the finance and banking systems], *Asahi Shimbun*, February 15, 2001.

31. Some BOJ members saw that QE would make a flexible and preferable monetary policy instrument; it would allow the BOJ to raise the target ceiling indefinitely, compared to the ZIRP that is theoretically bound at zero (Kamikawa 2014, 80–82; Suda 2014). For others such as Deputy Governor Yamaguchi Yutaka, the concern over QE is that it gives the illusion of infinite possibility for additional easing (BOJ transcript from the Policy Board meeting on March 19, 2001, 77).

32. Under the QE policy, the BOJ stopped using the changes in uncovered overnight call rate as its monetary policy target, but as the BOJ's current account balance target expanded, the interest rate moved close to or to zero, hence it is virtual ZIRP.

33. BOJ transcript from Policy Board meeting on March 19, 2001, esp. 57, 58, 100.

The government had been slow to respond to the domestic financial crisis that emerged from Japan's nonperforming loan (NPL) problem, which began in the mid-1990s and continued into the first years of the 2000s. Prime Minister Koizumi came into office with an economic reform agenda, but the first minister of state and financial services, Yanagisawa Hakuo, was hesitant to inject funds into the financial sector, insisting that the major banks were robust and healthy (Kamikawa 2014, 90–91). Concerns over the country's financial health were further heightened by the partial removal of the deposit payoff guarantee (the so-called "payoff"), which came into effect in April 2002. Finally, a solution to the NPL problem came first with Prime Minister Koizumi's instruction to resolve the NPL problem in early September. Takenaka Heizō took over leadership of the FSA late in that September, and the Financial Revitalization Program (the so-called "Takenaka Plan") was implemented the following month. This plan addressed the NPL problem by forcing the banks to reassess their balance sheets and by providing a mandatory injection of public funds to the weaker banks through the Deposit Insurance Law. Meanwhile, it also helped nonfinancial corporations by providing financial support.[34]

The BOJ encouraged and supported these moves. In particular, the BOJ Policy Board took a significant step on September 18, 2002. It decided to expand its unconventional monetary policy of purchasing non-JGB assets by focusing on stocks owned by Japan's financial institutions.[35] This not only provided a buffer against declining stock prices, but it also allowed the government to engage in financial restructuring without negatively affecting the real sector during a time when the stock market was experiencing a major downturn.[36] This BOJ stock purchase scheme was widely used by the banks and helped support stock prices and disentangle cross-shareholding practices among former *keiretsu* companies (Shimizu 2004).[37]

---

34. For the announcement of the "Financial Revitalization Program," see http://webcache. googleusercontent.com/search?q=cache:4oMp3zvLlcwJ:www.fsa.go.jp/news/newsj/14/ginkou/ f-20021031-1.pdf+&cd=2&hl=en&ct=clnk&gl=us.

35. Purchasing equity is "prohibited (*kinjite*)" in principle by the New BOJ Law, which only allows the BOJ to make loans "against collateral in the form of negotiable instruments, national government securities and other securities, or electronically recorded claims (Article 33 (2))," unless "the Bank has obtained authorization from the Minister of Finance and the Prime Minister" (Article 43 (1)).

36. Due to Japan's *keiretsu* conglomerates and the main bank system that prevailed throughout the country's rapid growth era, the banks held a disproportionately large amount of stocks of their own conglomerate companies based on cross-shareholding, which affected the banks' capital base as share prices declined in the early 2000s.

37. Meanwhile, the BOJ also opened its purchase scheme to ABS in June 2003 to support development of the ABS market, but the scheme did not have much impact on the overall stimulus or in developing the market (Umeda 2011).

The timing illustrates that the BOJ used unconventional monetary policy to help tackle the problems in the financial sector and thus facilitate a solution to the NPL problem (Shimizu 2004; Umeda 2011). During the September Policy Board meeting, many board members reiterated how important it was to tackle the NPL issue due to the critical role banks have occupied in the Japanese economic system.[38] The BOJ insisted that despite QE the money supply would not increase if the banks were not revived enough to increase lending (Wakatabe 2015, 32).[39] Furthermore, the BOJ coordinated its support of the government's measures by raising its QE target to ¥20 trillion on the same day the Takenaka Plan was announced.

In short, once pressure forced the BOJ Policy Board to try unconventional monetary policy, it expanded QE not to fight deflation or boost the economy directly, but to encourage and support the government's efforts to solve the NPL problem.[40] In fact, the Policy Board continued to believe that unconventional monetary policy would not revitalize the economy and that what was needed were structural reforms to revive the *supply side* of the economy (i.e., the productive sector) to generate economic growth (Umeda 2011). For this mechanism to work properly, the financial sector had to function smoothly in transmitting funds to the economy. The BOJ's logic differed from the theoretical work on QE, which suggested that QE could work through other channels, such as asset prices and portfolio rebalancing, as discussed in chapter 2.

QE under Governor Fukui

In the middle of the first QE, Prime Minister Koizumi appointed Fukui Toshihiko (March 2003–March 2008), self-proclaimed as a "deflation fighter," as BOJ governor.[41] He appeared to collaborate more closely with the Koizumi government by raising the current account reserve target four months in a row (March,

---

38. BOJ transcript from Policy Board meeting on September 17 and 18, 2002, esp. 48, 68, 70.

39. Ibid., esp. 71. The decision to implement a stock-purchasing scheme was discussed among the board members during the ordinary session following the first day of the Policy Board meeting on September 17. The details of it were disclosed by the *Nihon Keizai Shimbun* (several articles on September 19, 2002) and cited in Umeda 2011 and Shimizu 2004, 218.

40. Minister Yosano once asked Governor Fukui why he maintained the QE and zero interest rate. Governor Fukui responded that it was to help the financial institutions. Yosano Kaoru (former minister of finance and minister of state), in discussion with the authors, Tokyo, January 20, 2016.

41. Many argue that Governor Fukui was much less dogmatic and more flexible in his monetary policy implementation than Hayami or Shirakawa were. Nonetheless, as discussed by Kamikawa (2014, 144–54), Governor Fukui took an active posture toward easing despite his belief against these measures in order to improve the BOJ's reputation and allow more policy space.

April, May, and June 2003).[42] In actuality, however, the expansion of Japan's monetary base was relatively limited (chapter 2), as the BOJ purchase of JGBs increased slowly from ¥42.2 trillion in 2001 to ¥62.3 trillion in 2006.

During Fukui's term, the BOJ also tended to discount the effectiveness of QE and fixate on QE's negative effects. The first BOJ concern was the monetization of public debt and holding of risky assets. To safeguard against this danger, the BOJ Policy Board created an informal ceiling by developing the "banknote rule," which set an upper benchmark on how much the BOJ current account balance could be expanded.[43] The BOJ's holdings of JGBs also exposed it to the risk of capital losses from long-term interest rate movements. To minimize this risk, the Policy Board moved to compress the average period of maturity on the JGBs it owned from 5.5 years at the beginning of QE in February 2001 to 4.0 years in February 2006; the average maturity was the shortest in February 2005 at 3.8 years (Nakazawa and Yoshikawa 2011).[44] Holding assets other than JGBs with lower credit ratings posed additional risk for the BOJ. If the BOJ faced losses, Policy Board members and staff alike feared that it might have to be bailed out by the government (Suda 2014).

Second, as the duration of QE extended into its third year, the BOJ Policy Board members began to express several other concerns regarding QE's detrimental effects on the market. On the macroeconomic side, members of the Policy Board feared the creation of an asset bubble (Suda 2014). QE might also prevent Japan from engaging in serious structural reforms or resolving NPL issues by providing an artificially low interest-rate environment, a point echoed by the IMF (IMF Financial System Stability Assessment, cited in Suda 2014).[45] In addition, the collapse of the interest rate signal in the financial market became a concern. The rapidly expanding yen carry-trade, which was contributing to a global monetary imbalance, was another problem. By 2007, an estimated $1 trillion in funds was borrowed by foreign financial firms in Japan at extremely low interest rates, converted into dollars utilizing the relatively stable exchange rate, and invested in

---

42. Having learned from Governor Hayami's errors, Governor Fukui managed communications and political dynamics much more tactfully than the former governor had. A former member of the Council on Economic and Fiscal Policy, interview, Tokyo, June 28, 2016.

43. In 2001, the circulating banknotes in Japan amounted to ¥76 trillion, while the long-term JGBs outstanding totaled ¥46 trillion.

44. Meanwhile, the average period of maturity of JGB issues by the government increased during this time from four years and eleven months in 2001 to five years and four months in 2005. Data from Ministry of Finance, Debt Management Report 2006, 23, http://warp.ndl.go.jp/info:ndljp/pid/1282348/www.mof.go.jp/english/bonds/saimukanri/2006/saimu.htm.

45. This, in turn, allowed zombie firms to survive, leading to low productivity and depressed job creation (Caballero, Hoshi, and Kashyap 2008).

higher yielding assets, pushing up asset prices around the world (Umeda 2011). These capital outflows contributed to a relatively weak yen at the time, but its reversal would trigger large yen appreciation at the time of the global financial crisis (discussed below).

Despite all of these concerns, the Japanese economy gradually recovered during this period, helped by the global economic upturn. In response, the BOJ laid out plans for phasing out QE. The moves to lift QE and end the second phase of the "virtual ZIRP" began at the Policy Board meeting on October 10, 2003, when the BOJ specified three conditions for discontinuation: (1) the average CPI must increase above zero percent over the next several months, (2) there should be no foreseeable decline in CPI growth, and (3) there must be no other considerations that might require the continuation of QE. Governor Fukui then announced in July 2004 that the Japanese economy was on the verge of full recovery from a decade-long postbubble recession and warned about the re-emergence of an asset bubble (Kamikawa 2014, 122).

QE Phased Out

By the close of 2005 as the CPI began to climb,[46] the BOJ saw indications that all three conditions to stop QE had been met; there were also increasing concerns of asset bubbles in the economy. By October 2005, Governor Fukui along with the other Policy Board members viewed the real estate market in Tokyo as overheating.[47]

In order to judge the timing of the QE phaseout, the BOJ worked to establish its own benchmarks. To that end, the BOJ and its Policy Board engaged in an active debate over how to measure deflation and price stability. Since lifting the first ZIRP in the summer of 2000, the BOJ had struggled to define what it meant by "price stability." The first attempt at clarification was in its 2000 October report titled "On Price Stability."[48] The report ambiguously defined "price stability" as "a situation neither inflationary nor deflationary." As the Policy Board prepared to lift QE, a debate ensued with the government. Governor Fukui and the BOJ, on the one hand, focused on the core CPI data (which excludes perishable food, since

---

46. The BOJ's semiannual report on "Outlook for Economic Activity and Prices" in October 2005 reported this uptick from April 2005. The CPI (excluding fresh foods) rose from negative 0.1 percent to positive 0.1 percent, and the CPI forecast for 2006 projected higher increase of 0.5 percent (up from 0.3 percent in April). Report available at http://www.boj.or.jp/en/mopo/outlook/gor0510.htm/.

47. BOJ transcript from Policy Board meeting on October 12, 2005, 71.

48. The report available at the BOJ website, https://www.boj.or.jp/en/announcements/release_2000/k001013a.htm/.

their prices are volatile), while the government, led by Minister Takenaka, argued in support of considering the GDP deflator as the benchmark.[49] It is important to note that Japan's measure of core CPI at the time, in contrast to the practice of the United States and EU countries, included fuel, which is subject to relatively high price volatility. In fact, during this time, imported fuel prices spiked, which caused the CPI to overstate the underlying inflation. Nonetheless, the BOJ treated the rise of the core CPI (year-on-year) above zero by the end of 2005 as a sufficient reason for lifting QE. By contrast, the government focused on the 1.4 percent decline of the GDP deflator from the previous year.[50]

Despite opposition by the LDP's reflationary faction, represented by Takenaka and Abe Shinzō, the BOJ gained support for terminating QE from Yosano Kaoru,[51] then the minister of state for economic and fiscal policy and a fiscal conservative who had been wary of excessive QE. The proposal to end the QE was supported by all but one of the Policy Board members at the Policy Board meeting on March 9, 2006.[52] During the discussion, board members were explicit in their view that the QE program was an "anomalous (*i'reina*) monetary policy."[53] *Nihon Keizai Shimbun* (March 11, 2006) reported that lifting QE to restore the money market function is a part of the "BOJ's DNA."[54]

The lifting of the QE policy, nonetheless, seemed to be premature to many. Shirai (2017, 16), who served on the BOJ Policy Board from 2011 to 2016, criticizes the rushed normalization of the BOJ's monetary easing and attributes it to

---

49. The GDP deflator measures the prices of all new, domestically produced, final goods and services in an economy including not only consumer items but also capital investment. The BOJ's view behind rejecting the GDP deflator as the benchmark is its propensity for volatility because of the influence of the price of imported goods. For an extensive discussion on the topic, see Ugai and Sonoda 2006.

50. "Nichigin sōsai ryōteki kanwa kaijo Keizai kasseika unagasu: bukka purasu teichaku e" [Bank of Japan lifted the QE and urges economic revitalization: Aiming to continue positive prices], *Nihon Keizai Shimbun*, December 23, 2005. The Cabinet Office later in March 2006 submitted a memo to the upper house Committee on Budget to emphasize the importance of using multiple indicators—from GDP deflator, output gap to unit labor cost—in addition to the CPI to decide on when to declare the end of deflation (Kujiraoka 2017, 146–47).

51. "Kōbō ryōteki kanwa kaijo (part 2): Seifu shibonda kyōkōron maboroshino gokuhi kaigi" [Battle over lifting of QE (part 2): The government's shriveled hardline and the illusionary secret meeting], *Nihon Keizai Shimbun*, March 12, 2006.

52. The one opposition vote came from Nakahara Shin (not the same Nakahara who served on the Policy Board from 1998 to 2002). He noted that he generally agreed with the economic assessment put forward by others. But he voted against the proposal mainly because he thought the CPI data needed more analysis, and it would be better to wait till April after the end of fiscal year (BOJ Policy Board meeting minutes from March 9, 2006, meeting).

53. BOJ transcript from Policy Board meeting on March 9, 2006, esp. 79, 85, 90.

54. "Omoi gōgi hakuhō no gōi" [Heavy discussion, razor-thin agreement], *Nihon Keizai Shimbun*, March 11, 2006.

"upward bias of inflation expectations, perhaps reflecting the BOJ's constantly optimistic projections." Abe Shinzō, the chief cabinet secretary during the lifting of QE, vocally opposed the move and demanded a postponement of the vote. The MOF persuaded him that open disagreement between the BOJ and the government would potentially create negative market sentiment (Kamikawa 2014, 130). Although Abe backed down that time, this experience influenced Abe's later decision to go after the BOJ and replace the Policy Board's leadership in line with his reflationary view after he became prime minister in December 2012 (chapter 8).[55]

Following the lifting of QE in March, which shifted the BOJ's monetary policy target back to the call rate, the BOJ Policy Board members unanimously agreed to lift the "virtual" ZIRP by raising the call rate to 0.25 percent at the July 14, 2006, Policy Board meeting. For this meeting, the Policy Board relied on the core CPI (0.6 percent increase year-on-year at the time) based on the "2000-standard" calculation. Only one month after the decision, the Ministry of Internal Affairs and Communication, which was in charge of the CPI data, issued its revised core CPI based on the new "2005-standard." Using this measure, the CPI was much lower, at 0.1 percent (year-on-year), than the figure the BOJ used (Umeda 2009; Shirai 2017).[56] The Ministry of Internal Affairs and Communication revises the CPI data at regular intervals of five years, so the BOJ knew that a revision of the core CPI data was coming. Given the eagerness of the Policy Board to end QE, they did not wait for the revised CPI. Moreover, the Policy Board did not just freeze the level of the monetary base, it started the process of exiting QE by allowing the monetary base to contract rather than keeping the level steady by reinvesting bond repayments.

In sum, throughout the five years of QE, the BOJ's Policy Board focused on its specific goals other than the country's deflation or economic growth. Although the Policy Board adopted QE, its members were keenly sensitive to the costs of continuing, expanding and extending the QE program from the possible re-emergence of an asset bubble to monetization of public debt to the loss of the call rate as one of BOJ's monetary instruments. Then as soon as there were signs of economic recovery based on the BOJ's hawkish interpretation of economic data, the BOJ moved to exit QE.

---

55. A former policy board member, interview, September 14, 2015, and Honda Etsurō (a former adviser to Prime Minister Abe), in discussion with the authors, September 18, 2015.

56. Also supported by the former Council on Economic and Fiscal Policy member, interview, June 28, 2016.

Case 3: The BOJ's Responses to the Global Financial Crises and 3–11 (2008–2012)

During the "accidental" BOJ governorship of Shirakawa (April 2008–March 2013; see chapter 5 on his appointment process), the Japanese economy faced repercussions from a series of economic crises. They include the GFC from 2008 to 2009, the Dubai crisis of November 2009 triggered by the collapse of the investment company Dubai World, the European sovereign debt crisis in the early 2010s, and the March 11 ("3–11") triple disaster of 2011. During these years, the BOJ implemented new policies—such as "qualitative easing"[57] and lowering the call rate from 0.5 percent to virtually zero (virtual ZIRP)—but avoided aggressive QE (table 7.2).

The Policy Board's resistance to QE is particularly puzzling for this period. The United States, the United Kingdom, and later the ECB began aggressive monetary stimulus that included massive QE programs. While Japan was the first country to experiment with QE only a few years earlier, the BOJ avoided a large ramp-up of QE even as its economy fell back into deflation and recession. The aggressive monetary easing by other central banks while the BOJ stood its ground contributed to yen appreciation against other currencies including the dollar, pound, and euro, hurting Japanese exporters and intensifying their calls for easing.

Facing rising popular support for the opposition DPJ before the lower house election in August 2009, LDP prime minister Asō Tarō (September 2008–September 2009) pushed for policies to stimulate the economy. The DPJ, which had been sympathetic to BOJ policies and independence, prevailed in the historic election. But after taking control of the government (September 2009–December 2012), it intensified demands on the BOJ to reflate the economy. From all quarters, the BOJ came under attack for doing "too little, too-late" (Kamikawa 2014, 207–11; Suda 2014).

The response on the part of the BOJ facing the GFC reflects similar patterns from the cases of ZIRP and QE. The BOJ and its staff delayed the Policy Board's adoption of aggressive easing measures in the immediate aftermath of

---

57. Farmer (2012, 1) distinguishes *qualitative* easing (QuaE), which is "a shift in the composition of the assets of the central bank toward less liquid and riskier assets, holding constant the size of the balance sheet," from conventional *quantitative* easing (QE), which is "an increase in the size of the balance sheet of the central bank through an increase it is monetary liabilities." The "qualitative" element under Governor Kuroda's quantitative and qualitative easing (QQE) also includes purchases of JGBs at different length of maturity (Shirai 2016, 127).

TABLE 7.2 Japan's comprehensive monetary easing: 2008–2012

ANNOUNCEMENT DATE	UNCOLLATERALIZED OVERNIGHT CALL RATE	BASIC LOAN RATE	ASSET PURCHASE (¥100 BILLION)	MAIN COMPONENTS
October 31, 2008	(0.5 %→) 0.3 %	(0.75 %→) 0.5 %		In response to economic downturn resulting from GFC and coordinated interest rate reduction.
December 19, 2008	0.1 %	0.3 %	JGB: (12/month→) 14/month	Introduction of the "Special Funds-Supplying Operations to Facilitate Corporation Financing." Introduction of outright purchases of CP.
January 22, 2009			CP/ABCP: 30	
February 19, 2009			Corporate bonds: 10	Introduction of outright purchases of corporate bonds.
March 18, 2009			JGB: 18/month	
October 30, 2009				Decide to extend the expiration date of the "Special Funds-Supplying Operation."
December 1, 2009				Introduction of the "Fixed-Rate Funds-Supplying Operation against Pooled Collateral."
June 15, 2010				Introduction of the "Fund-Provisioning Measure to Support Strengthening the Foundations for Economic Growth."
August 30, 2010				Increase the amount of funds provided through the "Fixed-Rate Funds-Supplying Operation against Pooled Collateral."
October 5, 2010	Between 0 and 0.1 %			Introduction of the "Comprehensive Monetary Easing" policy. Introduction of outright purchases of ETFs and J-REITs.

October 28, 2010	Total: 350	Introduction of the "Asset Purchase Program."
March 14, 2011	Total: 400	
June 14, 2011		Establish a new line of credit for the "Fund-Provisioning Measure to Support Strengthening the Foundations for Economic Growth."
August 4, 2011	Total: 500	
October 27, 2011	Total: 550	
February 14, 2012	Total: 650	Introduction of the "Price Stability Goal in the Medium to Long Term."
March 13, 2012		Increase the amount of funds provided through the "Fund-Provisioning Measure to Support Strengthening the Foundations for Economic Growth," and extend the expiration date of this measure.
April 27, 2012	Total: 700	
September 19, 2012	Total: 800	
October 30, 2012	Total: 910	Introduction of the "Fund-Provisioning Measure to Stimulate Bank Lending."
December 20, 2012	Total: 1,010	
January 22, 2013		Introduction of the "Price Stability Target."Introduction of the "Open-Ended Asset Purchasing Method."

Source: BOJ home page (BOJ Policy Board minutes).

the Lehman shock despite a sharp economic contraction and severe deflation, arguing that it was unnecessary since Japan's financial sector remained relatively sound. Governor Shirakawa strongly believed in the *negative* side effects—the risks and the costs—of these measures (Shirakawa 2008). The BOJ's Policy Board also continued to worry about medium- and long-term damage to its legitimacy and independence that would arise from unconventional monetary policy measures, particularly monetization of public debt.

The BOJ's monetary policy response throughout these years of crisis can be divided into three major periods. The first period (October 2008–Summer 2009) was the crisis management phase, in which the BOJ tackled the onset of the GFC as the lender of last resort. After the governing party changed and the new DPJ government declared in November 2009 that Japan had once again entered deflation, the Policy Board began to focus more on stimulus during the second period, when the BOJ introduced comprehensive monetary easing (CME) in October 2010 (discussed below). The third period covers the time from the "3–11" triple disaster (earthquake, tsunami, and nuclear plant meltdown) that struck Japan's northeast (Tōhoku) area in March 2011 to roughly the end of 2012, when an election brought Abe to power a second time.

Post-GFC Crisis Management

In the immediate aftermath of the collapse of Lehman Brothers in September 2008, the BOJ was slow to lower its call rate from 0.5 percent, which at the time was high in real terms (Kamikawa 2014, 166).[58] The Japanese financial sector, which had only recently recovered from the NPL problem after extensive restructuring in the mid-2000s, was not exposed to the toxic assets that plagued American and European financial institutions. The BOJ was therefore quite optimistic about the health of the Japanese economy at the beginning of this "North Atlantic" crisis, so much so that the BOJ did not participate in coordinated interest rate reductions among the six central banks of Europe and the United States on October 6 and 7, 2008. Governor Shirakawa was cautious about monetary easing, even as the crisis persisted and the majority of the Policy Board members began calling for lowering the overnight call rate at the end of October, following similar decisions made by the other central banks a few weeks earlier. At the Policy Board meeting on October 31, 2008, four out of five nonexecutive Policy Board members supported lowering the call rate to 0.2 percent, but Governor

---

58. The BOJ report produced on October 8, 2008, reflected this optimistic reading of the economic conditions. http://www.boj.or.jp/mopo/gp_2008/index.htm/.

Shirakawa insisted on limiting the call rate reduction to 0.3 percent. Shirakawa's rationale for supporting a smaller rate reduction was his concern that lowering the rate too much would be negative for the interest rate signal function (Kamikawa 2014, 169).[59] Even immediately prior to the next board meeting, Governor Shirakawa and the BOJ Secretariat remained adamant about keeping the rate at 0.3 percent (Kamikawa 2014, 173–74).[60]

As it turned out, the BOJ's optimistic view of Japan's economy at the start of the GFC proved to be far off the mark. Although Japan's financial sector was little affected, the crisis hit Japan heavily through three other channels. The first channel was massive yen appreciation, as the $1 trillion in yen carry-trade was reversed and other advanced countries began aggressive monetary easing. During this period, central banks in the United States and the United Kingdom moved aggressively to stimulate their economies by applying very low interest rates and implementing assorted versions of QE (Umeda 2011; King 2016). The second channel was the dramatic contraction of global consumption, particularly in the United States and Europe, where Japan's high-tech manufacturing firms accrued most of their export income (Kawai and Takagi 2009). Finally, foreign net selling of Japanese stocks hit Japan hard, as stock prices plummeted 42 percent from September 10 to October 27, reaching a twenty-six-year low of 7,162 on October 28.[61] Furthermore, it was also feared that this share price decline would hit the private banks' capital positions, causing a subsequent domestic credit crunch (Ueda 2009).

Under these circumstances, the BOJ functioned as a lender of last resort to tackle capital market disruptions and the credit crunch. Because the crisis made it increasingly difficult for Japanese firms to raise funds from the financial market, the BOJ supported cash flow to firms by purchasing commercial paper (CP) with relaxed collateral requirements via the "Special Funds-Supplying Operations to Facilitate Corporation Financing" (Suda 2014). Furthermore, in December 2008, the BOJ decided to start the purchase of private assets such as CP and ABCP (asset-backed commercial papers) as a crisis management measure. The

---

59. The vote was tied at 4 to 4, as the Policy Board was one member short due to the difficulty of having the proposals approved through the divided government at the time (chapter 5). Governor Shirakawa, acting as a tie-breaker in accordance with Article 18.2 of the New BOJ Law, tipped the vote in favor of 0.3 percent. This was the first time in postwar BOJ history that the tie-breaking power of the governor was used.

60. But the executive members of the Policy Board compromised this time to avoid repeat of the split vote at the December 2008 meeting ("Kin'yū kiki to Chūō Ginkō" [Financial crisis and central bank], *Asahi Globe*, December 22, 2008). The call rate was reduced to 0.1 percent by a 7 to 1 vote.

61. Around this time, 65 percent of Japan's annual stock transaction value was attributed to foreign investors (Shirai 2009).

measure, largely implemented after January 2009, included the purchase of corporate bonds (Suda 2014).[62] Citing the need to avoid moral hazard and excessive reliance on BOJ purchases, the BOJ's purchases were designed as temporary interventions with a specific end date.

During this time, the government used fiscal measures to revive the economy. In April 2009, Prime Minister Asō's LDP government launched a ¥56.8 trillion fiscal stimulus package through a mid-year supplemental budget financed by increased issuance of JGBs. Later, the newly elected DPJ government passed three subsequent stimulus packages totaling ¥55.3 trillion in 2009 and 2010.[63]

At the same time, the government stepped up its calls for QE,[64] but Governor Shirakawa, a well-known skeptic of QE, consistently steered the Policy Board to reject this policy path. Not only did he oppose the expansion of QE when he was the BOJ executive director in charge of monetary policy under Governor Fukui,[65] he also made clear his view that QE was ineffective in his book published in 2008, just before the GFC (Shirakawa 2008, 367). In the BOJ's own assessment, the last QE had positive effects in stabilizing the country's financial system, but no effect in boosting the economy (Shiratsuka 2010). Furthermore, the Japanese government's deteriorating fiscal position intensified the BOJ's concerns over debt monetization. To deflect pressure to buy more JGBs, the BOJ continued to cite the "banknote rule" from March 2001 (see above; Kamikawa 2014, 178–79).

Tackling Deflation with Comprehensive Monetary Easing

On November 20, 2009, the DPJ deputy prime minister and minister of state for economic and fiscal policy at that time, Kan Naoto, declared that Japan was once again entering deflation.[66] Japan was then hit by a stock market downturn and yen appreciation following the Dubai shock on November 25, 2009.

During this deflationary phase, the Policy Board implemented multiple "qualitative easing" measures with limited duration while eschewing aggressive QE. In spring 2010, the BOJ adopted a ¥3 trillion funding measure to

---

62. BOJ minutes from January 22, 2009 meeting.

63. Cabinet Office, Japan, http://www2.ttcn.ne.jp/~honkawa/5090.html; Takayama 2009.

64. "Tsuika kin'yū kanwa nichigin nimo atsuryoku, seifu yotō ni kitaikan" [Additional monetary easing; pressure on the BOJ, expectation from the leading party], *Nihon Keizai Shimbun*, December 18, 2008.

65. "Gurōbu 6 gō Kin'yū kiki to chuō ginkō: Shirakawa-ryū Jōshiki o utagau jōshiki jin" [Globe #6: Financial crisis and central bank: Shirakawa style; a plain common-sense man who doubts common sense], *Asahi Shimbun*, December 22, 2008.

66. "Defure Taisaku: Nichigin to Kyōchō" [Tackling deflation; coordination with the Bank of Japan], *Asahi Shimbun*, Nov. 21, 2009.

support Japanese firms in eighteen sectors, including R&D and entrepreneurship, through special loans ("Fund Provisioning Measure to Support Strengthening the Foundations for Economic Growth").[67] The CME policy was unveiled after the Policy Board meeting on October 5, 2010. This program was made up of three major policy components: the "virtual" ZIRP as the BOJ encouraged the call rate to stay between 0 and 0.1 percent; a forward guidance policy;[68] and a new asset purchase program covering purchases of JGBs, CP, corporate bonds, T-bills, exchange-traded funds (ETFs) and J-REITs (Japan Real Estate Investment Trust).[69] With the CME, the BOJ ventured into the realm of "credit easing" by purchasing private assets—a measure taken much earlier by the other central banks under the crisis—in order to lower the risk premium and encourage lending and investment. The BOJ Policy Board also viewed these collective measures as a way to jump-start lending and investment (BOJ Policy Board meeting minutes from October 30, 2010). Even though the announced call rate with the CME was 0 to 0.1 percent in 2010, the BOJ made sure to keep the call rate above zero through the Complementary Deposit Facility (Umeda 2011).[70]

The CME included the instruments that were later implemented on a much larger scale by Governor Kuroda's quantitative and qualitative easing (QQE) in 2013. The CME measures, however, were relatively ineffective in stimulating economic growth due to the BOJ's ambivalence and lack of commitment.[71] First, the BOJ's communication signaled its reluctance. For example, despite announcing that the BOJ would "do its utmost as central bank to overcome deflation,"[72] Governor Shirakawa contradicted the BOJ's own announcement by insisting that the lack of potential for growth in Japan was not a monetary

---

67. The program's details were announced in June 2010.

68. The virtual ZIRP was set to last until the Policy Board reached an "understanding of medium- to long-term price stability."

69. Shirai (2014, 13–14) argues that CME differs from QE in three ways: (a) it covers a wider range of financial assets, (b) CME is aimed at lowering longer-term interest rates and risk premiums through asset purchases, and (c) the complementary deposit facility included under CME bears a positive interest rate of 0.1 percent.

70. The Complementary Deposit Facility introduced by the BOJ Policy Board on October 31, 2008, committed the BOJ to pay 0.1 percent interest on deposits that financial institutions maintain with the BOJ above their required reserve (Kamikawa 2014, 168). This device allows the BOJ to maintain positive interest rate, as no banks would be willing to reduce the interest rates they charge on the market below this set rate with the BOJ.

71. Shirai (2014, 16) lists three sources of the CME's ineffectiveness. First, the CME was too complex. Second, the BOJ lacked credibility due to the piecemeal way the program was expanded. Third, it was perceived that monetary easing had already hit its limit and the policy lacked credibility.

72. BOJ announcement, "On Strengthened Monetary Easing," December 1, 2009, https://www.boj.or.jp/mopo/mpmsche_minu/minu_2009/g091201.pdf).

phenomenon. He frequently said that deflation came instead from fundamental structural problems, such as demographic change, that prevented people from investing and consuming (Kamikawa 2014, 206). Ultimately, the BOJ's monetary easing announcement was seen by the market as half-hearted and disappointing.[73]

Second, the BOJ's policies focused more heavily on avoiding moral hazard and market distortion than fighting deflation (Umeda 2011; Suda 2014). The CME had several measures attached to safeguard the BOJ by allowing it to exit from these temporary measures. As the BOJ extended its asset purchase program to include purchases of private assets through the CME, it established separate "funds" for these operations with only limited purchases of risk assets, and it inserted time limits for the duration of these measures.[74] Furthermore, although the Policy Board decided to treat the bank's purchase of long-term JGBs under the CME outside of the banknote rule, such purchases expanded only incrementally.[75]

Finally, the BOJ was concerned about the medium and long-term consequences of these unconventional monetary measures, especially those arising from phasing out and exiting its programs. An unsuccessful phaseout, like lifting of ZIRP, and potential balance sheet losses due to its purchase of riskier assets, carried risks for the BOJ. BOJ losses might lead to bailouts by the government, which would not only damage its reputation, but also endanger its independence.[76] The BOJ also believed losses might call into question the BOJ's accountability in the context of Japan's democratic system (Okina 2015).

In sum, the BOJ was reluctant to engage in aggressive monetary easing in the immediate aftermath of the GFC given the relative health of the financial sector. Subsequently, economic conditions deteriorated, and although the BOJ introduced multiple measures to tackle Japan's post-GFC economic downturn, these measures and the reluctant ways that they were implemented continued to reflect the BOJ's underlying policy ideas.

---

73. "Nichigin no hyōhen tsuika kanwa kettei" [Drastic change in policy by the BOJ toward monetary easing], *Asahi Shimbun*, December 2, 2009.

74. As expected, the asset purchase under the CME proved to be difficult to phase out. The DPJ government argued against phasing out these measures by noting the difficulty that small and medium enterprises were having in raising funds (Kamikawa 2014, 200–201).

75. By March 2012, the total amount of the BOJ banknote was ¥80.8 trillion, while the combination of short-term JGBs (¥64.4 trillion) and long-term JGBs purchased through the Special Fund (¥19 trillion) went over that amount (Reuters, April 12, 2012).

76. There was a precedent. The BOJ lost more than one billion dollars (¥111 billion) when it provided special loans to Yamaichi securities in the late 1990s.

Responding to "3–11"

In addition to the economic challenges described in the previous section, Japan experienced a devastating earthquake in the northern Tōhoku area, which triggered a large tsunami and a nuclear power plant meltdown in Fukushima on March 11, 2011. The economy experienced a major shock and the yen appreciated against the dollar, pound, and euro.[77] Yet again, the Policy Board responded with relatively conservative measures.

The BOJ focused on disaster-management measures first, including guaranteeing that the afflicted regions had access to banknotes and credit and installing exceptional measures to support small businesses facing end-of-fiscal-year adjustments when most of the business accounts are settled. In early April, the BOJ Policy Board voted to support a low-interest loan program for financial institutions in the area affected by the 3–11 triple disaster.

During the critical time right after the triple disaster, however, the BOJ, for two reasons, did not deploy monetary easing measures in support of the recovery effort. First, the BOJ was concerned yet again about government pressure to absorb more government bonds. When the ruling DPJ began discussion of additional tax to support Tōhoku reconstruction, opponents of the BOJ within the DPJ and from other parties insisted that the government should issue "reconstruction bonds" instead and suggested that they wanted the BOJ to absorb these bonds directly (Kujiraoka 2017, 215–20). Governor Shirakawa unequivocally opposed the idea.[78]

Second, the BOJ believed that monetary easing would be insufficient to boost the country's economy in the face of the tremendous supply-side shocks wrought by the disaster. The view expressed by the BOJ governor during this period was that the economic aftershocks of the disaster, emerging largely from physical damage and power shortages, could not be addressed by monetary policy; only when demand for funds increased after reconstruction would monetary policy be effective.[79] This sentiment, which had been repeatedly asserted by the BOJ in

---

77. The speculation was that the market reacted to the possibility that Japanese insurance companies would soon be selling foreign assets to recoup yen in order to respond to the massive demand for funds ("kikika no engai susumu: en saikōchini semaru nihon shikin kanryūno shiwaku" [Yen purchase increase under the crisis: Proceeding to reach the highest value of the yen as speculation of Japanese money returning to the country], *Nikkei Shimbun*, March 17, 2011). But in reality, it came largely from the betting on the part of currency speculators to move the yen higher first to dump it later (Kamikawa 2014, 216).

78. "Nichigin sōsai mitōshi" [The outlook by the BOJ governor], *Nihon Keizai Shimbun*, April 8, 2011. The BOJ had an ally here, as the MOF also insisted that such measure would not be implemented (BOJ minutes from Policy Board meeting on May 9, 2011).

79. Shirakawa's speech at IMES international conference on May 30, 2011. In this speech, Shirakawa also noted that there could be a sudden price increase once the supply conditions improve. https://www.boj.or.jp/announcements/press/koen_2011/ko110601a.htm/.

times of economic downturn, reflected the "BOJ Theory" that monetary policy could not restore economic growth unless there was adequate demand for funds.

In sum, despite the quick actions the BOJ made in response to the triple disaster to stabilize financial transactions and help those directly affected by the crisis, the BOJ Policy Board, in particular Governor Shirakawa, was not willing to engage in additional monetary easing. The Policy Board did not believe that monetary easing via QE would work to tame deflation and that doing so would compromise its position by having to monetize debt.

These three cases of BOJ monetary policymaking illustrate how policy ideas remained stable throughout the period between April 1998 and December 2012, despite changes in the economic and political context. As this context shifted, the BOJ Policy Board did not always get its way; indeed, at critical junctures, it had to acquiesce to political realities, in particular when it launched its first experiment with QE. Still, the cases underscore the durability of the policy ideas guiding the BOJ Policy Board. The tendency to zoom in on any signs of inflation despite Japan's long-running bouts with deflation, its obsession with independence, the specter of political entrapment (which QE would inevitably involve), the persistence of the "BOJ Theory," and the ever-present concern that unconventional monetary policies might trigger price inflation and an asset bubble continually animated the discussions of monetary policy. Indeed, the BOJ (as well as the MOF) saw some of these threats in inflation targeting as well, which was considered by then a mainstream conventional policy that central banks across the world had been using for years.

The Policy Board adopted ZIRP in good part to avoid QE. Then the BOJ consistently pushed for premature tightening, as it did first with lifting ZIRP and then when it moved to end its first experiment with QE, not just by freezing monetary base expansion but also allowing it to wind down. Most surprisingly, the BOJ resisted unconventional monetary policy as economic conditions deteriorated sharply after the GFC, even as other central banks launched massive QE programs, the yen appreciated, and political pressure on the BOJ to reflate the economy intensified sharply. Ultimately, the status quo proved politically untenable, as the next chapter discusses.

Chapter 8

ABENOMICS AND THE BREAK WITH THE BOJ ORTHODOXY

> I trust that many of you are familiar with the story of Peter Pan, in which it says, "the moment you doubt whether you can fly, you cease forever to be able to do it." Yes, what we need is a positive attitude and conviction.

—Kuroda Haruhiko, Governor of Bank of Japan, June 2015

> In these documents, there was a table listing a menu of conventional and unconventional policies. These were documents were from when I was still at the BOJ, in other words about twenty years ago [1997]. At that time, these unconventional policies were only an "idea on the desk," but they're now all being implemented. The only ones that haven't are government notes (currency issued not by central banks but by governments) and perfect amalgamation (monetary policies conducted under a fully unified central bank and government). Back then if you were to have even brought up the amalgamation approach, you would have been called crazy. Now such an approach is a natural part of the conversation.

—Ōtsuka Kōhei, Member of House of Councillors and former BOJ official, 2017

The reticence of the BOJ Policy Board to embrace bold, unconventional monetary measures came to an abrupt end. Since the start of 2013, the BOJ agreed to an inflation target of 2 percent and set an ambitious timeline for achieving it;[1] implemented large-scale quantitative easing (QE); targeted assets with longer-term maturities to drive down long-term interest rates; employed negative interest rates, and experimented with yield curve control (setting long-term interest rate targets). Table 8.1 summarizes the developments of what the BOJ has described as Quantitative Qualitative Easing (QQE). Unlike with the FRB or BOE, it was

---

Epigraph 1: "Opening Remark" at the 2015 BOJ-IMES Conference hosted by the IMES, Bank of Japan, June 4, 2015.

Epigraph 2: Ōtsuka Kōhei, in discussion with the author, May 18, 2017.

1. The initial time frame was two years, but it was revised after this target was not achieved.

TABLE 8.1 Chronology of policy changes since late 2012

2013	
Jan. 11	The government announced "Emergency Economic Measures for the Revitalization of the Japanese Economy" and mentioned revitalizing financial and capital markets in it.
Jan. 22	The Bank of Japan (BOJ) (1) introduced the "price stability target," at 2 percent in terms of the year-on-year rate of change in the consumer price index (CPI) and (2) introduced the "open-ended asset purchasing method" from January 2014. The government and BOJ released the joint statement ("accord") titled "Joint Statement of the Government and the Bank of Japan on Overcoming Deflation and Achieving Sustainable Economic Growth."
March 19	Kuroda Haruhiko started BOJ governorship along with two new deputy governors, Iwata Kikuo and Nakaso Hiroshi
April 4	BOJ adopted the "quantitative and qualitative monetary easing."
April 18	BOJ revised the "Outline of Outright Purchases of Japanese Government Bonds" and frequency of purchases becomes approximately eight times (business days) per month.
May 10	LDP Japan Economic Revival Headquarters announced its midterm proposal.
May 22	BOJ announced a revision of the way of purchasing Japanese government bonds (JGBs) and swiftly conduct money market operations in order to keep stable long-term interest rate.
May 30	BOJ changed the frequency of the outright purchases of JGBs from approximately eight times to approximately eight to ten times (business days) per month.
June 14	The government announced "Japan Revitalization Strategy."
Dec. 5	The government announced "Economic Measures for Realization of Virtuous Cycles" and committed to enhancing financial functions and reviewing the management of public and semipublic funds.
2014	
Feb. 18	BOJ doubled the scale of (i) the Fund-Provisioning Measure to Stimulate Bank Lending (hereafter "Stimulating Bank Lending Facility") and (ii) the Fund-Provisioning Measure to Support Strengthening the Foundations for Economic Growth (hereafter "Growth-Supporting Funding Facility"), and to extend the application period for these facilities by one year. Specifically, under the Stimulating Bank Lending Facility, financial institutions will be able to borrow funds from the bank up to an amount that is twice as much as the net increase in their lending. As for the Growth-Supporting Funding Facility, the maximum amount of the bank's fund provisioning under the main rules will be doubled from 3.5 trillion yen to 7 trillion yen.
May 23	LDP Japan Economic Revival Headquarters announced "Japan Revival Vision."
June 24	The government announced "Japan Revitalization Strategy—Revised 2014."
Oct. 31	BOJ expanded the QQE policy (1) to accelerate the pace of increase in the monetary base at an annual pace of about 80 trillion yen (an addition of about 10–20 trillion yen compared with the past) and to (2) to increase asset purchases (80 trillion yen (an addition of about 30 trillion yen compared with the past)) and extend the average remaining maturity of JGB purchases (seven to ten years (an extension of about three years at maximum compared with the past)).

Dec. 27	The government announced "Immediate Economic Measures for Extending Virtuous Cycles to Local Economies" and expected BOJ to achieve the price stability target of 2 percent at the earliest possible time.

2015

Jan. 21	BOJ extended the application period for the Stimulating Bank Lending Facility and the Growth-Supporting Funding Facility by one year, and introduced a new framework for enabling financial institutions, which do not have a current account at the Bank, to use these facilities through their central organizations. With regard to the main rules for the Growth-Supporting Funding Facility, the bank will increase the maximum amount of funds that it can provide to each financial institution from 1 trillion yen to 2 trillion yen, and also increase the maximum amount outstanding of its fund-provisioning as a whole from 7 trillion yen to 10 trillion yen.
April	BOJ extended the projection of the time to reach 2 percent inflation target from April 2015 (two years) to the first half of 2016 (extension 1)
June 30	The government decided "Basic Policy on Economic and Fiscal Management and Reform 2015" and "Japan Revitalization Strategy—Revised 2015."
October	BOJ extended the projection of the time to reach 2 percent inflation target to the second half of 2016 (extension 2)
Dec 18	BOJ adopted supplementary measures for quantitative and qualitative monetary easing (i.e., measures to support firms' investment in physical and human capital and to facilitate smooth implementation of quantitative and qualitative monetary easing).

2016

Jan. 29	BOJ introduced "Quantitative and Qualitative Monetary Easing with a Negative Interest Rate." BOJ extended the projection of the time to reach 2 percent inflation target to the first half of 2017 (extension 3)
April	BOJ extended the projection of the time to reach 2 percent inflation target to within 2017 (extension 4)
June 30	The government announced "Japan Revitalization Strategy—Revised 2016."
July 29	BOJ increased the ETF purchase from ¥3.3 trillion to ¥6 trillion.
September 21	BOJ announced "The QQE with Yield Curve Control" where the BOJ purchase JGBs so that ten-year JGB yields will remain at around 0 percent. Inflation-overshooting commitment also announced and a stringent timeline to achieve 2 percent inflation target abandoned.
November	BOJ extended the projection of the time to reach 2 percent inflation target to sometime around 2018 (extension 5)

2017

July	BOJ extended the projection of the time to reach 2 percent inflation target to sometime around 2019 (extension 6)

Source: Kin'yu seisaku no Sui'i [Changes in monetary policy], Prepared by Division 4 (Committee on Financial Affairs), Committee Department, Secretariat of the House of Representatives. Based on Cabinet Office "Report on Economic and Fiscal Policy" (various issues), and sources from the Bank of Japan.

not Policy Board members accepting new economic ideas that drove the process of adopting these policies. Instead, a change in leadership with the LDP's electoral victory in December 2012 led to the introduction of new ideas and policies.

In the lead-up to the election, the LDP and its leader, Abe Shinzō, campaigned explicitly on a commitment to overcoming deflation and using monetary policy to do so. The politicization of monetary policy in Japan is quite remarkable. Of the advanced industrial democracies no other party leader has made monetary policy such a central part of its electoral campaign since the GFC. In his first months as prime minister, Abe Shinzō appointed a new governor, Kuroda Haruhiko, and two deputy governors to the BOJ Policy Board. As the terms of other nonexecutive members expired on a rolling basis, Abe then eliminated resistance to his monetary policy agenda by replacing all the remaining Policy Board members with supporters of his policy agenda by the summer of 2017.

The Politics of Monetary Policy and the 2012 Election

The lower house election in December 2012 brought the LDP and Abe Shinzō to power, but even before the election, all indications were that the next government was going to push the BOJ Policy Board to pursue an aggressive reflationary monetary policy. The question was how much change there would be. As discussed in chapter 7, tension had been building between the government and the BOJ going back to 2000, surfacing when the BOJ ended its zero interest rate policy in 2000 and again when it wound down its QE in 2006. After the DPJ came to power in 2009, the government had expected greater cooperation from the BOJ since the party had played a critical role in the selection of Governor Shirakawa, but it felt betrayed by the BOJ's intransigence.[2] As the government's frustration grew, it applied greater pressure for greater monetary easing, particularly in the face of the FRB's aggressive monetary easing through 2011. As political pressure mounted, the BOJ Policy Board adopted an "inflation goal" (avoiding the word "target") of 1 percent (year-on-year rate of increase in the CPI).[3] Nevertheless, the BOJ's actions fell short of government expectations, and some DPJ members began to call for revision of the New BOJ Law, including considering

---

2. House of Councillors member from the DPJ, who had previously been a BOJ official, interview, September 16, 2015.

3. "The price stability goal in the medium to long term." Bank of Japan, February 14, 2012, https://www.boj.or.jp/en/announcements/release_2012/k120214b.pdf, accessed August 5, 2017. In the press conference after the announcement, Governor Shirakawa stated it was not appropriate to call this "goal" an inflation targeting (Miwa and Maruyama 2012, 1).

a change to allow the government to dismiss the BOJ governor.[4] The DPJ was particularly focused on monetary easing since Prime Minister Noda had committed to raising the consumption tax the following year, whose implementation would have been virtually impossible under deflation. In October 2012, the minister of economic and fiscal policy, Maehara Seiji, pressured the BOJ to issue the first-ever joint statement with the government: "Measures Aimed at Overcoming Deflation" (Kamikawa 2014, 235).[5] The statement committed the BOJ to work toward achieving inflation of 1 percent. Reflecting the long-standing concerns within the BOJ, the statement also adhered to the view that structural factors in the Japanese economy contributing to deflation needed to be addressed and that financial imbalances from easing would have to be monitored.

Monetary policy became a major campaign issue for the December 2012 lower house election, with both of the major parties—and several minor ones as well—calling for steps to end deflation and reverse the strengthening of the yen. The timing of this election was crucial, as the five-year terms of the governor and deputy governors at the BOJ were set to expire in early 2013. The next elected government thus would have the chance to appoint three new executives to the BOJ Policy Board relatively soon after the election.

Abe himself had been a long and vocal critic of the BOJ. As deputy cabinet secretary, he along with Cabinet Secretary Nakagawa opposed the lifting of ZIRP, and upon learning of the BOJ's denial of the government's request that the BOJ postpone its vote, he called BOJ's decision "mistaken" (Kujiraoka 2017, 74). Then again in 2006 when he was chief cabinet secretary he viewed the BOJ's decision to lift QE as a serious policy mistake. During his first stint as prime minister from 2006 to 2007, he then sparred with the BOJ as the Policy Board considered raising interest rates. Abe's critical view of the BOJ was reinforced by his key economic advisers—including Nakagawa Hidenao, Nakahara Nobuyuki, Takenaka Heizo, and Takahashi Yōichi—who supported reflationary policies (Wakatabe 2015, 46). Abe eventually came to believe that deflation would have been avoided if the BOJ had continued its policy of monetary easing in the late 2000s.[6]

---

4. "Nichigin hō kaisei an matomaru (Revision Proposal of the BOJ Law Reached)," *Nihon Keizai Shimbun*, June 1, 2012.

5. "ANALYSIS: Govt Puts BOJ In Unprecedented 'Collaboration,'" *The Nikkei*, October 31, 2012.

6. "Abe To Forge Govt-BOJ Alliance Via Economic Panel," *The Nikkei*, December 25, 2012. Prime Minister Abe's conviction as "reflationist" was also influenced by his personal relationship, especially during the time after he stepped down from the prime ministership in 2007, with reflationists such as Yamamoto Kōzō (LDP diet member), Takahashi Yōichi (Kaetsu University Professor), Hamada Kōichi (Emeritus Professor, Yale University) and Honda Etsuro (former Shizuoka University Professor and current ambassador to Switzerland). "Miezaru Te o Okasu—Zaimushō o shinjinai Shushō" [Challenging the invisible hand; the prime minister does not trust Ministry of Finance], *Nihon Keizai Shimbun*, October 12, 2016.

The LDP staked out the most aggressive antideflation position. In its official party manifesto, the LDP listed defeating deflation as one of its first priorities and called for a 2 percent inflation target, bold monetary easing, and consideration of revision of the BOJ Law in order to facilitate better cooperation with the government.[7] The manifesto also called for cooperation between the BOJ and the MOF to establish a special fund to purchase foreign bonds to deal with yen appreciation (which ultimately never came to fruition). In addition, the LDP's president, Abe Shinzō, publicly called for the BOJ to buy all new issues of JGBs and to pursue monetary easing without any preset limit.

The DPJ's 2012 electoral campaign manifesto also listed ending deflation by 2014 as an explicit policy goal. The DPJ, though, claimed that its joint statement from October 2012 would be the basis for its monetary policy coordination. Differentiating the DPJ approach from the LDP, the DPJ prime minister, Noda Yoshihiko, asserted that the goal of 1 percent inflation would be more realistic than the 2 percent inflation target suggested by the LDP.

Abe and Kuroda's Takeover of Monetary Policymaking

The LDP won a landslide victory in this 2012 election and with its junior coalition partner, Kōmeito, controlled just over two-thirds of the seats of the lower house. Upon coming to power, Prime Minister Abe launched his Abenomics agenda based on a strategy of "three arrows": expansionary monetary policy, flexible fiscal policy (stimulus followed by longer-term fiscal consolidation), and supply-side focused structural reforms.

During the election, Governor Shirakawa had publicly opposed Abe and the LDP's platform, thus turning the election into a public verdict on monetary policy (Kujiraoka 2017, 270). The resounding victory gave Abe a strong political mandate to pursue his economic policies, and Abe immediately drew on his political capital in dealing with the BOJ. Abe pressured the BOJ to issue a joint statement with the government in January 2013, and ultimately Shirakawa capitulated. Under the so-called accord, the BOJ set an inflation target of 2 percent and committed to using monetary easing to achieve this target "at the earliest possible time."[8]

---

7. "Kokumin to Jimin to no Yakusoku" [Contract between the people and the LDP], Liberal Democratic Party, 2012, https://jimin.ncss.nifty.com/pdf/seisaku_ichiban24.pdf, accessed March 3, 2015.

8. "Joint Statement of the Government and the Bank of Japan on Overcoming Deflation and Achieving Sustainable Economic Growth," Bank of Japan, January 22, 2013, https://www.boj.or.jp/en/announcements/release_2013/k130122c.pdf, accessed March 3, 2015.

Breaking Up the Policy Network

To push his agenda further and to lock changes in, Prime Minister Abe changed the leadership at the BOJ. The term of the governor was set to expire in early April, but Governor Shirakawa resigned a few weeks early to make way for a quicker transition.[9] In preparation for the transition, Prime Minister Abe took direct charge with a hands-on approach to selecting the next leadership of the policy board. He created his own brain trust composed of well-known and outspoken reflationists, including Hamada Kōichi (Professor Emeritus at Yale University), Itō Takatoshi (then at University of Tokyo), Nakahara Nobuyuki, and others. Reflecting their desire to infuse the BOJ with ideas that broke with the BOJ orthodoxy, Dr. Hamada commented frankly in an interview, "what we don't want is someone who would be under the thumb of the BOJ's own people."[10]

After having several names floated for the BOJ governorship, Prime Minister Abe appointed Kuroda Haruhiko, a former MOF vice minister of international affairs who had long been an outspoken critic of the BOJ. As governor, Kuroda was the first head of the BOJ since the creation of the new policy board in 1998 who had not been a "true blood" (*haenuki*) career BOJ official. During his confirmation hearing, Kuroda noted that the BOJ's policies had been insufficient and placed clear blame on the BOJ for Japan's unsuccessful attempts to overcome deflation, commenting, "Responsibility lies with the central bank."[11] As widely reported in the media, Kuroda also commented that he would do "whatever it takes" as governor to escape deflation and suggested a two-year time frame for reaching the 2 percent inflation target.

Prime Minister Abe also selected Iwata Kikuo, an economist from Gakushūin University. As discussed in chapter 4, Iwata had been a vocal critic of the BOJ's policies and had publicly called for more aggressive quantitative easing to overcome deflation, in some cases suggesting his own concrete numerical targets for doing so. Even more controversially, Iwata had also supported revising the New BOJ Law to mandate that the central bank do whatever possible to achieve an inflation target. Prime Minister Abe, though, did not totally shut out the BOJ. He appointed one BOJ insider, Nakaso Hiroshi, as the second deputy governor to maintain a channel to the BOJ, perhaps also as an olive branch. Nakaso was a *haenuki* BOJ career official who was credited for overseeing the unwinding of the first QE in

---

9. His resignation on March 19 was timed to coincide with the expiration of terms of the two deputy governors so that the three executives would change all at once.

10. "Key Abe Adviser Favors Putting Jobs, Growth Under BOJ's Writ," *The Nikkei*, January 17, 2013.

11. "'We'll do whatever we can,' Kuroda vows—Shoe-in for BOJ's Top Job Shows Antideflation Determination in Diet," *Nikkei Weekly*, March 11, 2013.

2006 without disrupting the financial market when he was the head of Financial Markets Department (Shimizu 2016, 233–34). His appointment was also important to maintain morale among the BOJ staff and to indicate some continuity in their future career prospects.[12]

Upon becoming governor, Kuroda quickly set a new tone. He brought together all the BOJ officials and declared that it was an embarrassment that Japan was the only country that had suffered from deflation for such a long period and made it clear that raising prices was the number one goal.[13] Governor Kuroda moved the Policy Board to embrace an aggressive approach to combating deflation. At first, the Policy Board members went along with his direction. Within two weeks of his appointment, Kuroda announced an "extraordinary monetary easing" (*ijigen no kin'yū kanwa*) to achieve a target CPI rate of 2 percent through doubling the monetary base in two years. From April 2013 through September 2014, all the votes on monetary policy operations introduced by Kuroda passed unanimously (see chapter 5 appendix). There were some minor dissenting votes and alternative proposals, but these largely pertained to language on the official central bank view of future prices and the economy as well as the wording over the time frame for achieving the inflation target.

Over time, however, opposition to additional monetary easing grew within the Policy Board. In response to the consumption tax increase in April 2014, Governor Kuroda proposed increasing the pace of monetary expansion from ¥60 to 70 trillion per year to ¥80 trillion, lengthening the average maturity of JGB purchases by about three years, and expanding purchases of ETFs and J-REITs. This proposal barely passed the Policy Board meeting in October by a vote of 5 to 4. Every member who had been appointed before Prime Minister Abe except one— Shirai Sayuri—voted against the proposal. In subsequent Policy Board meetings, one of the four opponents, Kiuchi Takahide, a chief economist from Nomura Securities, continually voted against the chair's monetary policy proposal, bringing to an end the period of consensus voting.

The close votes from the Policy Board meeting of October 2014 underscored one of the challenges of establishing credibility under deflation: the difficulty central banks face in convincing markets that they will stay committed to monetary easing. Prime Minister Abe responded to resistance to Kuroda's proposals within the Policy Board by gradually replacing opponents as their terms expired, in effect removing the vestiges of the old BOJ monetary regime.[14] In

---

12. Former BOJ official, interview, Tokyo, June 20, 2016.

13. Former BOJ official present at the meeting, interview, Tokyo, April 5, 2016.

14. It is ironic that two board members, Kiuchi Takahide and Satō Takehiro, who were appointed in July 2012 because they were seen as sympathetic to monetary easing during the DPJ rule, began to cast opposing votes against Governor Kuroda's proposals of aggressive monetary easing from October 2014 (chapter 5 appendix).

2015, he replaced two previous members, Morimoto (who opposed the October 2014 monetary easing) and Miyao, with Funo Yukitoshi, a Toyota executive, and Harada Yutaka, an economist from the Economic Planning Agency (since 2012 a fixed-term professor at Waseda University). Harada was well known for his advocacy of reflationist policies and had published several books criticizing the BOJ's monetary policy (before Kuroda). He had also coauthored work with other reflationists, such as Hamada Kōichi and Iwata Kikuo. These appointments proved to be crucial when Kuroda proposed a negative interest rate policy for the first time in January 2016. The measure barely passed, 5 to 4. All five of the supporters were Abe appointees, while the four dissenters, Shirai, Ishida, Satō, and Kiuchi, predated Abe.

In 2016, Abe replaced two of these dissenters, Shirai and Ishida, when their five-year terms ended. On April 1, Sakurai Makoto, an economist and friend of Hamada Kōichi, one of Abe's key monetary policy advisers, was appointed. Sakurai was also an acquaintance of Yamamoto Kōzō, one of the most vocal reflationists within the LDP. Sakurai was reportedly so unknown in monetary policy circles that the BOJ had to scramble to find out who he was when his name was announced.[15] Later that year in June, Masai Takako, a supporter of Kuroda, was appointed as another member of the board.[16] Finally, in July 2017, the terms of the last two remaining pre-Abe Policy Board members, Satō and Kiuchi, expired. Abe replaced them with Kataoka Gōshi, an economist, and Suzuki Hitoshi, a former vice president of the Bank of Tokyo-Mitsubishi UFJ. Kataoka has been well known for his support for aggressive monetary easing and qualitative easing, and Suzuki had publicly supported Kuroda's policy.[17]

The Unfolding of the BOJ's Unconventional Monetary Policy

Governor Kuroda and the Policy Board announced a new QQE program that mixed an aggressive QE with "qualitative" monetary policies that focused on the composition of asset purchases to drive up targeted asset prices and lower term

---

15. "Nichigin jin'ji someta 'abe-iro'" [Appointments of BOJ board members colored in 'Abe color'], *Asahi Shimbun*, June 10, 2016.

16. "Mainasu kin'ri fueru shijiha nichigin shingi iin ni Masai-shi, katachidakeno giron kenen mo" [Increase in support for the negative interest rate; Masai becomes the board member, discussion merely for form's sake], *Asahi Shimbun*, July 1, 2016.

17. "Nichigin Iin ni Kanwa Sekkyoku-ha" [Pro-monetary easing members appointed to the BOJ Policy Board], *Nihon Keizai Shimbun*, April 19, 2017 (at the time of their nomination).

premia. For the first two years of QQE, the stock market rallied, the yen depreciated, and core inflation[18] rose.

The government then proceeded with its plan to increase the consumption tax rate from 5 percent to 8 percent in April 2014, which produced a one-time jump in prices (due to higher taxes) but also weakened demand, leading to a sharp drop in output. In response, the Policy Board voted (5 to 4), in favor of expanding the monetary base from ¥60 to 70 trillion to ¥80 trillion, and expanding the average maturity of the JGB purchased by the BOJ. Still, from mid-2015 core inflation moderated and at times hovered just above zero.

Governor Kuroda and the BOJ Policy Board then suddenly introduced their negative interest rate policy at the end of January 2016 in another 5 to 4 vote. The move surprised many since Kuroda had suggested shortly before that he was not considering a negative interest rate. While introducing this new policy, the BOJ continued using quantitative targets (¥80 trillion net JGB purchase per year) and qualitative measures, such as the purchase of longer-maturity JGBs and other assets (ETFs, J-REIT, and corporate bonds).[19]

The introduction of the negative interest rate policy signaled a shift from a focus on a quantity target (buying a set amount of the JGBs) to the interest rate. This shift was spurred in part by concern that large-scale asset purchases might not be sustainable since the BOJ could run out of JGBs to purchase at some future point. Some applauded the new step taken by the BOJ, but banks and some lawmakers reacted negatively to the introduction of the negative interest rate policy. Legislators in the House of Councillors criticized Governor Kuroda for introducing a negative interest rate policy only eight days after he had clearly denied his intention to do so at the Audit Committee meeting.[20] Despite the small share of deposits affected by the negative interest rate (between ¥10 and 30 trillion out of ¥250 trillion in deposits),[21] banks complained that the policy decreased the profit margin on their lending.

Initially, in the wake of the negative interest rate policy announcement, the stock market rallied and the yen depreciated, but the tide then reversed. Shirai (2016, 140–41) suggests that the negative reaction might have been due to awareness of the surprisingly small scope of the negative interest rate and the

---

18. The BOJ defines the core inflation rate by excluding fresh food from its inflation rate calculation, while the "core core inflation rate" excludes food and energy.

19. See Shirai 2017 for detailed explanation of the evolution of BOJ monetary policy from the late 2000s into early 2017.

20. House of Councillors staff, interview, Tokyo, July 19, 2017. The Audit Committee meeting was on January 21, 2016.

21. The BOJ created a three-tier system of the interest rates, so that negative interest rates only affected one tier.

complexity of how it was applied. Banks intensified their criticism, pointing to how the BOJ had failed to reach its 2 percent inflation target. By then, Kuroda and the BOJ had extended the date for reaching the inflation target four times.[22]

To take stock of its efforts, on September 21, 2016, the BOJ released its comprehensive assessment of its QQE policy. The report painted a relatively optimistic picture of the success of the last two and a half years, proclaiming that "Japan's economy is no longer in deflation."[23] The report ascribes the failure to achieve its inflation target in the previous three years mostly to external factors including declining oil prices, the impact of the tax increase on domestic consumption, and the slowdown of emerging market economies. The report concludes that it might take longer than expected to achieve its inflation target.[24]

During the same September meeting, the Policy Board also decided to introduce an additional measure focusing on the long-term interest rate in order to raise prices. This new policy of "QE with yield curve control" targets not only the short-term but also the long-term interest rate, specifically an interest rate around zero for ten-year JGBs. In contrast to QE, as described in chapter 2, the BOJ bases its purchases of assets on achieving a specific yield curve rather than a quantitative monetary base target. In addition, the BOJ publicly committed to overshooting its inflation target until "the observed CPI exceeds the price stability target of 2 percent and stays above the target in a stable manner."[25]

Assessing the Effects of the BOJ's New Monetary Policy

Since the start of Governor Kuroda's much bolder deployment of unconventional monetary policy, a number of economic measures have shown improvement. As of early 2018, the economy has grown for eight straight quarters, the longest expansion in thirty years. A broad class of assets, such as land and stocks, has seen significant price rises. Moreover, the yen has depreciated and long-term interest rates have fallen. The overall price level has risen since the end of 2012, and the BOJ has had more consecutive months of price increases (year-on-year)

---

22. The target announced in April 2016 was "within the year 2017."

23. Here the BOJ refers to the "core inflation rate," while the "core core inflation rate" of CPI had been in negative territory since early 2016.

24. "Comprehensive Assessment: Developments in Economic Activity and Prices as well as Policy Effects since the Introduction of Quantitative and Qualitative Monetary Easing (QQE)" available from the BOJ at http://www.boj.or.jp/en/mopo/mpmdeci/state_2016/index.htm/.

25. "New Framework for Strengthening Monetary Easing: Quantitative and Qualitative Monetary Easing with Yield Curve Control," Bank of Japan, September 21, 2016, available at https://www.boj.or.jp/en/mopo/mpmdeci/state_2016/index.htm/.

than any other period since 1998. Perhaps most significantly, the unemployment rate has declined steadily reaching 2.4 percent at the start of March 2018, its lowest rate in twenty-four years. There are also signs that private consumption is slowly trending upwards.

The empirical studies on the macroeconomic impacts of the BOJ's aggressive monetary policy under Kuroda also provide a relatively positive picture. Research has found that the BOJ's monetary policy has increased output and inflation (Hausman and Wieland 2014, 2015; Dekle and Hamada 2015; Miyao and Okimoto 2017). The existing work highlights a number of channels through which the BOJ's monetary policy has worked, such as the interest term premia (Rogers, Scotti, and Wright 2014; Fukunaga, Kato, and Koeda 2015; Kimura and Nakajima 2016), inflation expectations (De Michelis and Iacoviello 2016), yen depreciation (Dekle and Hamada 2015; Hausman and Wieland 2015; Lam 2015), and stock prices (Hausman and Wieland 2015).

Some research, though, has found more mixed results. Hausman and Weiland (2014) initially find an effect on consumption, but in subsequent work (2015), they find no effect. Work has also noted that the effect of yen depreciation on exports has been weak (Hausman and Wieland 2015; Fukuda and Doita 2016). Ueda (2013) attributes the temporary boom after the QQE to speculative investments by foreign investors, which he argues is bound to be ephemeral.

By one metric, the BOJ's QQE policies have not succeeded: the BOJ has not achieved its inflation target despite first setting a two-year time frame for doing so and then periodically extending this time frame. Of course, this time frame is self-imposed and one can debate the usefulness of this benchmark. Other central banks, such as the FRB and ECB, did not set specific time frames for achieving these targets nor have they met their targets yet. Low inflation seems part of a broader trend toward a lower natural real interest rate or "r-star." The r-star for Japan is extremely low, perhaps even negative due to combination of factors such as "secular stagnation" (due to a shrinking workforce, low productivity growth, etc.) and an excess of savings (Bernanke 2017b). This complicates reflation, but in such circumstances, central banks can still attempt to increase inflation expectations. In the case of Japan, however, inflation expectations seem to be relatively unresponsive to the BOJ's signals (Bank of Japan 2016). This may have to do with how inflation expectations in Japan are formed[26] and the deep deflationary mindset that has taken hold in Japan (Shirai 2017). Still others have suggested that the problem may partly be due to the credibility of the BOJ itself (Hausman

---

26. Bernanke (2017b) discusses these explanations.

and Wieland 2015; De Michelis and Iacoviello 2016). Whatever the cause, the failure to achieve its target within the BOJ Policy Board's shifting time frame has invited sharp criticism from opponents of the BOJ's monetary experiment.

Beyond the failure to achieve the inflation target, there have been other concerns about the BOJ's monetary policy and unconventional monetary policy more generally. Some have pointed out that such policies can potentially create excessive risk taking and reduce the liquidity of bond markets if QE becomes quite large (for instance see OECD 2017). The search for yield and an asset boom in turn could lead to financial instability, a claim that has been echoed by critics of QE in the United States as well. This view, however, is contested by others. Bernanke, for instance, notes that the level of risk taking in Japan is quite low, and he is skeptical that Japan has reached the point where these potential costs outweigh the macroeconomic benefits of the BOJ's monetary easing.[27]

Another issue is the sustainability of the BOJ's QE program. As of 2017, the BOJ holds about 40 percent of all JGBs. In the future, some have argued, the BOJ could run out of JGBs to purchase. The BOJ has turned to ETFs and other assets as well, but that in turns has invited additional criticism that the government should not take such significant ownership of the private sector, an argument with a normative dimension. The BOJ's yield curve control program, however, could alleviate concerns about the sustainability of balance sheet expansion. By targeting the ten-year interest rate, the BOJ can talk down interest rates. Moreover, the smaller share in private hands should make it easier for the BOJ to control the yield curve through a *lower* level of JGB purchases (Bernanke 2017b).

Another hotly contested issue is the challenge of exiting QE. The BOJ's holding of debt is high in comparative terms, and the monetary base is approaching 100 percent of the country's GDP (compared to between 20 to 30 percent in the United States and Europe).[28] The BOJ's holdings potentially expose the bank to losses, which some worry could damage its precarious fiscal position, with the government debt level at 250 percent of the country's GDP. Others worry that even if QQE succeeds in boosting the economy, the BOJ may be forced to keep long-term interest rates low so that the government can manage its debt (Suzuki 2014, 501). As discussed in chapter 2, central balance sheet losses are a possibility, though the growth and higher inflation that might lead to such losses should

27. Ben Bernanke (former chairman of the Federal Reserve), in discussion with the author, August 31, 2017.

28. Economic Survey; Japan, OECD, April 2017, 16, available at https://webcache.googleusercontent.com/search?q=cache:NWrGZBCez5oJ:https://www.oecd.org/economy/surveys/Japan-2017-OECD-economic-survey-overview.pdf+&cd=6&hl=en&ct=clnk&gl=us.

improve the government's overall fiscal position by generating enough tax revenue to more than offset such losses.[29] Since the start of Abenomics, the annual budget deficit has dropped and the government's overall debt level has stabilized.

The Future of the BOJ

The BOJ has embarked on a significantly new course in the five years from 2013 to 2018 under Governor Kuroda. What this means for the future of the BOJ is, however, less clear. Most significantly, Prime Minister Abe has not pushed to amend the New BOJ Law to limit future independence, although his key economic advisers and allies such as Honda Etsurō and Yamamoto Kōzō have advocated doing so. Prime Minister Abe's success in reorienting monetary policy without such a change rests in part on good timing and political longevity. He not only had the luck of getting to appoint a new executive team at the BOJ early in his administration, but he also has had a long tenure—very long by Japanese standards—that has allowed him to make all the six nonexecutive policy board member selections as well. Of course, Abe's ability to stay in power is at least partly due to his economic policies that have revived economic growth. Prime Minister Abe has been in power longer than the terms of all of the Policy Board members, and in February 2018 he renominated Kuroda for a second term as governor and Wakatabe Masazumi and Amamiya Masayoshi as deputy governors. These appointments, confirmed in March 2018, keep the BOJ Policy Board on the same course. Wakatabe, an economic historian from Waseda University, has been a vocal advocate of reflation and wrote a book very critical of the BOJ's past policies (Wakatabe 2015). Keeping with the tradition of appointing one BOJ insider, Amamiya was a career BOJ official. Known as "Mr. BOJ," Amamiya played a key role in implementing the Policy Board's unconventional monetary policies.

Prime Minister Abe has also continued to exert close control over the process of selecting new leadership. The Cabinet Office reportedly coordinated the process in consultation with Prime Minister Abe and Asō Tarō, whose serves as his deputy prime minister, finance minister, minister of state and financial services, and minister in charge of overcoming deflation.[30] Not surprisingly, all of the people supposedly considered for the governorship—including Takatoshi Itō and Honda Etsurō—were strong supporters of Abe's reflationary goals. The

---

29. Ben Bernanke, personal communication, August 31, 2017.
30. "Nichigin jin'ji sorezore no tatakai (2)" [The battles over BOJ appointments, 2], *Nihon Keizai Shimbun*, February 21, 2018.

process was controlled so tightly that LDP executives reportedly complained that they were not consulted despite the need for approval by the Diet.[31]

Future prime ministers may not have the same serendipitous timing or long tenures that allow them to influence the Policy Board. Still, the case of Prime Minister Abe illustrates that if a prime minister does have the chance to select the leadership of the BOJ, he or she can shift monetary policy relatively quickly and dramatically. Formal power in this case can easily trump informal influence.

At the same time, elements of the old policy network remain and with it, elements of the pre-existing worldview. While within the BOJ organization there is growing support for Kuroda's reflationary policy, some within the BOJ reportedly feared the appointment of Honda Etsurō to either governor or deputy governor viewing the former MOF official as too radical a reflationist; MOF also disliked his calls for more aggressive fiscal expansion to spur higher inflation.[32] There is also, as discussed above, a high degree of concern among influential BOJ alumni about the large-scale QQE, and some have publicly called for limiting it.[33] Former "true blood" deputy governor Yamaguchi Yutaka, echoing the old BOJ orthodoxy, criticizes QQE without structural reform as "pouring water into a bucket with a big hole" (2015, 7). Furthermore, it is not clear that the BOJ staff has entirely abandoned its traditional worldview. Many within the BOJ as well as alumni fret that although Abe and Kuroda are responsible for QQE, it is the reputation of independence and credibility of the BOJ that are at stake. Many have voiced concerns that something could go terribly wrong—large balance sheet losses, out-of-control inflation, financial instability, and so forth—and that the BOJ will be left as the scapegoat. There is also concern that in the event of a shock, even one that is relatively contained, the BOJ will not have any other monetary measures left for further easing, a criticism that is also frequently raised in the United States and euro area as well. Such a shock might result from the consumption tax increase scheduled in October 2019 or post-Olympic slump in 2020. In fact, depending on the circumstances, it is plausible that advocates of the BOJ orthodoxy may regain some degree of influence, particularly if Abe and Kuroda's monetary experiments are deemed a failure in the future.

---

31. "Nighin jin'ji sorezore no tatakai (4)" [The battles over BOJ appointments, 4], *Nihon Keizai Shimbun*, February 23, 2018.

32. "Nichigin jin'ji sorezore no tatakai (1)" [The battles over BOJ appointments, 1], *Nihon Keizai Shimbun*, February 20, 2018. "Nichigin jin'ji sorezore no tatakai (2)" [The battles over BOJ appointments, 2], *Nihon Keizai Shimbun*, February 21, 2018.

33. For instance, the former executive director of the BOJ, Hideo Hayakawa, has made such public comments. See "Bank of Japan Should Quit While It Is Ahead Says Hayakawa," *Bloomberg News*, October 14, 2014, http://www.bloomberg.com/news/articles/2014-10-14/bank-of-japan-should-quit-while-it-s-ahead-says-hayakawa, accessed on March 3, 2015.

Chapter 9

CONCLUSION

Monetary Policy, Networks, and the Diffusion of Ideas

> **It is . . . quite literally a prehistoric argument in monetary terms to assert that central banks are engaged in experimental, unprecedented, or somehow scandalous and dangerous policy maneuvers today—we should stop giving such trumped-up rhetoric any credence. . . . The idea that there are somehow pristine, virgin central banks, expected by the public to be like a vestal priesthood, that will be tainted forever by intervening in a given financial market, is . . . a truly primitive and antirational way of thinking about both economics and the beliefs of the general public.**
>
> —Adam Posen, President of the Peterson Institute for International Economics and former MPC member at BOE, 2012

> **[QE] is 'unconventional' monetary policy and should not be needed under normal business cycle conditions in the future**
>
> —Martin Feldstein, Professor of Economics at Harvard University, 2017

The Japanese economy has suffered chronic bouts of deflation since the late 1990s, and it is the only country to have been trapped in a prolonged deflation since the end of World War II. Throughout this period, Japan confronted several major economic shocks including the GFC and "3–11" triple disaster. Yet in the face of these challenges, the BOJ showed a reluctance to embrace bold, unconventional measures to overcome deflation despite growing calls from economists dating back to the end of the 1990s. Within Japan, political pressure mounted steadily on the BOJ to pursue a reflationary policy. In retrospect, given these pressures, the BOJ's reluctance to use monetary policy to more actively combat deflation is remarkable.

In this book, we have argued that Japan's reluctance to embrace unconventional monetary policy is a result of entrenched ideas within Japan's monetary policy network. These ideas originated in the BOJ's long institutional experience

---

Epigraph 1: From Irwin 2013, 337.

prior to its de jure independence. Formative experiences—especially with inflation during the 1970s, the asset bubble during the later half of the 1980s, and
its painful collapse—informed the BOJ's worldview. The BOJ put a premium
on a stringent definition of price stability, held a belief in independent action,
and viewed activist monetary policy with skepticism. Legislation vested policymaking authority in a new independent Policy Board in 1998, but in practice
the relatively closed informal monetary policy network centered around the BOJ
bureaucratic apparatus allowed the BOJ worldview to predominate. The policy
network was stable for many years, but as deflation and economic stagnation
persisted, political pressure for change grew, culminating in a wholesale attack on
the BOJ and its Policy Board. By the end of 2012, monetary policy emerged as
one of the central electoral campaign issues in the LDP's policy platform, a development without parallel among the advanced democracies. With the launch of
Abe's second term in office after a landslide LDP victory, the new prime minister
overturned the BOJ orthodoxy by forcing the hand of the BOJ, starting from
the appointments of the governor and the two deputy governors in March 2013
and systematically overhauling the entire membership of the Policy Board by the
summer of 2017.

In this conclusion, we draw out some of the larger implications of our study
in three areas: (1) the role of ideas in monetary policy, (2) the role of policy networks in determining ideational coherence and salience, and (3) the process of
ideational change.

Ideas, Interests, and Monetary Policy

That ideas matter has been demonstrated by a body of work that has explored
their impact on a variety of monetary issues: monetary union (McNamara 1998),
capital controls (Chwieroth 2010), IMF lending (Chwieroth 2013; Nelson 2014),
and the diffusion of central bank independence (Verdun 1999; King 2005). In
this book, we show that ideas matter in the realm of monetary policy setting, and
more specifically in influencing decisions about using unconventional monetary
policies to fight deflation in Japan.

Ultimately monetary politics is largely about the politics of ideas. As others have noted, economics and monetary policy more specifically are complex
fields where causal relationships are only intelligible in reference to pre-existing
policy ideas, which themselves may be contested. When one set of policies ideas
become dominant, as in Japan prior to Abenomics, they privilege a set of policies that have specific economic and distributional consequences. In this sense
ideas *determine* the politics of monetary policies. In the Japanese case, strong

beliefs about the appropriate role of monetary policy, price stability, and how, if at all, monetary policy could be used to address deflation played a decisive role in monetary policy choices. In practice, these choices imposed costs on a variety of different actors: workers suffering from weak labor markets due to an output gap as well as exporters experiencing a strengthening yen. When policy ideas and those that support them lose authority, the politics of monetary policy become battles fought self-consciously over policy ideas themselves; this is exactly what happened in Japan.

This finding suggests the need for a rethinking of the concept of central bank independence (CBI). Central bank independence has been largely conceived as the independence of technocratic central bankers on the one hand and voters, interest groups, and politicians on the other, with their relationship mediated by different legal and political institutions. Indeed, this is the explicit logic behind the economic theory of CBI. Many political scientists have adopted this framework when focusing on the question of political control in the context of delegation of monetary policy authority to independent central banks. Viewed from this perspective, the actors that matter are the ones with some material interest at stake and a formal channel for expressing these preferences: voters' right to choose politicians, politicians' formal authority to curtail or revoke a central bank's independence, etc.

If ideas do matter, as we demonstrate, then a whole additional set of influences must be taken into account that bring into question the adequacy of the rationalist approach's thin description of independence. We need to consider central bankers themselves and the wider multitude of ideational influences on them. Rationalist approaches largely overlook policy choices as driven largely by the relative degree of external influences on them with essentially no theorization of central banker preferences. This is ironic in two senses for materialist approaches. First, central bankers have been delegated formal policymaking authority in most industrialized democracies, and second, despite relying on material incentives, central bankers themselves have no such obvious incentives from which one can assume policy preferences. Although Adolph (2014) is an exception in arguing that central bankers have material incentives to secure central bank posttenure employment, he too finds support for the effect of career socialization in shaping central banker preferences.

Given that policy ideas do matter, and indeed are central to the politics of monetary policy, scholars need to understand the policy ideas that embody specific goals, priorities, and judgments about monetary policy as well as the conduits through which these ideas ultimately reach policymakers. In this study, we locate the development of the BOJ's policy ideas in the BOJ itself and its experiences over its organizational history. These ideas were reinforced through recruitment and organizational socialization. The wider monetary policy network served as a vehicle for creating ideational dominance within the *formally independent* Policy Board since 1998.

While this study focuses on the Japanese case, all policy boards are embedded in networks of overlapping institutions and ideational influences. In many cases, these networks are open to greater ideational diversity and thus less likely to see a dominant set of ideas emerge. Even so, the differences debated in policy boards are largely over competing sets of ideas. Moreover, the BOJ is not the only organization where a coherent and influential set of policy ideas emerged. The Bundesbank has long been known for its monetary conservatism, and the Bank for International Settlements has come to embrace a specific worldview as well.

This is not to say that material interests do not matter. To what extent will a central banker be guided by perceived political pressure or by his or her policy worldview? This is an open empirical question. In studying monetary politics, however, it behooves researchers to consider both ideational factors and material incentives. We substantiate our claim empirically—through text analysis and case studies—and show that ideas matter even when controlling for alternative explanations based on material incentives.

Policy Networks and Ideas

Scholars have found that ideas have the greatest influence when they have greater coherence and less heterogeneity (Chwieroth 2007; Ban 2016). In studying the impact of ideas, then, one must understand how such coherence is created. Ban (2016) suggests that cohesion is generated when like-minded experts occupy key policy positions with few challengers. For this book, we highlight the role of policy networks as the means by which ideas travel to key policymaking positions, generating varying levels of coherence depending on policy network attributes. One analytical value of drawing on policy networks is that it provides a framework for understanding the specific hierarchy of ideational processes that shape outcomes. As we discuss in chapter 3, the broad literature on ideas has highlighted a variety of processes that lead to ideational reproduction and path dependence, ideational diffusion, and ideational change; this work, though, has not always provided a clear framework to understand the conditions that determine which processes become operative and how these processes determine which ideas predominate and which do not.

It is important to stress that the dominant policy ideas within the BOJ, while having certain distinctive characteristics and a specific evolutionary trajectory, had points of overlap with policy views outside of Japan. The Bundesbank is well known for its overriding commitment to price stability (King 1993) and strong norm against monetization of debt, which can be traced back to its historical experience with hyperinflation during the Weimar Republic (Irwin 2013). This view is likely why many within the Bundesbank vociferously opposed unconventional policies such as quantitative easing. Similarly, the BOJ's view in some ways mirrored the so-called BIS view. While amorphous, the BIS view includes a hawkish commitment to price stability, a belief that monetary tightening should be used to prevent asset bubbles, and a view that the appropriate way out of a recession is through monetary and fiscal austerity in order to deleverage balance sheets. The BIS has also suggested that QE is not effective and argued strongly for central banks to unwind QE programs.[1]

Within the Federal Reserve System as well, several of the presidents of the regional reserve banks were well-known hawks that opposed QE.[2] Even Bernanke ally Kevin Warsh opposed the second round of QE on the grounds that the real problem for the US economy was the problem of foreclosures, high debt of households, and fiscal retrenchment (Irwin 2013). Within the ECB, Axel Weber, the well-known German economist, stridently opposed ECB purchases of government debt (quantitative easing), arguing that it would undermine financial stability.

The key difference in Japan's monetary experience prior to Abenomics was the coherence and salience of the BOJ's specific policy ideas in shaping monetary policy for such a long period. While similar ideas existed in other contexts, they were not nearly as dominant as in Japan. We argue that the key to understanding the degree of impact of policy ideas depends on the nature of the policy network. All policy boards are embedded in policy networks. Thus the challenge, as Conti-Brown (2016) notes regarding the FRB, is as follows: "To understand more, we need to specify the insider, the outsider, the mechanism of influence, and the policy goal" (Conti-Brown 2016, 6–7). Looking comparatively, Japan's monetary policy network—until it was disrupted by Prime Minister Abe—was exceptional in that it was highly *centralized* and *stable*. Both of these characteristics created a relatively closed circuit through which the BOJ's policy ideas flowed without significant challenges from other policy ideas.

---

1. See for example the Bank of Settlements 84th Annual Report, April 1, 2013 to March 2014, available at http://www.bis.org/publ/arpdf/ar2014e.pdf. For critical discussions, see Brad DeLong's blogpost, "Trying and Failing to Understand the 84th BIS Annual Report: Monetarist, Deleveraging, Fiscalist, and ??? Understandings of Our Current Dilemmas: The Honest Broker for the Week of July 5, 2014," at http://www.bradford-delong.com/2014/07/trying-and-failing-to-understand-the-84th-bis-annual-report-monetarist-deleveraging-fiscalist-and-understandings-of-o.html.

2. These include Richard Fisher, Jeffrey Lacker, Charles Plosser, and Tom Hoenig.

Japan's policy network was centralized in the sense that influence within the network was relatively concentrated. The key institution was the BOJ organization itself. As covered in chapters 4 and 5, the overarching organization housed the BOJ worldview, which developed over its long history. All central banks tend to be hierarchical and bureaucratic organizations. In the case of the BOJ, its practices tended to emphasize internal socialization over specialized training and nurture a strong sense of what it means to be an insider. There is of course a high level of technical expertise within the BOJ, with many well-regarded researchers with and without doctorates in economics. Many of its economists, however, tend to be concentrated in the central bank's internal think tank, which is relatively removed from policymaking.

While the BOJ's central position in the monetary policy network gave it greater influence, this influence was also contingent on the stability of the network itself. In Japan, the key institutions in the network were relatively constant. For nominations for executive positions for the Policy Board, the BOJ had a seat at the metaphoric table. The Prime Minister's Office consulted with the BOJ, the MOF, and former officials from both. As discussed in chapter 5, the MOF's views largely accorded with those of the BOJ at least with regard to unconventional monetary policy and inflation targeting, which served to further shift outcomes toward the BOJ's policy ideas. While these consultations alone did not determine the final outcomes, they played a role in the remarkable pattern of having all three BOJ governors from 1998 to early 2013 being drawn from the ranks of the former career BOJ officials. The BOJ had even greater influence in the selection of the nonexecutive members of the Policy Board. Thus these members seldom threatened the BOJ consensus view. Moreover, internal practices within the BOJ provided opportunities for BOJ staff members to influence the views of Policy Board members.

Policy Networks and Competing Ideational Processes

A body of literature has focused on the issue of ideational change suggesting specific processes that can contribute to such change (DiMaggio and Powell 1983; Haas 1992; Legro 2000; Simmons, Dobbin, and Garrett 2006, 2008; Blyth 2007; Chwieroth 2010). Why, until the launch of Abenomics, did these processes seem to have limited impact and why did processes of ideational reproduction prevail? The case of Japan's monetary policy until the launch of Abenomics demonstrates that attributes of policy networks can be decisive in influencing which of these processes become salient and which do not. A closed policy network creates a bias toward ideational reproduction and limits the impact of processes that generate ideational change.

The literature identifies various processes that generate ideational change, including professionalization, recruitment, learning, and emulation (Simmons, Dobbin, and Garrett 2006, 2008; Chwieroth 2010). Starting with professionalization, scholars have found that professional fields, such as economics, can be a powerful vehicle for ideational change. The movement of people with specific professional training into policymaking positions can serve as a means to introduce new ideas. This effect has been documented in a wide range of economic policy areas as scholars have highlighted the power of economics as a professional field. Chwieroth (2010) finds, for instance, that professionalization served as a means by which new ideas about the benefit of liberalizing capital controls gradually influenced norms within the IMF, and Nelson (2014) contends that economics training shapes beliefs that ultimately influence IMF lending decisions. Others have shown how global neoliberal ideas have been spread by economists (Domínguez 1997 Babb 2001; Ban 2016).

While this link existed in the Japanese context as well, the impact of the profession of economics was refracted through Japan's relatively closed policy network, resulting in a stronger influence of the BOJ's internal "house" worldview. More specifically, the closed network limited the impact of professionalization in two ways. First, within the BOJ bureaucratic apparatus, the influence of the profession was in part mitigated by recruitment and career socialization practices. As discussed in chapter 5, the BOJ recruits economics majors but usually as undergraduates who then go through intensive on-the-job training that emphasizes general over specialized technical training. While some hires on the elite track later are sent for advanced degrees, this is after they have already been socialized into the organization. The number of those with PhDs in economics is also relatively low and their influence also tends to be limited. The PhDs tend to be concentrated in the BOJ's internal think tank, and with a few notable exceptions (such as Okina Kunio), most of the influential career track civil servants do not have PhDs. Second, while there have been a number of economists with PhDs on the Policy Board, there have not been many experts in monetary policy (arguably four, excluding the BOJ *haenuki* insiders, out of two dozen). This lack of expertise meant in practice that the Policy Board did not function effectively as a strong counterweight to BOJ's worldview until the start of Abenomics.

Chwieroth finds that recruitment can contribute to ideational change when "organizational and professional beliefs become decoupled" (2010, 49). The case of the BOJ prior to Abe, however, shows that a closed network can block the effect of this decoupling. Over the years, influential economists[3] began to

---

3. For example, Ben Bernanke, Itō Takatoshi, Paul Krugman, Bennett McCallum, Adam Posen, Lars Svensson, and many others.

articulate new ideas that suggested that unconventional monetary policies could be effective under deflation. Japan's experience with deflation provided a real-world reference point that further animated the debate. While these professional beliefs about the viability of unconventional policies were far from hegemonic at the start of the 2000s, by later in the decade these policy ideas were increasingly widespread and influential, with major central banks including the FRB and the BOE undertaking policy experiments on the basis of these ideas. As a gradual professional consensus emerged, so too did the gap between these ideas and the BOJ's policy ideas. Yet the BOJ's recruitment had no significant effect on ideational change.

Many of the studies looking at recruitment and the wider role of the economics profession have tended to focus specifically on the recruitment of PhDs from Anglo-American economics departments, which has served as a vehicle for the diffusion of neoliberal ideas. As the Japanese case shows, however, the impact of recruitment on ideational change is contingent, since (1) recruitment selection can be endogenous to existing organizational practices, and (2) organizational socialization works in conjunction with recruitment selection to shape policy views. Regarding the first point, organizations can target very different kinds of recruits, which ultimately can be decisive in determining whether recruitment will lean toward ideational path dependence or ideational change. In the Japanese case, very unlike the IMF, the BOJ has not recruited from this same pool, again preferring to recruit undergraduates and not those who already have advanced degrees from Anglo-American economics departments.

Another potential route to ideational change is through *learning* (Hall 1993; Legro 2000; Simmons, Dobbin, and Garrett 2008; Chwieroth 2010). Learning is a process through which actors change their beliefs. Learning can refer to a change in beliefs about the best way to achieve a goal,[4] or a more fundamental shift in beliefs that entails a change in the nature of the goals. In Japan, the closed monetary policy network privileged pre-existing beliefs in a way that reinforced its worldview and limited learning. The BOJ's policy beliefs were not static, but they fluctuated around a relatively narrow band. At times, the BOJ seemed lackadaisical about deflation. At some points, for instance, Policy Board members referred even to "good deflation." At other times, the BOJ viewed deflation as problematic but remained skeptical that monetary policy would be effective in overcoming it without negative side effects. These views heavily shaped the lessons it drew from its own experiences. Due to the political backlash against what was perceived as an excessive and premature monetary tightening—with the lifting of its ZIRP in

---

4. Chwieroth (2010) categorizes this as adaptation rather than learning.

2000—the BOJ was backed into accepting QE reluctantly. Yet the lesson it drew from this experience was that QE was not effective even though the output gap closed steadily and other economists found that the QE did have positive effects.[5] In fact, this view was reflected and reinforced by papers published by BOJ economists in their in-house think tank's journal.[6]

Ideational change might also have occurred through *emulation*. Policymakers cannot always make decisions based on evidence, and judging between options can be characterized by uncertainty (Simmons, Dobbin, and Garrett 2006). Under such circumstances, policymakers may look to the practices of others. To some extent, emulation overlaps with learning since decisions seldom can be made solely on the basis of evidence, particularly in the field of economics. In the Japanese case, there were conditions for emulation. The FRB, followed by the BOE, moved decisively toward large-scale QE interventions with the onset of the GFC. Moreover, these central bank interventions had adverse consequences on Japan, for instance through yen appreciation. Then Japan suffered another external shock: the disastrous events of the earthquake, tsunami, and nuclear crisis of March 2011. Throughout this period, though, the monetary policy network remained stable and so too did the underlying policy ideas since the BOJ Policy Board tended to view Japan's position—with less exposure to the crisis in its banking sector—as dissimilar from the US and UK experience.

Policy Paradigms and Ideational Change

The foregoing discussion addresses the path dependence of policy ideas within the monetary policy network. To reiterate, the closed nature of the policy network limited the influence of multiple potential sources of ideational change. Yet ultimately the ideas guiding policy did change radically. Prime Minister Abe brought with him new policy ideas when he came to power for a second time at the end of 2012. He committed to an unabashed reflationary agenda and appointed Kuroda and two new deputy governors in 2013 to launch an aggressive, unconventional monetary policy to achieve this goal. He consolidated this process of ideational transformation by then replacing every single one of the other six remaining Policy Board positions by the summer of 2017, effectively removing all opposition to his monetary policy vision. Under Kuroda, the Policy Board embraced an

---

5. See discussion in chapter 2 for list of specific papers.

6. Interestingly, with the appointment of Kuroda in 2013, papers published by the BOJ's economists suddenly reached the opposite conclusion: QE was in fact effective.

unprecedented quantitative easing program and introduced a variety of other unconventional policies, such as negative interest rates and yield curve control.

What drove Japan's path to change, and what does it tell us about the politics of monetary policy? The shift in monetary policy ideas in Japan closely conforms to Hall's influential theory of policy paradigms (1993). Borrowing from Kuhn (1970), Hall distinguishes between incremental changes that occur largely within an existing paradigm—i.e., normal science—versus more radical changes that result from a "paradigm shift." One can argue that within Japan, Prime Minister Abe helped give rise to a paradigm shift that redefined priorities—establishing reflation as an urgent priority—and articulated a belief that monetary policy could be used to achieve that goal. In accordance with Hall's theory, ideational change occurred through a breakdown in the ability of existing policy ideas to describe reality, thereby inviting wider political intervention beyond state actors. Social learning thus occurred through the *political process* (rather than the relatively closed policy network) where the pursuit of power drove attempts to articulate a new answer to a policy problem. By the end of 2012, both major political parties were calling for a new, more reflationary monetary policy and calling on the BOJ to use new instruments to achieve this goal. As described in chapter 8, Prime Minister Abe made reflationary monetary policy a central pillar of his party's electoral campaign to win power. This pattern accords with what Hall observes about the process of paradigm shift as it moves decision making out of the realm of state institutions. Hall notes, "Politicians compete for office precisely by propounding new solutions to collective problems which appeal to the electorate. . . . The competition for power can itself be a vehicle for social learning" (Hall 1993, 289).

The Wider Context

Though it seems to explain the Japanese case so well, the theory of policy paradigm does not fully explain why Prime Minister Abe and Governor Kuroda chose to replace the BOJ orthodoxy with the ideas that they did. The experiences of the FRB, BOE, and to a lesser extent ECB provided real-world examples that suggested that policy ideas that had been anathema within Japan's policy network might actually be effective or at a minimum not have the deleterious effects suggested by critics. Thus, there was learning eventually driven by political intervention. This, though, in turn raises the larger question about the context in which major central banks were moving toward unconventional monetary policy. This context contributed to the framing of the BOJ's monetary policy as a failure in combating deflation and reviving growth and suggested a specific alternative course.

Shifting the focus to other central banks, the role of an exogenous shock—the GFC—the role of economists within monetary policy networks, and the network structure contributed to the spread of policy ideas. The incorporation of professional economists within these policy networks has been an ongoing trend. Partly by happenstance, several economists at the time of the GFC who had been influential in articulating the ideas behind unconventional policy were on monetary policy boards. One of the most consequential cases is Ben Bernanke, an authority on economic crises who had been appointed chairman of the FRB before the GFC. As an academic economist, his work examined the causes of the Great Depression, analyzed the Japanese case of deflation, and evaluated policy options in a deflationary environment (Bernanke, Reinhart, and Sack 2004). There were others too, notably Lars Svensson, an influential academic economist whose research also examines the challenge of deflation and the role of unconventional monetary policy. Like Bernanke, he had also been a public critic of the BOJ's policy choices and vociferously called for bolder monetary policy. Svensson was appointed deputy governor of the Swedish Riksbank just before the GFC. After the onset of the crisis, Adam Posen, a US-based economist who had written extensively about deflation as well as Japan's experience with it, was appointed to the Bank of England MPC. The GFC and spread of deflation provided an opportunity to apply policy ideas these economists had been pioneers in developing.

The case of the FRB is a clear case where the influence of the economics profession shaped its receptiveness to unconventional policy. Ben Bernanke as the Federal Reserve chairman had the most direct impact, but the FRB staff also played a role. As discussed in chapter 5, the FRB employs a high number of PhDs in economics, and the environment is an academic one in which research is valued. A PhD is more or less a requirement in practice to occupy the top positions related to policy at the FRB. At the time Ben Bernanke first joined the FRB in 2002 as a governor after spending over twenty years in academia (mainly at Stanford University and Princeton University), he recalls that about nine or ten of his former students were working as staff members there. At the outbreak of the GFC, the FRB's staff economists were well-versed in the literature on unconventional policies and were prepared to implement QE. Indeed, Bernanke notes that during the deliberations, FRB economists, particularly from the Washington DC board headquarters and New York Federal Reserve, played an active role in contributing ideas about how such policies could be used. Not only were they conversant with the policies and theories behind them, they were on balance supportive of deploying such policies. Bernanke recalled the following about the FRB staff: "They [FRB staff economists] followed their responsibility to try and evaluate proposals from both the pro and the con side. But they very much took on board the idea that given the environment of 2008, 2009, and 2010 that some aggressive and creative programs were going to be needed and they played a very important role in developing and advocating for those policies."[7]

While the monetary policy network in the United States and other countries have had strong ties to the economics profession, these connections alone were not decisive. Many economists were and are skeptical of unconventional policies, and a number of monetary policy board members at the FRB were reluctant to use such policies. The resistance to unconventional monetary policy, however, was not as cohesive within other policy boards as it was in Japan, and it ultimately reflected a minority of board members at the FRB.

The case of the BOE provides an interesting contrast with the FRB and the BOJ. Initially, the BOE's MPC was slow to accept that the unfolding financial crisis in 2008 would require that it shift its goal from fighting inflation to combating recession and deflation, but when the MPC decided to use QE they did so decisively, as discussed in chapter 2. Before the collapse of Lehman Brothers in September 2008, the MPC debated whether interest rates should in fact be hiked. Danny Blanchflower, an MPC external member and economist at Dartmouth University, argued that the threat of recession called for aggressive monetary easing. At the time, Blanchflower's view, though, was in the minority. Throughout this period, Blanchflower recalls being isolated and excluded at the BOE for challenging the prevailing consensus view within the MPC.[8] After being on the losing end of a vote in August 2008, the difference in assessments between Blanchflower and Governor Mervyn King came into clear public view. After the MPC meeting, Blanchflower reached out to the media and laid out his grim assessment for the UK economy, reportedly angering the governor for violating the BOE's unwritten rules of conduct (Irwin 2013, 138). The debate later spilled over to the Treasury Committee of the House of Commons, where Blanchflower and Mervyn King presented their conflicting views. As financial crisis spread and the economy deteriorated rapidly, Blanchflower threatened to hold a press conference to criticize Governor King if he did not accept greater easing, which reportedly forced King to accept a larger interest rate reduction (Irwin 2013, 162).

While the MPC had its share of inflation hawks at the time, unlike with the BOJ, there was no systematic and ingrained opposition to QE. Once the MPC

---

7. Ben Bernanke (former chairman of the Board of Governors of the Federal Reserve System and distinguished fellow in residence, Brookings Institution), in discussion with the author, August 31, 2017.

8. David Blanchflower (former member Monetary Policy Committee, Bank of England), in discussion with the author, September 7, 2017. According to Blanchflower, the BOE did not assign him staff members, so he initially had to find someone outside of the BOE to hire. He recalls not being invited to meetings where other MPC members separately discussed monetary policy.

fully grasped the extent of the financial crisis and its consequences for the UK's economy, the MPC accepted the necessity of QE. There was some resistance to QE, as Adam Posen, former MPC member (2009 to 2012) and current president of Peterson Institute for International Economics, notes, but that it "shouldn't be exaggerated."[9]

The reluctance within the MPC to use QE a second time in 2010 was greater. Posen, a vocal advocate of QE, found himself on the losing end of some votes. He notes, though, that the nature of the arguments against QE were over more technical matters and not ideological in nature. Posen recalls in response to some of the opposition he faced: "I found myself quite outraged and surprised . . . but again it was a very different argument than the argument I had with people at the BOJ previously or at the ECB at the same time . . . it was primarily a debate inside the MPC about the forecast. A little bit about the inflation risks. But it was not about is QE effective, is this going to compromise independence, is this going to cause a bubble."[10] Posen also recalls that the MPC discussion was very open and conducive to "intellectual risk taking and debate," perhaps more so than at the FRB or ECB, and that it was not uncommon for members to dissent from or even outvote the governor openly.[11]

The nature of the UK's larger monetary policy network helps explain to some degree why the MPC was more open to the QE in the first place. The process of applying to the MPC is open: a formal job listing is publicly posted, and anyone can apply although in some cases candidates are invited to apply. Her Majesty's Treasury (HM Treasury) oversees the process, and then final candidates are reviewed by a committee of three that includes two officials from HM Treasury and one former member of the BOE. The chancellor of the exchequer then must approve the selection. While superficially the role of HM Treasury and the BOE in interviewing candidates resembles the consultative role of the BOJ and the MOF in Japan, at least until Prime Minister Abe, there are differences. The selection process is not driven by a specific ideological view of the "correct" monetary policy and tends to focus on credentials and experience.[12]

The process still may be prone to certain kinds of groupthink given the regularity of the process; indeed, Danny Blanchflower believes there is a bias

---

9. Adam Posen (former member Monetary Policy Committee, Bank of England and president of the Peterson Institute for International Economics), in discussion with the author, October 7, 2017.

10. Ibid.

11. Ibid.

12. Ibid. Posen notes that the process is open to a variety of views. His immediate predecessor had a more conservative view of QE, although he was also appointed under a Labour government. Being at the extreme end in terms of policy worldview, though, would likely disqualify one from consideration.

toward theoretical economics due to the heavy recruitment of MPC members from Oxford, Cambridge, and the London School of Economics.[13] This question, though, is beyond the scope of the book. Regardless, what is clear is that the process was open enough to ensure critical diversity on the MPC, and at a minimum, it did not work to exclude those sympathetic to QE. Danny Blanchflower notes that Prime Minister Gordon Brown advocated for his nomination to the MPC to provide a counterweight to Governor King.[14] In the case of Adam Posen, his supportive views of QE were abundantly clear prior to his nomination. He had worked previously with Prime Minister Gordon Brown and Chancellor of the Exchequer Alistair Darling. Posen also had written extensively on unconventional policy, deflation, and Japan's monetary policy mistakes. Indeed, media reports in the United Kingdom suggested that Posen was selected in part because of his knowledge of the Japanese case, which would help him steer the BOE away from making similar mistakes. Posen himself, though, is unsure to what extent this in fact figured into his selection.[15]

The ECB is the central bank that at the time of the GFC had the most vociferous skeptics of unconventional monetary policy, in particular central bank bond purchases. This was not a coincidence but rather reflected the strong influence of Germany and the Bundesbank in the creation of the ECB and the appointment of an inflation hawk, Jean-Claude Trichet, as its first president. Trichet, it was said, "spoke French with a German accent," alluding to his strong commitment to price stability (Irwin 2013, 115). These views carried into the ECB's initial assessment of the unfolding crisis and its response. Trichet called for "expansionary austerity," a position in line with the BIS view. According to this view, austerity would inspire market confidence and aid in recovery. This conservatism infused the ECB's aversion to the large-scale purchase of government debt.

Yet despite some initial similarities with the Japanese case, the path of the ECB illustrates how the looser monetary policy network eventually contributed to change. The Bundesbank, as the largest economy, was the principal driver of monetary conservativism, yet despite its outsized influence, the Bundesbank was not as able to dominate the network like the BOJ did. Over time the views within the ECB Governing Council shifted—due in large part to the crisis engulfing the PIGS (Portugal, Ireland, Greece, and Spain)—and Trichet and the majority of Governing Council members backed QE through the purchase of government

---

13. David Blanchflower (former member Monetary Policy Committee, Bank of England), in discussion with the author, September 7, 2017.

14. Ibid.

15. Adam Posen (former member Monetary Policy Committee, Bank of England and president of the Peterson Institute for International Economics), in discussion with the author, October 7, 2017.

debt. The two German members of the Governing Council—Axel Weber, president of the Bundesbank, and Jürgen Stark, an ECB Executive Board member and former Bundesbank official—vociferously objected, but they were overruled. With the replacement of Trichet with Mario Draghi, the ECB moved even further from the Bundesbank's worldview.

Considering the various paths to ideational change, one interesting aspect is how rapidly new ideas about monetary policy can spread. This is in part due to the nature of central banks. One person can have a significant impact, particularly if that person is appointed to the top position in a policy board. In practice, this influence depends on the formal power of the governor as well as informal practices, such as whether there is consensus voting or not. This aspect of monetary policy contrasts with the diffusion of ideas related to fiscal policy, such as Keynesianism. A much thicker set of political institutions govern fiscal policy, thus requiring wider buy-in. By contrast, policy boards that decide on monetary policy have less institutional friction. Even the ECB, which had higher institutional barriers to QE and was modeled on the Bundesbank, shifted quickly under Mario Draghi. In the case of Japan, once the prime minister committed to overturning the BOJ orthodoxy and had the chance to appoint new leadership, change happened rapidly. Ultimately, formal power trumps informal influence when the two are at odds. In the Japanese case, network stability ultimately rested on deference to process and the reputational authority of the BOJ, both of which were eroded by policy failure.

A New Policy Paradigm?

Although the BOJ was late to the game of aggressive unconventional monetary easing, the extent to which many of the largest central banks appear to be converging on a new economic view of the world is remarkable. At the time of this writing, there is growing (although far from complete) consensus that deflation and low inflation, rather than inflation, are the principal challenges of the time, and that new economic theories provide a sound basis for trying bold and in some cases unprecedented unconventional monetary policies. The world's major central banks—the FRB, BOJ, ECB—and a host of others including the Danish Nationalbank, Swedish Riksbank, and Swiss Nationalbank, have all deployed various unconventional policies. Indeed, one can arguably describe these trends as part of a new global policy paradigm. Within this new paradigm, Kuhn's normal science proceeds apace with empirical studies examining the effects of various unconventional policies that further bolster or make modifications to the emerging social consensus.

While the consensus is spreading, the jury is still out. There has been some political backlash against unconventional monetary policies. For instance, politicians and commentators on the right in the United States have assailed what they view as the debasement of the currency. Some voice concerns about the potential for inflation, and a number of commentators lament the intrusion of the state into the market and the negative effects this has had on risk taking. Others, such as the BIS, have questioned the effectiveness of QE. These arguments alone are unlikely to shift the consensus in a new direction, but the longer-term consequences of QE are unclear; it remains to be seen, for instance, whether central banks can unwind their QE programs, and there is not necessarily any agreement on whether they even need to do so. If, however, problems do arise that might be attributable to unconventional monetary policies, there are certainly actors and institutions—including many in Japan—waiting in the wings with an explanation of what went wrong and ready to enter the fray in the battle over monetary policy ideas.

Currency and Foreign Exchange Rates

Over the coverage of our research, the Japanese yen exchange rate vis-à-vis US dollars changed. The following is the conversion rate that we use in this book to convert the yen to US dollars.

YEAR	¥$ FX RATE
1971	348
1972	303
1973	271
1974	292
1975	297
1976	296
1977	268
1978	210
1979	219
1980	227
1981	220
1982	249
1983	237
1984	238
1985	238

(Continued)

(Continued)

YEAR	¥$ FX RATE
1986	168
1987	145
1988	128
1989	138
1990	145
1991	135
1992	127
1993	111
1994	102
1995	94
1996	109
1997	121
1998	131
1999	114
2000	108
2001	122
2002	125
2003	116
2004	108
2005	110
2006	116
2007	118
2008	103
2009	94
2010	88
2011	80
2012	80
2013	98
2014	106
2015	121
2016	109
2017 (by September)	112

The annual average is determined by taking monthly yen/dollar foreign exchange rates to make a twelve-month average.

Source: Board of Governors of the Federal Reserve System (US), Japan/U.S. Foreign Exchange Rate [EXJPUS], retrieved from FRED, Federal Reserve Bank of St. Louis; https://fred.stlouisfed.org/series/EXJPUS, September 8, 2017.

Appendix to Chapter 5

TABLE 5A-1   Monetary policy voting data from 1998 through 2016

YEAR	DATE	CHAIR'S PROPOSAL	PRO	CON	COUNTER PROPOSAL
1998	Jan.16	UOCR—slightly below ODR.	4	0	
	Feb. 13		4	0	
	Feb. 26		4	0	
	Mar. 13		4	0	
	Mar. 26		4	0	
	Apr. 9		9	0	
	Apr. 24		9	0	
	May 19		9	0	
	Jun. 12		7	2 Miki:[E] N. Nakahara:[E]	Miki: reduce the average amount of required reserves by \ 1 trillion N. Nakahara: UOCR— around 0.40% Goto: UOCR—0.40–0.50%

(Continued)

TABLE 5A-1 (Continued)

YEAR	DATE	CHAIR'S PROPOSAL	PRO	CON	COUNTER PROPOSAL
	Jun. 25		8	1 N. Nakahara:[E]	N. Nakahara: as above
	Jul. 16		8	1 N. Nakahara:[E]	N. Nakahara: UOCR— around 0.35%
	Jul. 28		8	1 N. Nakahara:[E]	N. Nakahara: as above
	Aug. 11		8	1 N. Nakahara:[E]	N. Nakahara: UOCR— around 0.25%
	Sep. 9	[E] UOCR— around 0.25%	8	1 Shinotsuka:[T]	Shinotsuka: keep the status quo Miki: UOCR—around 0.25% / reduce the average amount of required reserves by \ 1 trillion
	Sep. 24		8	1 Shinotsuka:[T]	Shinotsuka: UOCR—0.4–0.5%
	Oct. 13		8	1 Shinotsuka:[T]	
	Oct. 28		7	2 N. Nakahara:[E] Shinotsuka:[T]	N. Nakahara: Change the wording
	Nov. 13		8	1 Shinotsuka:[T]	
	Nov. 27		7	2 N. Nakahara:[E] Shinotsuka:[T]	N. Nakahara: UOCR— around 0.15%
	Dec. 15		7	2 N. Nakahara:[E] Shinotsuka:[T]	N. Nakahara: UOCR— around 0.10%
1999	Jan. 19		7	2 N. Nakahara:[E] Shinotsuka:[T]	N. Nakahara: as above

YEAR	DATE	CHAIR'S PROPOSAL	PRO	CON	COUNTER PROPOSAL
	Feb. 12	[E] UOCR—as low as possible (initially around 0.15% and subsequently further decline)	8	1 Shinotsuka:[T]	N. Nakahara: UOCR—as low as possible (first at 0.10% and then further decline)
	Feb. 25		7	2 N. Nakahara:[E] Shinotsuka:[T]	N. Nakahara: 1% annual increase in CPI
	Mar. 12		7	2 N. Nakahara:[E] Shinotsuka:[T]	N. Nakahara: as above
	Mar. 25		7	2 N. Nakahara:[E] Shinotsuka:[T]	N. Nakahara: as above
	Apr. 9		7	2 N. Nakahara:[E] Shinotsuka:[T]	N. Nakahara: as above
	Apr. 22		7	2 N. Nakahara:[E] Shinotsuka:[T]	N. Nakahara: as above Shinotsuka: UOCR—around 0.03%
	May 18		7	2 N. Nakahara:[E] Shinotsuka:[T]	N. Nakahara: as above Shinotsuka: UOCR—around 0.25%
	Jun. 14		7	2 N. Nakahara:[E] Shinotsuka:[T]	N. Nakahara: as above Shinotsuka: as above
	Jun. 28		7	2 N. Nakahara:[E] Shinotsuka:[T]	N. Nakahara: as above Shinotsuka: as above
	Jul. 16		7	2 N. Nakahara:[E] Shinotsuka:[T]	N. Nakahara: 0.5–2.0% annual increase in CPI Shinotsuka: as above

(Continued)

TABLE 5A-1 (Continued)

YEAR	DATE	CHAIR'S PROPOSAL	PRO	CON	COUNTER PROPOSAL
	Aug. 13		7	2 N. Nakahara:[E] Shinotsuka:[T]	N. Nakahara: as above Shinotsuka: as above
	Sep. 9		7	2 N. Nakahara:[E] Shinotsuka:[T]	N. Nakahara: as above
	Sep. 21		7	2 N. Nakahara:[E] Shinotsuka:[T]	N. Nakahara: as above
	Oct. 13	[E] UOCR— as low as possible	6	2 N. Nakahara:[E] Shinotsuka:[T]	N. Nakahara: as above
	Oct. 27		6	2 N. Nakahara:[E] Shinotsuka:[T]	N. Nakahara: as above
	Nov. 12		6	2 N. Nakahara:[E] Shinotsuka:[T]	N. Nakahara: as above Shinotsuka: as above
	Nov. 26		6	2 N. Nakahara:[E] Shinotsuka:[T]	N. Nakahara: as above Shinotsuka: as above
	Dec. 17		6	2 N. Nakahara:[E] Shinotsuka:[T]	N. Nakahara: as above Shinotsuka: as above
2000	Jan. 17		7	2 N. Nakahara:[E] Shinotsuka:[T]	N. Nakahara: as above Shinotsuka: as above
	Feb. 10		7	2 N. Nakahara:[E] Shinotsuka:[T]	N. Nakahara: as above Shinotsuka: as above
	Feb. 24		7	2 N. Nakahara:[E] Shinotsuka:[T]	N. Nakahara: as above Shinotsuka: as above
	Mar. 8		7	2 N. Nakahara:[E] Shinotsuka:[T]	N. Nakahara: as above Shinotsuka: as above

YEAR	DATE	CHAIR'S PROPOSAL	PRO	CON	COUNTER PROPOSAL
	Mar. 24		7	2 N. Nakahara:[E] Shinotsuka:[T]	N. Nakahara: as above Shinotsuka: as above
	Apr. 10		7	2 N. Nakahara:[E] Shinotsuka:[T]	N. Nakahara: as above Shinotsuka: as above
	Apr. 27		7	2 N. Nakahara:[E] Shinotsuka:[T]	N. Nakahara: as above Shinotsuka: as above
	May 17		7	2 N. Nakahara:[E] Shinotsuka:[T]	N. Nakahara: as above Shinotsuka: as above
	Jun. 12		7	2 N. Nakahara:[E] Shinotsuka:[T]	N. Nakahara: as above Shinotsuka: as above
	Jun. 28		7	2 N. Nakahara:[E] Shinotsuka:[T]	N. Nakahara: as above Shinotsuka: as above
	Jul. 17		7	2 N. Nakahara:[E] Shinotsuka:[T]	N. Nakahara: as above Shinotsuka: as above
	Aug. 11	[T] UOCR— around 0.25%	7	2 N. Nakahara:[E] Ueda:[E]	N. Nakahara: as above
	Sep. 14		8	1 N. Nakahara:[E]	N. Nakahara: as above
	Oct. 13		8	1 N. Nakahara:[E]	N. Nakahara: as above
	Oct. 30		8	1 N. Nakahara:[E]	N. Nakahara: as above
	Nov. 17		8	1 N. Nakahara:[E]	N. Nakahara: as above
	Nov. 30		8	1 N. Nakahara:[E]	N. Nakahara: as above

(Continued)

TABLE 5A-1 (Continued)

YEAR	DATE	CHAIR'S PROPOSAL	PRO	CON	COUNTER PROPOSAL
	Dec. 15		8	1 N. Nakahara:[E]	N. Nakahara: as above
2001	Jan. 19		8	1 N. Nakahara:[E]	N. Nakahara: as above
	Feb. 9	(1)[status quo] UOCR—around 0.25%	6	3 N. Nakahara:[E] Ueda:[E] Taya:[E]	N. Nakahara: as above Taya: UOCR—around 0.10%
		(2)[E] ODR—0.35%	8	1 Shinotsuka:[T]	
	Feb. 28	(1)[E] UOCR— around 0.15%	7	2 N. Nakahara:[E] Shinotsuka:[T]	N. Nakahara: UOCR— as low as possible / ODR—0.10% Shinotsuka: UOCR— around 0.25%
		(2)[E] ODR—0.25%	7	2 N. Nakahara:[E] Shinotsuka:[T]	
	Mar. 19	(1)[E] Change the operating target to OB-CA. Continue the operations until CPI registers a 0% or an increase.	8	1 Shinotsuka:[T]	N. Nakahara: 0.5–2.0% annual increase in CPI Shinotsuka: UOCR— around 0.15%
		(2)[E] OB-CA— around \ 5 trillion	8	1 Shinotsuka:[T]	
	Apr. 12/13		9	0	
	Apr. 25		9	0	
	May 17/18		9	0	
	Jun. 14/15		9	0	
	Jun. 28		9	0	
	Jul. 12/13		9	0	

YEAR	DATE	CHAIR'S PROPOSAL	PRO	CON	COUNTER PROPOSAL
	Aug. 13/14	[E] OB-CA— around \ 6 trillion	8	1 N. Nakahara:[E]	N. Nakahara: 0% or more in CPI / OB-CA—around \ 7 trillion
	Sep. 18	(1)[E] OB-CA— above \ 6 trillion	8	1 N. Nakahara:[E]	N. Nakahara: CPI at 99.1 / OB-CA— around \ 8 trillion
		(2)[E] ODR—0.10%	8	1 N. Nakahara:[T]	
	Oct. 11/12		8	1 N. Nakahara:[E]	N. Nakahara: CPI at 99.1 / OB-CA— around \ 10 trillion
	Oct. 29		8	1 N. Nakahara:[E]	N. Nakahara: as above
	Nov. 15/16		8	1 N. Nakahara:[E]	N. Nakahara: as above
	Nov. 29		7	1 N.Nakahara:[E]	N. Nakahara: as above
	Dec. 18/19	[E] OB-CA— around \ 10–15 trillion	8	1 N. Nakahara:[E]	N. Nakahara: CPI at 99.2 / OB-CA— around \ 15 trillion
2002	Jan. 15/16		8	1 N. Nakahara:[E]	N. Nakahara: as above
	Feb. 7/8		8	1 N. Nakahara:[E]	N. Nakahara: CPI at 1.0–3.0% / OB-CA— around \ 18 trillion
	Feb. 28		8	1 N. Nakahara:[E]	N. Nakahara: CPI at 1.0–3.0% / OB-CA— around \ 20 trillion
	Mar. 19/20		8	1 N. Nakahara:[E]	N. Nakahara: as above
	Apr. 10/11		9	0	
	Apr. 30		9	0	
	May 20/21		9	0	

(Continued)

YEAR	DATE	CHAIR'S PROPOSAL	PRO	CON	COUNTER PROPOSAL
	Jun. 11/12		9	0	
	Jun. 26		9	0	
	Jul. 15/16		9	0	
	Aug. 8/9		9	0	
	Sep. 17/18		9	0	
	Oct. 10/11		9	0	
	Oct. 30	[E] OB-CA— around \ 15–20 trillion	9	0	
	Nov. 18/19		9	0	
	Dec. 16/17		9	0	
2003	Jan. 21/22		9	0	
	Feb. 13/14		9	0	
	Mar. 4/5	[E] OB-CA— around \ 15–20 trillion / from Apr.1 \ 17–22 trillion	9	0	
	Mar. 25		9	0	
	Apr. 7/8		8	1 Fukuma:[E]	Fukuma: OB-CA—around \ 25–30 trillion
	Apr. 30	[E] OB-CA— around \ 22–27 trillion	9	0	
	May 19/20	[E] OB-CA— around \ 27–30 trillion	7	2 Taya:[T] Suda:[T]	
	Jun. 10/11		9	0	
	Jun. 25		9	0	
	Jul. 14/15		9	0	
	Aug. 7/8		9	0	
	Sep. 11/12		8	1 Fukuma:[E]	Fukuma: OB-CA—around \ 30–35 trillion

YEAR	DATE	CHAIR'S PROPOSAL	PRO	CON	COUNTER PROPOSAL
	Oct. 9/10	[E] OB-CA— around \ 27–32 trillion	6	3 Ueda:[T] Taya:[T] Suda:[T]	
	Oct. 31		9	0	
	Nov. 20/21		9	0	
	Dec. 15/16		9	0	
2004	Jan. 19/20	[E] OB-CA— around \ 30–35 trillion	7	2 Taya:[T] Suda:[T]	
	Feb. 4/5		9	0	
	Feb. 26		9	0	
	Mar. 15/16		9	0	
	Apr. 8/9		9	0	
	Apr. 28		9	0	
	May 19/20		9	0	
	Jun. 14/15		9	0	
	Jun. 25		9	0	
	Jul. 12/13		9	0	
	Aug. 9/10		9	0	
	Sep. 8/9		9	0	
	Oct. 12/13		9	0	
	Oct. 29		9	0	
	Nov. 17/18		9	0	
	Dec. 16/17		9	0	
2005	Jan. 18/19		9	0	
	Feb. 16/17		9	0	
	Mar. 15/16		9	0	
	Apr. 5/6		8	1 Fukuma:[T]	Fukuma: OB-CA— around \ 27–32 trillion

(Continued)

YEAR	DATE	CHAIR'S PROPOSAL	PRO	CON	COUNTER PROPOSAL
	Apr. 28		7	2 Fukuma:[T] Mizuno:[T]	Fukuma: as above
	May 19/20		7	2 Fukuma:[T] Mizuno:[T]	Fukuma: as above
	Jun. 14/15		7	2 Fukuma:[T] Mizuno:[T]	Fukuma: as above Mizuno: OB-CA—around \ 25–30 trillion
	Jul. 12/13		7	2 Fukuma:[T] Mizuno:[T]	Fukuma: as above Mizuno: as above
	Jul. 27		7	2 Fukuma:[T] Mizuno:[T]	Fukuma: as above Mizuno: as above
	Aug. 8/9		7	2 Fukuma:[T] Mizuno:[T]	Fukuma: as above Mizuno: as above
	Sep. 7/8		7	2 Fukuma:[T] Mizuno:[T]	Fukuma: as above Mizuno: as above
	Oct. 11/12		7	2 Fukuma:[T] Mizuno:[T]	Fukuma: as above Mizuno: as above
	Oct. 31		7	2 Fukuma:[T] Mizuno:[T]	Fukuma: as above Mizuno: as above
	Nov. 17/18		7	2 Fukuma:[T] Mizuno:[T]	Fukuma and Mizuno: OB-CA—around \ 27–32 trillion
	Dec. 15/16		7	2 Fukuma:[T] Mizuno:[T]	Fukuma and Mizuno: as above
2006	Jan. 19/20		7	2 Fukuma:[T] Mizuno:[T]	Fukuma and Mizuno: as above

YEAR	DATE	CHAIR'S PROPOSAL	PRO	CON	COUNTER PROPOSAL
	Feb. 8/9		7	2 Fukuma:[T] Mizuno:[T]	Fukuma and Mizuno: as above
	Mar. 8/9	[T] Change the operating target to UOCR. UOCR—0%	7	1 S. Nakahara:[E]	
	Apr. 10/11		9	0	
	Apr. 28		9	0	
	May 18/19		9	0	
	Jun. 14/15		9	0	
	Jul. 13/14	(1)[T] UOCR—around 0.25%	9	0	
		(2)[T] BDR/BLR—0.4%	6	3 Suda:[T] Mizuno:[T] Noda:[T]	Mizuno: BDR/BLR—0.5%
	Aug. 10/11		9	0	
	Sep. 7/8		9	0	
	Oct. 12/13		9	0	
	Oct. 31		9	0	
	Nov. 15/16		9	0	
	Dec. 18/19		9	0	
2007	Jan. 17/18		6	3 Suda:[T] Mizuno:[T] Noda:[T]	Suda, Mizuno and Noda: UOCR—around 0.5%
	Feb. 20/21	(1)[T] UOCR—around 0.5%	8	1 Iwata:[E]	
		(2)[T] BDR/BLR—0.75%	8	1 Iwata:[E]	

(Continued)

TABLE 5A-1 (Continued)

YEAR	DATE	CHAIR'S PROPOSAL	PRO	CON	COUNTER PROPOSAL
	Mar. 19/20		9	0	
	Apr. 9/10		9	0	
	Apr. 27		9	0	
	May 16/17		9	0	
	Jun. 14/15		9	0	
	Jul. 11/12		8	1 Mizuno:[T]	Mizuno: UOCR—around 0.75%
	Aug. 22/23		8	1 Mizuno:[T]	Mizuno: as above
	Sep. 18/19		8	1 Mizuno:[T]	Mizuno: as above
	Oct. 10/11		8	1 Mizuno:[T]	Mizuno: as above
	Oct. 31		8	1 Mizuno:[T]	Mizuno: as above
	Nov. 12/13		8	1 Mizuno:[T]	Mizuno: as above
	Dec. 19/20		9	0	
2008	Jan. 21/22		9	0	
	Feb. 14/15		9	0	
	Mar. 6/7		9	0	
	Apr. 8/9		7	0	
	Apr. 30		7	0	
	May 19/20		7	0	
	Jun. 12/13		7	0	
	Jul. 14/15		7	0	
	Aug. 18/19		7	0	
	Sep. 16/17		7	0	
	Sep. 18		6	0	
	Sep. 29		7	0	
	Oct. 6/7		7	0	

YEAR	DATE	CHAIR'S PROPOSAL	PRO	CON	COUNTER PROPOSAL
	Oct. 14		7	0	
	Oct. 31	(1)[E] UOCR—around 0.3%	4	4 Suda:[E] Nakamura: [E] Kamezaki:[E] Mizuno:[T]	Suda, Nakamura, and Kamezaki: UOCR—around 0.25%
		(2)[E] BDR/BLR—0.5%	8	0	
	Nov. 20/21		8	0	
	Dec. 2		8	0	
	Dec. 18/19	(1)[E] UOCR—around 0.1%	7	1 Noda:[T]	
		(2)[E] BDR/BLR—0.3%	8	0	
2009	Jan. 21/22		8	0	
	Feb. 18/19		8	0	
	Mar. 17/18		8	0	
	Apr. 6/7		8	0	
	Apr. 30		8	0	
	May 21/22		8	0	
	Jun. 15/16		8	0	
	Jul. 14/15		8	0	
	Aug. 10/11		8	0	
	Sep. 16/17		8	0	
	Oct. 13/14		8	0	
	Oct. 30		8	0	
	Nov. 19/20		8	0	
	Dec. 1		7	0	
	Dec. 17/18		7	0	

(Continued)

TABLE 5A-1 (Continued)

YEAR	DATE	CHAIR'S PROPOSAL	PRO	CON	COUNTER PROPOSAL
2010	Jan. 25/26		7	0	
	Feb. 17/18		7	0	
	Mar. 16/17		7	0	
	Apr. 6/7		8	0	
	Apr. 30		8	0	
	May 10		7	0	
	May 20/21		8	0	
	Jun. 14/15		8	0	
	Jul. 14/15		9	0	
	Aug. 9/10		9	0	
	Aug. 30		9	0	
	Sep. 6/7		9	0	
	Oct. 4/5	[E] UOCR—around 0–0.1%	9	0	
	Oct. 28		9	0	
	Nov. 4/5		9	0	
	Dec. 20/21		9	0	
2011	Jan. 24/25		9	0	
	Feb. 14/15		9	0	
	Mar. 14		9	0	
	Apr. 6/7		9	0	
	Apr. 28		9	0	
	May 19/20		9	0	
	Jun. 13/14		9	0	
	Jul. 11/12		9	0	
	Aug. 4		9	0	
	Sep. 6/7		9	0	
	Oct. 6/7		9	0	
	Oct. 27		9	0	
	Nov. 15/16		9	0	

YEAR	DATE	CHAIR'S PROPOSAL	PRO	CON	COUNTER PROPOSAL
	Nov. 30		8	0	
	Dec. 20/21		9	0	
2012	Jan. 23/24		9	0	
	Feb. 13/14		9	0	
	Mar. 12/13		9	0	
	Apr. 9/10		7	0	
	Apr. 27		7	0	
	May. 22/23		7	0	
	Jun. 14/15		7	0	
	Jul. 11/12		7	0	
	Aug. 8/9		9	0	
	Sep. 18/19		9	0	
	Oct. 4/5		9	0	
	Oct. 30		9	0	
	Nov. 19/20		9	0	
	Dec. 19/20		9	0	
2013	Jan. 21/22		9	0	
	Feb. 13/14		9	0	
	Mar. 6/7		9	0	
	Apr. 3/4	[E] Change the operating target to MB. MB—increases at an annual pace of \ 60–70 trillion.	9	0	
	Apr. 26		9	0	
	May 21/22		9	0	
	Jun. 10/11		9	0	
	Jul. 10/11		9	0	

(Continued)

TABLE 5A-1 (Continued)

YEAR	DATE	CHAIR'S PROPOSAL	PRO	CON	COUNTER PROPOSAL
	Aug. 7/8		9	0	
	Sep. 4/5		9	0	
	Oct. 3/4		9	0	
	Oct. 31		9	0	
	Nov. 20/21		9	0	
	Dec. 19/20		9	0	
2014	Jan. 21/22		9	0	
	Feb. 17/18		9	0	
	Mar. 10/11		9	0	
	Apr. 7/8		9	0	
	Apr. 30		9	0	
	May 20/21		9	0	
	Jun. 12/13		9	0	
	Jul. 14/15		9	0	
	Aug. 7/8		9	0	
	Sep. 3/4		9	0	
	Oct. 6/7		9	0	
	Oct. 31	MB—increases at an annual pace of \ 80 trillion.	5	4 Morimoto:[T] Ishida:[T] Satō:[T] Kiuchi:[T]	
	Nov. 18/19		8	1 Kiuchi:[T]	
	Dec. 18/19		8	1 Kiuchi:[T]	
2015	Jan. 20/21		8	1 Kiuchi:[T]	
	Feb. 17/18		8	1 Kiuchi:[T]	
	Mar. 16/17		8	1 Kiuchi:[T]	

YEAR	DATE	CHAIR'S PROPOSAL	PRO	CON	COUNTER PROPOSAL
	Apr. 7/8		8	1 Kiuchi:[T]	Kiuchi: MB—increases at an annual pace of \ 45 trillion.
	Apr. 30		8	1 Kiuchi:[T]	Kiuchi: as above
	May 21/22		8	1 Kiuchi:[T]	Kiuchi: as above
	Jun. 18/19		8	1 Kiuchi:[T]	Kiuchi: as above
	Jul. 14/15		8	1 Kiuchi:[T]	Kiuchi: as above
	Aug. 6/7		8	1 Kiuchi:[T]	Kiuchi: as above
	Sep. 14/15		8	1 Kiuchi:[T]	Kiuchi: as above
	Oct. 6/7		8	1 Kiuchi:[T]	Kiuchi: as above
	Oct. 30		8	1 Kiuchi:[T]	Kiuchi: as above
	Nov. 18/19		8	1 Kiuchi:[T]	Kiuchi: as above
	Dec. 17/18		8	1 Kiuchi:[T]	Kiuchi: as above
2016	Jan. 28/29	(1)[status quo] MB —increases at an annual pace of \ 80 trillion.	8	1 Kiuchi:[T]	Kiuchi: as above
		(2)[E] PR— minus 0.1% to the Policy Rate Balances in current accounts.	5	4 Shirai:[T] Ishida:[T] Satō:[T] Kiuchi:[T]	

(Continued)

TABLE 5A-1 (Continued)

YEAR	DATE	CHAIR'S PROPOSAL	PRO	CON	COUNTER PROPOSAL
	Mar. 14/15	(1)[status quo] MB	8	1 Kiuchi:[T]	Kiuchi: as above
		(2)[status quo] PR	7	2 Satō:[T] Kiuchi:[T]	Sato: PR—0.1%
	Apr. 27/28	(1)[status quo] MB	8	1 Kiuchi:[T]	Kiuchi: as above
		(2)[status quo] PR	7	2 Satō:[T] Kiuchi:[T]	
	Jun. 15/16	(1)[status quo] MB	8	1 Kiuchi:[T]	Kiuchi: as above
		(2)[status quo] PR	7	2 Satō:[T] Kiuchi:[T]	

Notes:
E: monetary easing
T: monetary tightening
BDR/BLR: basic discount rate/basic loan rate
CPI: consumer price index
MB: monetary base
ODR: official discount rate
OB-CD: outstanding balance of the current accounts at the Bank of Japan
PR: policy rate
UOCR: uncollateralized overnight call rate

Period: From January–April 1998 to July 2016.

Covered proposals: The policy proposals on the instruments of monetary policy implementation (I.e., the proposals on the guideline for money market operations, on the official discount rate/basic discount rate and the basic loan rate, and on the reserve requirement ratio).

Source: Bank of Japan, "Minutes of the Monetary Policy Meeting."

Appendix to Chapter 6

FIGURE 6A-1. Histograms of the four indexes

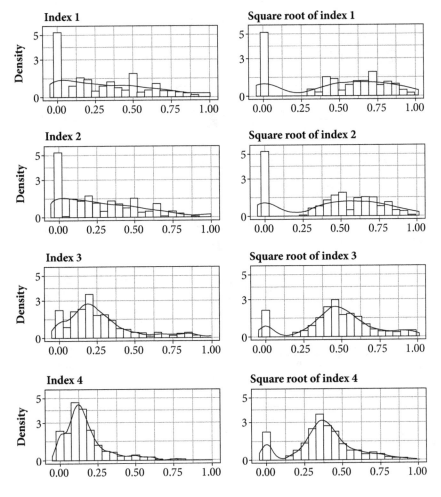

TABLE 6A-1 Regression models with interaction term

	INDEX 1	INDEX 2	INDEX 3	INDEX 4
Intercept	1430.09(***)	1468.84(***)	1341.05(***)	1240.82(***)
	(468.37)	(473.91)	(472.20)	(469.13)
BOJ ideas	−336.38(***)	−377.55(***)	−319.14(**)	338.41
	(118.56)	(131.00)	(141.76)	(1044.04)
Abe 2 dummy	1314.30	1165.62	284.65	−350.62(*)
	(1010.39)	(998.01)	(1062.68)	(189.07)
Monetary base	0.49	0.53	0.81	0.84
	(0.60)	(0.58)	(0.60)	(0.60)
Economic growth	−69.65	−71.36	−66.91	−65.49
	(50.37)	(50.55)	(50.44)	(50.41)
Change in CPI	−5701.39	−5395.92	−4579.89	−4512.94
	(4232.76)	(4181.92)	(4300.59)	(4346.09)
Debt	−1.36	−1.48	−1.50	−1.43
	(0.97)	(0.97)	(0.95)	(0.94)
Political business cycle	5.67	1.53	45.17	44.08
	(65.78)	(67.72)	(93.73)	(93.46)
Legislative veto points	494.19(**)	516.95(**)	501.27(**)	481.20(**)
	(227.05)	(226.13)	(222.79)	(223.26)
Abe 1 dummy	377.58(*)	391.48(*)	310.50	309.15
	(223.12)	(223.22)	(216.62)	(215.39)
Partisan control of the government	−668.16(**)	−673.83(**)	−725.77(***)	−713.39(***)
	(281.60)	(276.23)	(267.76)	(267.76)
Fukushima dummy	−515.89(*)	−510.67(*)	−619.83(**)	−632.56(**)
	(308.05)	(309.16)	(303.55)	(304.81)
GFC dummy	−229.43(***)	−232.18(***)	−208.54(**)	−203.24(**)
	(88.86)	(88.12)	(97.96)	(98.09)
Fukui dummy	−182.06	−175.87	−264.86	−281.03
	(164.82)	(162.56)	(169.57)	(171.26)
Shirakawa dummy	−96.99	−66.99	−204.56	−216.88
	(248.50)	(251.45)	(244.79)	(244.49)
Kuroda dummy	57.42	55.74	−485.48	−448.77
	(609.52)	(604.94)	(714.48)	(656.76)
BOJ Ideas X Abe dummy	299.20	531.78	3116.25	3481.12
	(1346.03)	(1423.26)	(2829.56)	(3237.83)
Num. obs.	242	243	247	248
R2	0.39	0.39	0.39	0.39
Adj. R2	0.35	0.35	0.35	0.35
L.R.	120.22	121.30	122.35	121.95

Robust standard errors; ***$p < 0.01$, **$p < 0.05$, *$p < 0.1$

TABLE 6A-2 Regression models: Lagged economic variables

	INDEX 1	INDEX 2	INDEX 3	INDEX 4
Intercept	1255.42(***)	1283.77(***)	1205.37(**)	1134.81(**)
	(472.69)	(479.78)	(480.96)	(469.18)
BOJ ideas	−370.65(***)	−400.43(***)	−360.34(***)	−420.01(**)
	(120.24)	(135.98)	(138.43)	(186.01)
Monetary base (lag)	−0.27	−0.22	−0.11	−0.11
	(0.50)	(0.49)	(0.51)	(0.51)
Economic growth (lag)	−67.81	−66.92	−59.80	−57.34
	(52.72)	(52.58)	(52.16)	(52.19)
Change in CPI (lag)	−7204.02	−7097.97	−7053.44	−7482.12(*)
	(4406.76)	(4428.37)	(4364.79)	(4274.56)
Debt (lag)	−0.48	−0.60	−0.46	−0.38
	(0.91)	(0.91)	(0.91)	(0.90)
Political business cycle	45.71	40.01	87.60	85.08
	(114.61)	(118.48)	(136.21)	(135.48)
Legislative veto points	282.28	303.88	295.78	283.67
	(210.56)	(212.22)	(213.79)	(212.04)
Abe 1 dummy	212.49	223.18	95.16	86.38
	(196.29)	(198.67)	(186.18)	(183.67)
Abe 2 dummy	1505.23(***)	1484.10(***)	1377.92(***)	1379.89(***)
	(491.79)	(489.28)	(473.63)	(474.76)
Partisan control of	−428.07(*)	−432.40(*)	−494.26(**)	−485.20(**)
government	(229.42)	(225.21)	(227.30)	(224.76)
Fukushima dummy	−520.06	−518.01	−613.39(*)	−621.21(*)
	(320.95)	(322.61)	(316.60)	(317.87)
GFC dummy	−391.80(***)	−394.58(***)	−377.62(***)	−379.30(***)
	(125.21)	(125.01)	(128.96)	(129.04)
Fukui dummy	−96.69	−92.83	−160.48	−164.15
	(174.60)	(174.59)	(182.78)	(183.05)
Shirakawa dummy	123.67	155.28	5.14	1.28
	(250.52)	(254.84)	(261.70)	(264.22)
Kuroda dummy	648.84	682.61	448.23	428.10
	(618.01)	(618.17)	(618.04)	(618.70)
Num. obs.	241	242	246	247
R2	0.39	0.39	0.38	0.38
Adj. R2	0.35	0.35	0.34	0.34
L.R.	119.60	120.23	118.53	118.61

Robust standard errors; ***$p < 0.01$, **$p < 0.05$, *$p < 0.1$

TABLE 6A-3 Regression models: Lagged economic variables plus lagged DV

	INDEX 1	INDEX 2	INDEX 3	INDEX 4
Intercept	721.36(*)	740.64(*)	687.21(*)	626.03
	(397.08)	(404.19)	(399.81)	(388.12)
Lagged DV	0.41(***)	0.41(***)	0.42(***)	0.42(***)
	(0.10)	(0.10)	(0.10)	(0.10)
BOJ ideas	−272.13(**)	−290.34(**)	−239.11(**)	−259.23
	(108.87)	(121.02)	(119.19)	(158.84)
Monetary base (lag)	−0.47	−0.43	−0.34	−0.34
	(0.42)	(0.42)	(0.43)	(0.43)
Economic growth (lag)	−59.39	−58.54	−53.79	−51.88
	(49.63)	(49.57)	(48.92)	(48.99)
Change in CPI (lag)	−3818.66	−3742.75	−3915.91	−4230.87
	(4045.83)	(4059.46)	(3922.64)	(3814.22)
Debt (lag)	0.18	0.09	0.17	0.23
	(0.70)	(0.71)	(0.69)	(0.69)
Political business cycle	54.92	50.65	79.62	75.63
	(76.32)	(76.47)	(77.52)	(77.80)
Legislative veto points	104.11	120.14	112.35	103.30
	(184.64)	(187.32)	(186.89)	(185.90)
Abe 1 dummy	75.12	82.44	−6.83	−11.61
	(149.50)	(152.07)	(142.13)	(141.36)
Abe 2 dummy	1190.61(***)	1175.25(***)	1100.67(***)	1103.59(***)
	(411.86)	(409.27)	(395.03)	(395.18)
Partisan control of government	−230.18	−234.98	−283.18	−279.21
	(209.20)	(206.70)	(208.99)	(207.05)
Fukushima dummy	−479.80	−479.44	−548.78(*)	−554.76(*)
	(311.00)	(312.45)	(307.63)	(309.09)
GFC dummy	−295.87(***)	−297.18(***)	−284.64(***)	−282.61(***)
	(105.76)	(105.49)	(109.85)	(109.54)
Fukui dummy	−54.19	−52.53	−99.71	−107.71
	(147.39)	(147.40)	(152.31)	(152.93)
Shirakawa dummy	83.26	104.19	−3.99	−15.57
	(206.92)	(208.26)	(219.17)	(221.02)
Kuroda dummy	168.94	189.90	9.33	−19.37
	(529.69)	(526.77)	(531.59)	(530.93)
Num. obs.	241	242	246	247
R2	0.49	0.49	0.49	0.49
Adj. R2	0.46	0.46	0.45	0.45
L.R.	163.32	163.97	164.46	164.71

Robust standard errors; ***$p < 0.01$, **$p < 0.05$, *$p < 0.1$

TABLE 6A-4 Regression models: Change in the monetary base, ratio indexes

	INDEX 1	INDEX 2	INDEX 3	INDEX 4
Intercept	1378.98(***)	1396.53(***)	1259.81(***)	1224.01(***)
	(486.85)	(495.09)	(478.38)	(466.69)
BOJ ideas	−179.08(**)	−191.35(**)	−113.92	−168.97
	(79.79)	(84.14)	(75.63)	(139.41)
Monetary base	0.47	0.53	0.63	0.66
	(0.66)	(0.63)	(0.62)	(0.60)
Economic growth	−80.59	−78.06	−66.17	−65.05
	(52.43)	(52.29)	(50.76)	(50.71)
Change in CPI	−6326.25	−6094.02	−5467.32	−5685.50
	(4912.13)	(4816.57)	(4352.80)	(4226.74)
Debt	−1.30	−1.38	−1.30	−1.21
	(1.00)	(1.00)	(0.98)	(0.96)
Political business cycle	24.77	5.76	29.01	31.65
	(74.96)	(83.55)	(102.60)	(101.83)
Legislative veto point	512.76(**)	516.35(**)	497.13(**)	483.45(**)
	(235.75)	(237.16)	(229.40)	(228.07)
Abe 1 dummy	326.52	358.83	266.75	266.15
	(230.37)	(229.67)	(223.45)	(218.35)
Abe 2 dummy	1489.43(***)	1477.58(***)	1352.05(***)	1390.44(***)
	(478.94)	(474.91)	(462.69)	(462.35)
Partisan control of	−667.33(**)	−679.81(**)	−695.32(**)	−726.94(***)
government	(295.88)	(282.06)	(279.99)	(271.73)
Fukushima dummy	−526.09(*)	−529.76(*)	−623.45(**)	−624.23(**)
	(307.74)	(309.66)	(301.36)	(302.78)
GFC dummy	−196.58	−191.30	−256.29(**)	−219.11(**)
	(126.37)	(124.23)	(113.41)	(101.25)
Fukui dummy	−205.04	−216.39	−269.21	−281.50
	(175.15)	(169.76)	(171.61)	(172.41)
Shirakawa dummy	−130.39	−129.35	−193.46	−254.58
	(285.79)	(273.54)	(260.66)	(254.98)
Kuroda dummy	92.57	78.57	−96.63	−179.85
	(624.26)	(601.63)	(597.65)	(592.22)
Num. obs.	227	232	244	248
R2	0.38	0.38	0.38	0.38
Adj. R2	0.34	0.34	0.34	0.34
L.R.	109.34	111.16	117.11	118.56

Robust standard errors; ***p < 0.01, **p < 0.05, *p < 0.1

TABLE 6A-5 Regression models: Lagged economic variables, ratio indexes

	INDEX 1	INDEX 2	INDEX 3	INDEX 4
Intercept	1198.97(**)	1226.66(**)	1086.01(**)	1059.20(**)
	(493.81)	(503.07)	(479.06)	(462.83)
BOJ ideas	−196.31(***)	−206.31(**)	−130.13(*)	−224.32(*)
	(73.29)	(83.64)	(70.78)	(133.78)
Monetary base (lag)	−0.26	−0.19	−0.09	−0.08
	(0.52)	(0.51)	(0.52)	(0.51)
Economic growth (lag)	−70.53	−69.33	−56.27	−54.92
	(56.51)	(56.24)	(55.00)	(52.41)
Change in CPI (lag)	−7527.11	−7189.24	−7190.44	−7576.48(*)
	(4805.29)	(4866.73)	(4514.60)	(4299.36)
Debt (lag)	−0.45	−0.55	−0.47	−0.38
	(0.93)	(0.93)	(0.92)	(0.91)
Political business cycle	65.89	45.76	60.84	66.39
	(129.79)	(133.68)	(143.59)	(140.75)
Legislative veto points	298.88	305.83	294.53	280.74
	(220.58)	(222.08)	(215.08)	(212.88)
Abe 1 dummy	177.52	204.14	97.21	91.75
	(193.45)	(198.88)	(190.01)	(185.52)
Abe 2 dummy	1471.91(***)	1466.86(***)	1340.45(***)	1375.77(***)
	(498.16)	(494.31)	(474.29)	(472.47)
LDP dummy	−427.54(*)	−450.01(*)	−452.03(*)	−477.50(**)
	(249.98)	(239.73)	(237.37)	(226.27)
Fukushima dummy	−540.46(*)	−545.22(*)	−629.71(**)	−627.60(**)
	(319.68)	(322.17)	(315.53)	(316.93)
GFC dummy	−377.96(**)	−368.50(**)	−412.92(***)	−378.99(***)
	(148.54)	(148.48)	(137.00)	(131.65)
Fukui dummy	−128.12	−139.63	−189.97	−194.21
	(179.15)	(177.25)	(181.29)	(182.10)
Shirakawa dummy	92.00	87.42	32.47	−17.81
	(287.92)	(282.54)	(271.42)	(268.75)
Kuroda dummy	653.51	627.86	443.66	380.75
	(630.74)	(618.68)	(617.38)	(619.47)
Num. obs.	226	231	243	247
R2	0.38	0.38	0.38	0.38
Adj. R2	0.34	0.34	0.34	0.34
L.R.	108.42	110.05	115.71	117.36

Robust standard errors; ***$p < 0.01$, **$p < 0.05$, *$p < 0.1$

TABLE 6A-6 Regression models: Lagged economic variables plus lagged DV, ratio indexes

	INDEX 1	INDEX 2	INDEX 3	INDEX 4
Intercept	653.77	668.28	582.45	560.35
	(421.74)	(432.53)	(399.69)	(383.68)
Lagged DV	0.42(***)	0.42(***)	0.42(***)	0.42(***)
	(0.10)	(0.10)	(0.10)	(0.10)
BOJ ideas	−136.58(*)	−140.81(*)	−77.55	−117.10
	(72.61)	(80.71)	(68.67)	(119.57)
Monetary base (lag)	−0.42	−0.37	−0.32	−0.30
	(0.45)	(0.43)	(0.44)	(0.43)
Economic growth (lag)	−63.50	−61.75	−50.36	−50.21
	(53.57)	(53.37)	(51.75)	(49.18)
Change in CPI (lag)	−4304.05	−4109.65	−3933.75	−4274.87
	(4452.80)	(4491.62)	(4070.02)	(3823.01)
Debt (lag)	0.21	0.13	0.18	0.24
	(0.71)	(0.71)	(0.70)	(0.69)
Political business cycle	67.99	53.35	60.62	61.30
	(84.77)	(81.25)	(78.97)	(79.41)
Legislative veto points	102.02	108.91	108.32	99.33
	(194.36)	(196.12)	(187.90)	(186.30)
Abe 1 dummy	65.25	77.48	−5.84	−6.57
	(149.98)	(152.85)	(144.86)	(142.48)
Abe 2 dummy	1172.76(***)	1165.95(***)	1078.54(***)	1104.67(***)
	(415.45)	(412.08)	(395.23)	(392.82)
Partisan control of government	−243.19	−260.94	−258.48	−279.60
	(224.02)	(215.98)	(215.29)	(207.76)
Fukushima dummy	−499.72	−503.80	−559.61(*)	−559.54(*)
	(310.66)	(313.29)	(307.62)	(308.80)
GFC dummy	−272.32(**)	−264.19(**)	−298.37(***)	−275.55(**)
	(122.55)	(122.66)	(115.34)	(111.09)
Fukui dummy	−89.06	−97.97	−127.15	−133.68
	(150.67)	(149.08)	(151.23)	(152.44)
Shirakawa dummy	27.51	21.35	−3.52	−42.93
	(233.89)	(226.85)	(225.90)	(224.86)
Kuroda dummy	138.69	112.57	−23.01	−75.67
	(536.11)	(519.85)	(529.74)	(531.59)
Num. obs.	226	231	243	247
R2	0.49	0.48	0.49	0.48
Adj. R2	0.45	0.45	0.45	0.45
L.R.	150.33	153.20	161.34	163.86

Robust standard errors; ***p < 0.01, **p < 0.05, *p < 0.1

References

Abdelal, Rawi, Mark Blyth, and Craig Parsons. 2010. "Introduction." In *Constructing the International Economy*, edited by Rawi Abdelal, Mark Blyth, and Craig Parsons. Ithaca, NY: Cornell University Press.

Achen, Christopher H. 2001. "Why Lagged Dependent Variables Can Suppress the Explanatory Power of Other Independent Variables." Center for the Study of Democratic Politics, Princeton University, November 2, 2001.

Adolph, Christopher. 2014. *Bankers, Bureaucrats, and Central Bank Politics: The Myth of Neutrality*. New York: Cambridge University Press.

Akerlof, George A., William T. Dickens, and George L. Perry. 1996. "The Macroeconomics of Low Inflation." *Brookings Papers on Economic Activity* 1:1–76.

Alesina, Alberto. 1987. "Macroeconomic Policy in a Two-Party System as a Repeated Game." *The Quarterly Journal of Economics* 102 (3): 651–78.

Alesina, Alberto, Nouriel Roubini, and Gerald D. Cohen. 1997. *Political Cycles and the Macroeconomy*. Cambridge, MA: MIT Press.

Alesina, Alberto, and Lawrence H. Summers. 1993. "Central Bank Independence and Macroeconomic Performance: Some Comparative Evidence." *Journal of Money, Credit and Banking* 25 (2): 151–62.

Alesina, Alberto, and Guido Tabellini. 1988. "Credibility and Politics." *European Economic Review* 32 (2): 542–50.

Amyx, Jennifer Ann. 2004. *Japan's Financial Crisis: Institutional Rigidity and Reluctant Change*. Princeton, NJ: Princeton University Press.

Ansell, Christopher. 2008. "Network Institutionalism." In *The Oxford Handbook of Political Institutions*, edited by Rod A. W. Rhodes, Sarah A. Binder, and Bert A. Rockman, 75–89. New York: Oxford University Press.

Arita, Tetsufumi. 2007. "Bound by a Hidden Agenda: The Birth and Consequences of the Bank of Japan's Quantitative Monetary Easing." Walter H. Shorenstein Asia-Pacific Research Center Working Paper, Stanford University.

Baba, Naohiko, Shinichi Nishioka, Nobuyuki Oda, Masaaki Shirakawa, Kazuo Ueda, and Hiroshi Ugai. 2005. "Japan's Deflation, Problems in the Financial System and Monetary Policy." BIS Working Paper (188).

Babb, Sarah L. 2001. *Managing Mexico: Economists from Nationalism to Neoliberalism*. Princeton, NJ: Princeton University Press.

Baig, Taimur. 2003. "Understanding the Costs of Deflation in the Japanese Context." International Monetary Fund Working Paper (3/215).

Baig, Taimur, Jörg Decressin, Tarhan Feyzioglu, Manmohan S. Kumar, and Chris Faulkner-MacDonagh. 2003. "Deflation: Determinants, Risks, and Policy Options." International Monetary Fund Occasional Paper (221).

Ban, Cornel. 2016. *Ruling Ideas: How Global Neoliberalism Goes Local*. New York: Oxford University Press.

Bank of Japan. 2004. *Atarashii Nippon Ginkō Sono Kinō to Gyōmu* [The new Bank of Japan: Its functions and operations]. Tokyo: Yūhikaku.

Bank of Japan. 2016. Comprehensive Assessment: Developments in Economic Activity and Prices as well as Policy Effects since the Introduction of Quantitative and Qualitative Monetary Easing (QQE), September 21, 2016. https://www.boj.or.jp/en/announcements/release_2016/k160921b.pdf.

Barnett, Michael N., and Martha Finnemore. 1999. "The Politics, Power, and Pathologies of International Organizations." *International Organization* 53 (4): 699–732.

Barro, Robert J., and David B. Gordon. 1983. "Rules, Discretion and Reputation in a Model of Monetary Policy." *Journal of Monetary Economics* 12 (1): 101–21.

Baumgartner, Frank R. 2014. "Ideas, Paradigms and Confusions." *Journal of European Public Policy* 21 (3): 475–80.

Berkmen, Pelin S. 2012. "Bank of Japan's Quantitative and Credit Easing: Are They Now More Effective?" IMF Working Papers (12/2).

Berman, Sheri. 2001. "Ideas, Norms, and Culture in Political Analysis." *Comparative Politics* 33 (2): 231–50.

Berman, Sheri. 2013. "Ideational Theorizing in the Social Sciences since "Policy Paradigms, Social Learning, and the State." *Governance* 26 (2): 217–37.

Bernanke, Ben S. 1999. "Japanese Monetary Policy: A Case of Self-Induced Paralysis?" Presented at ASSA meetings, Boston, MA, January 9, 2000.

Bernanke, Ben S. 2003. "Some Thoughts on Monetary Policy in Japan: Remarks before the Japan Society of Monetary Economics." Speech at the Japan Society of Monetary Economics, Tokyo, Japan, March 31, 2003. https://www.federalreserve.gov/boarddocs/speeches/2003/20030531.

Bernanke, Ben S. 2004. "The Great Moderation." In *The Taylor Rule and the Transformation of Monetary Policy*, edited by Evan F. Koenig, Robert Leeson, and George A. Kahn. Stanford, CA: Hoover Institute Press Publication.

Bernanke, Ben S. 2015. *The Courage to Act: A Memoir of a Crisis and Its Aftermath.* New York: W. W. Norton & Company.

Bernanke, Ben S. 2016. "What Tools Does the Fed Have Left? Part 2: Targeting Longer-Term Interest Rates." Brookings Institution (blog). https://www.brookings.edu/blog/ben-bernanke/2016/03/24/what-tools-does-the-fed-have-left-part-2-targeting-longer-term-interest-rates

Bernanke, Ben S. 2017a. "Shrinking the Fed's Balance Sheet." Brookings, January 26, 2017. https://www.brookings.edu/blog/ben-bernanke/2017/01/26/shrinking-the-feds-balance-sheet/.

Bernanke, Ben S. 2017b. "Some Reflections on Japanese Monetary Policy." Brookings, May 23, 2017. https://www.brookings.edu/blog/ben-bernanke/2017/05/23/some-reflections-on-japanese-monetary-policy/.

Bernanke, Ben S., and Vincent R. Reinhart. 2004. "Conducting Monetary Policy at Very Low Short-Term Interest Rates." *The American Economic Review* 94 (2): 85–90.

Bernanke, Ben S., Vincent Reinhart, and Brian Sack. 2004. "Monetary Policy Alternatives at the Zero Bound: An Empirical Assessment." *Brookings Papers on Economic Activity* 2004 (2): 1–100.

Blinder, Alan S. 2007. "Monetary Policy by Committee: Why and How?" *European Journal of Political Economy* 23 (1): 106–23.

Blyth, Mark. 2001. "The Transformation of the Swedish Model: Economic Ideas, Distributional Conflict, and Institutional Change." *World Politics* 54 (1): 1–26.

Blyth, Mark. 2002. *Great Transformations: Economic Ideas and Institutional Change in the Twentieth Century*. New York: Cambridge University Press.

Blyth, Mark. 2003. "Structures Do Not Come with an Instruction Sheet: Interests, Ideas, and Progress in Political Science." *Perspectives on Politics* 1 (4): 695–706.

Blyth, Mark. 2007. "Beyond the Usual Suspects: Ideas, Uncertainty, and Building Institutional Orders." *International Studies Quarterly* 51 (4): 761–77.

Blyth, Mark. 2013. *Austerity: The History of a Dangerous Idea*. New York: Oxford University Press.

Boivin, Jean, Michael T. Kiley, and Frederic S. Mishkin. 2010. "How Has the Monetary Transmission Mechanism Evolved Over Time?" NBER Working Paper No. 15879.

Bordo, Michael, and Arunima Sinha. 2016. "A Lesson from the Great Depression That the Fed Might Have Learned: A Comparison of the 1932 Open Market Purchases with Quantitative Easing." NBER Working Paper No. 22581.

Borio, Claudio, and Haibin Zhu. 2012. "Capital Regulation, Risk-Taking and Monetary Policy: A Missing Link in the Transmission Mechanism?" *Journal of Financial Stability* 8 (4): 236–51.

Boskin, Michael J., Ellen R. Dulberger, Zvi Griliches, Robert J. Gordon, and Dale Jorgensen. 1996. Toward a More Accurate Measure of the Cost of Living. Final report to the Senate Finance Committee for the Advisory Commission to study the Consumer Price Index.

Bowman, David, Fang Cai, Sally Davies, and Steven Kamin. 2011. "Quantitative Easing and Bank Lending: Evidence from Japan." Board of Governors of the Federal Reserve System International Finance Discussion Papers.

Caballero, Ricardo J., Takeo Hoshi, and Anil K. Kashyap. 2008. "Zombie Lending and Depressed Restructuring in Japan." *The American Economic Review* 98 (5): 1943–77.

Calder, Kent E. 1988. *Crisis and Compensation: Public Policy and Political Stability in Japan, 1949–1986*. Princeton, NJ: Princeton University Press.

Calza, Alessandro, Tommaso Monacelli, and Livio Stracca. 2013. "Housing Finance and Monetary Policy." *Journal of the European Economic Association* 11 (supp. 1): 101–22.

Campbell, John L., and Ove K. Pedersen. 2014. *The National Origins of Policy Ideas: Knowledge Regimes in the United States, France, Germany, and Denmark*. Princeton, NJ: Princeton University Press.

Cargill, Thomas F. 2000. "Monetary Policy, Deflation, and Economic History: Lessons for the Bank of Japan." IMES Discussion Paper Series No. 2000-E-30.

Cargill, Thomas F., and Jennifer Holt Dwyer. 2013. "New Management at the Bank of Japan, End of 'Independent' Bank of Japan and Implications for the Concept of Central Bank Independence." Walter H. Shorensen Asia-Pacific Research Center Working Paper.

Cargill, Thomas F., and Jennifer Holt Dwyer. 2015. "The Bank of Japan Experience: New Management and Lessons for Legal Central Bank Independence." *Journal of Contemporary Management* 4 (4), http://www.bapress.ca/jcm/jcm-article/1929-0136-2015-04-01-14.pdf#search=%27Cargill+and+Dwyer++The+Bank+of+Japan%27.

Cargill, Thomas F., and Michael M. Hutchinson. 1991. "Political Business Cycles with Endogenous Election Timing: Evidence from Japan." *The Review of Economics and Statistics* 73 (4): 733–39.

Cargill, Thomas F., Michael M. Hutchison, and Takatoshi Ito. 1997. *The Political Economy of Japanese Monetary Policy*. Cambridge, MA: MIT Press.

Cargill, Thomas F., Michael M. Hutchison, and Takatoshi Ito. 2000. *Financial Policy and Central Banking in Japan*. Cambridge, MA: MIT Press.

Carpenter, Daniel P. 2001. *The Forging of Bureaucratic Autonomy: Reputations, Networks, and Policy Innovation in Executive Agencies, 1862–1928*. Princeton, NJ: Princeton University Press.

Chang, Kelly H. 2003. *Appointing Central Bankers: The Politics of Monetary Policy in the United States and the European Monetary Union*. Cambridge: Cambridge University Press.

Chopin, Marc C., C Steven Cole, and Michael A. Ellis. 1996. "Congressional Influence on US Monetary Policy: A Reconsideration of the Evidence." *Journal of Monetary Economics* 38 (3): 561–70.

Chwieroth, Jeffrey M. 2007. "Testing and Measuring the Role of Ideas: The Case of Neoliberalism in the International Monetary Fund." *International Studies Quarterly* 51 (1): 5–30.

Chwieroth, Jeffrey M. 2010. *Capital Ideas: The IMF and the Rise of Financial Liberalization*. Princeton, NJ: Princeton University Press.

Chwieroth, Jeffrey M. 2013. "'The Silent Revolution:' How the Staff Exercise Informal Governance over IMF Lending." *The Review of International Organizations* 8 (2): 265–90.

Conti-Brown, Peter. 2016. *The Power and Independence of the Federal Reserve*. Princeton, NJ: Princeton University Press.

Cooper, Chris, and Kiyotaka Matsuda. 2016. "Japan Inc. Profits Head for Biggest Abe-Era Drop on Yen Gain." Bloomberg. https://www.bloomberg.com/news/articles/2016-04-13/japan-inc-profits-head-for-biggest-abe-era-drop-on-stronger-yen.

Copelovitch, Mark S., and David Andrew Singer. 2008. "Financial Regulation, Monetary Policy, and Inflation in the Industrialized World." *The Journal of Politics* 70 (3): 663–80.

Cukierman, Alex. 1992. *Central Bank Strategy, Credibility, and Independence: Theory and Evidence*. Cambridge, MA: MIT Press.

Cukierman, Alex. 1994. "Central Bank Independence and Monetary Control." *The Economic Journal* 104 (427): 1437–48.

Daigneault, Pierre-Marc. 2014. "Reassessing the Concept of Policy Paradigm: Aligning Ontology and Methodology in Policy Studies." *Journal of European Public Policy* 21 (3): 453–69.

De Haan, Jakob, and Willem J. Kooi. 2000. "Does Central Bank Independence Really Matter?: New Evidence for Developing Countries Using a New Indicator." *Journal of Banking & Finance* 24 (4): 643–64.

De Michelis, Andrea, and Matteo Iacoviello. 2016. "Raising an Inflation Target: The Japanese Experience with Abenomics." *European Economic Review* 88: 67–87. doi: 10.1016/j.euroecorev.2016.02.021.

Dekle, Robert, and Koichi Hamada. 2015. "Japanese Monetary Policy and International Spillovers." *Journal of International Money and Finance* 52: 175–99.

DiMaggio, Paul J., and Walter W. Powell. 1983. "The Iron Cage Revisited: Collective Rationality and Institutional Isomorphism in Organizational Fields." *American Sociological Review* 48 (2): 147–60.

DiMaggio, Paul J., and Walter W. Powell. 1991. *The New Institutionalism in Organizational Analysis*. Vol. 17. Chicago: University of Chicago Press.

Dobbin, Frank. 1994. *Forging Industrial Policy: The United States, Britain, and France in the Railway Age*. New York: Cambridge University Press.

Domínguez, Jorge. 1997. "Technopols: Freeing Politics and Markets in Latin America in the 1990s." In *Technopols: Freeing Politics and Markets in Latin America in the 1990s*, edited by Jorge Domínguez, 1–48. University Park: Pennsylvania State University Press.

Drazen, Allan. 2001. "The Political Business Cycle after 25 Years." In *NBER Macroeconomics Annual 2000*, edited by Ben S. Bernanke and Kenneth Rogoff, 75–138. Cambridge, MA: MIT Press.

Dwyer, Jennifer Holt. 2004. "Explaining Central Bank Reform in Japan." *Social Science Japan Journal* 7 (2): 245–62.

Dwyer, Jennifer Holt. 2012. "Explaining the Politicization of Monetary Policy in Japan." *Social Science Japan Journal* 15 (2): 179–200.

Economic and Social Research Institution. 2011. "Baburu/Defure ki no nihon keizai to keizai seisaku" [Japan's economy and economic policy in bubble/ deflation period]. Vol. 3. *The Record of the Japanese Economy—A Time Witness Testimony* (oral history).

Eggertsson, Gauti B., and Michael Woodford. 2004. "Policy Options in a Liquidity Trap." *The American Economic Review* 94 (2): 76–79.

Eijffinger, Sylvester C. W., and Jakob De Haan. 1996. "The Political Economy of Central-Bank Independence." Special Papers in International Economics 19: 1–82.

Elson, Sara Beth, Douglas Yeung, Parisa Roshan, Susan R. Bohandy, and Alireza Nader. 2012. *Using Social Media to Gauge Iranian Public Opinion and Mood after the 2009 Election*. Santa Monica, CA: Rand Corporation.

Epstein, David, and Sharyn O'halloran. 1999. *Delegating Powers: A Transaction Cost Politics Approach to Policy Making under Separate Powers*. New York: Cambridge University Press.

Farmer, Roger E. A. 2012. "Qualitative Easing: How It Works and Why It Matters." National Bureau of Economic Research No. 1821.

Faust, Jon, and John S. Irons. 1999. "Money, Politics and the Post-war Business Cycle." *Journal of Monetary Economics* 43 (1): 61–89.

Fawley, Brett W., and Christopher J. Neely. 2013. "Four Stories of Quantitative Easing." *Federal Reserve Bank of St. Louis Review* 95 (1): 51–88.

Fisher, Irving. 1933. "The Debt-Deflation Theory of Great Depressions." *Econometrica* 1 (4): 337–357.

Forder, James. 1996. "On The Assessment and Implementation of 'Institutional' Remedies." *Oxford Economic Papers* 48 (1): 39–51.

Fourcade, Marion. 2009. *Economists and Societies: Discipline and Profession in the United States, Britain, and France, 1890s to 1990s*. Princeton, NJ: Princeton University Press.

Franzese, Robert J., Jr. 1999. "Partially Independent Central Banks, Politically Responsive Governments, and Inflation." *American Journal of Political Science* 43 (3): 681–706.

Franzese Jr, Robert J. 2002. "Electoral and Partisan Cycles in Economic Policies and Outcomes." *Annual Review of Political Science* 5 (1): 369–421.

Friedman, Milton. 1969. *Optimum Quantity of Money and Other Essays*. Chicago, IL: Aldine Publishing Co.

Fujii, Yoshihiro. 2004. *Shibarareta kinyū seisaku: Kenshō nihon ginkō* [Bound financial policy: Examining the BOJ]. Tokyo: Nihon Keizai Shimbunsha.

Fujiki, Hiroshi, Kunio Okina, and Shigenori Shiratsuka. 2001. "Monetary Policy under Zero Interest Rate: Viewpoints of Central Bank Economists." *Monetary and Economic Studies* 19 (1): 89–130.

Fukuda, Shin-ichi, and Tsutomu Doita. 2016. "Unconventional Monetary Policy and its External Effects: Evidence from Japan's Exports." *The Developing Economies* 54 (1): 59–79.

Fukunaga, Ichiro, Naoya Kato, and Junko Koeda. 2015. *Maturity Structure and Supply Factors in Japanese Government Bond Markets*. Institute for Monetary and Economic Studies, Bank of Japan.

Funabashi, Yoichi. 1989. *Managing the Dollar: From the Plaza to the Louvre*. 2nd ed. Washington, DC: Peterson Institute for International Economics.

Gagnon, Joseph E. 2016. "Quantitative Easing: An Underappreciated Success." Peterson Institute for International Economics Policy Brief (16–4).

Gilpin, Robert. 2001. *Global Political Economy*. Princeton, NJ: Princeton University Press.

Goffman, Erving. 1959. *The Presentation of Self in Everyday Life*. New York: Anchor.

Goldstein, Judith. 1993. *Ideas, Interests, and American Trade Policy*. Ithaca, NY: Cornell University Press.

Goldstein, Judith, and Robert O. Keohane. 1993. *Ideas and Foreign Policy—Beliefs, Institutions, and Political Change*. Edited by Judith Goldstein and Robert O. Keohane. Ithaca, NY: Cornell University Press.

González-Bailón, Sandra, and Georgios Paltoglou. 2015. "Signals of Public Opinion in Online Communication: A Comparison of Methods and Data Sources." The ANNALS of the American Academy of Political and Social Science 659 (1): 95–107. doi: 10.1177/0002716215569192.

Gourevitch, Peter Alexis. 1986. *Politics in Hard Times: Comparative Responses to International Economic Crises*. Ithaca, NY: Cornell University Press.

Grier, Kevin B. 1991. "Congressional Influence on U.S. Monetary Policy: An Empirical Test." *Journal of Monetary Economics* 28 (2): 201–20.

Grilli, Vittorio, Donato Masciandaro, and Guido Tabellini. 1991. "Political and Monetary Institutions and Public Financial Policies in the Industrial Countries." *Economic Policy* 6 (13): 341–92.

Grimes, William W. 2002. *Unmaking the Japanese Miracle: Macroeconomic Politics, 1985–2000*. Ithaca, NY: Cornell University Press.

Haas, Peter M. 1992. "Introduction: Epistemic Communities and International Policy Coordination." *International Organization* 46 (1): 1–35.

Hall, Peter A. 1989. "Introduction." In *The Political Power of Economic Ideas: Keynesianism across Nations*, edited by Peter A. Hall, 3–26. Princeton, NJ: Princeton University Press.

Hall, Peter A. 1993. "Policy Paradigms, Social Learning, and the State: the Case of Economic Policymaking in Britain." *Comparative Politics* 25 (3): 275–96.

Hall, Peter A. 1997. "The Role of Interests, Institutions, and Ideas in the Comparative Political Economy of the Industrialized Nations." In *Comparative Politics: Rationality, Culture, and Structure*, edited by Mark Irving Lichbach and Alan S. Zuckerman, 174–207. New York: Cambridge University Press.

Hall, Peter A., and Robert J. Franzese. 1998. "Mixed Signals: Central Bank Independence, Coordinated Wage Bargaining, and European Monetary Union." *International Organization* 52 (3): 505–35.

Hall, Peter A., and Rosemary C. R. Taylor. 1996. "Political Science and the Three New Institutionalisms." *Political Studies* 44 (5): 936–57.

Hall, Rodney Bruce. 2008. *Central Banking as Global Governance: Constructing Financial Credibility*. New York: Cambridge University Press.

Hamada, Kōichi. 2012. *America wa Nihon Keizai no Fukkatsu wo shitte iru* [America knows the revival of the Japanese economy]. Tokyo: Kōdansha.

Hamada, Koichi. & Noguchi, A. 2005. "The Role of Preconceived Ideas in Macroeconomic Policy: Japan's Experiences in Two Deflationary Periods." *International Economics and Economic Policy* 2: 101–26.

Hausman, Joshua K., and Johannes F. Wieland. 2014. "Abenomics Preliminary Analysis and Outlook." *Brookings Papers on Economic Activity* (Spring): 1–76.

Hausman, Joshua K., and Johannes F. Wieland. 2015. "Overcoming the Lost Decades?: Abenomics after Three Years." *Brookings Papers on Economic Activity* (Fall): 385–413.

Heckel, Markus. 2014. "The Bank of Japan—Institutional Issues of Delegation, Central Bank Independence and Monetary Policy." PhD dissertation, Universität Duisburg-Essen.

Heclo, Hugh. 1978. "Issue Networks and the Executive Establishment." In *Public Administration: Concepts and Cases*, edited by Richard Stillman, 413. Boston: Wadsworth Publishing.

Heclo, Hugh, and Aaron B. Wildavsky. 1974. *The Private Government of Public Money: Community and Policy Inside British Politics*. Berkeley: University of California Press.

Henning, C. Randall. 1994. *Currencies and Politics in the United States, Germany, and Japan*. Washington, DC: Peterson Institute for International Economics.

Hibbs, Douglas A. 1977. "Political Parties and Macroeconomic Policy." *The American Political Science Review* 71 (4): 1467–87.

Holmes, Douglas R. 2013. *Economy of Words: Communicative Imperatives in Central Banks*. Chicago: University of Chicago Press.

Huber, John D., and Charles R. Shipan. 2002. *Deliberate Discretion?: The Institutional Foundations of Bureaucratic Autonomy*. New York: Cambridge University Press.

Irwin, Neil. 2013. *The Alchemists: Three Central Bankers and a World on Fire*. New York: Penguin Books.

Itō, Masanao, Ryoji Koike, and Masato Shizume. 2015. "1980 nendai ni okeru kin'yū un'ei ni tsuite: Ākaibu shiryō tou kara mita nihon ginkō no ninshiki wo Chūshin ni" [Financial policy administration in the 1980s: With a focus on the BOJ's perspectives in archival documents etc.]. *Nihon ginkō kin'yū kenkyū sho. Kinyū kenkyū (Monetary and Economic Studies)* 34 (2): 67–160.

Ito, Takatoshi. 1990. "The Timing of Elections and Political Business Cycles in Japan." *Journal of Asian Economics* 1 (1): 135–56.

Ito, Takatoshi. 2004. Inflation Targeting and Japan: Why Has the Bank of Japan not Adopted Inflation Targeting? In NBER Working Paper.

Ito, Takatoshi, and Frederic S. Mishkin. 2006. "Two Decades of Japanese Monetary Policy and the Deflation Problem." In *Monetary Policy with Very Low Inflation in the Pacific Rim, NBER-EASE*, vol. 15, edited by Takatoshi Ito and Andrew K. Rose, 131–202. Chicago: University of Chicago Press.

Ito, Takatoshi, and Jin Hyuk Park. 1988. "Political Business Cycles in the Parliamentary System." *Economics Letters* 27 (3): 233–38.

Iversen, Torben. 1999. "Erratum: The Political Economy of Inflation: Bargaining Structure or Central Bank Independence?" *Public Choice* 101 (3): 285–306. doi: 10.1023/a:1018730513366.

Iwata, Kikuo. 2003. *Mazu defure wo tomeyo* [Stop deflation first]. Tokyo: Nihon Keizai Shinbunsha.

Iwata, Kikuo. 2011. *Defure to Chō endaka* [Deflation and the super high yen]. Tokyo: Kodansha Gendai Shinsho.

Janis, Irving Lester. 1982. *Groupthink: Psychological Studies of Policy Decisions and Fiascoes*. 2nd ed. Boston: Houghton Mifflin.

Jockers, Matthew L. 2013. *Macroanalysis: Digital Methods and Literary History*. Urbana: University of Illinois Press.

Johnson, Juliet. 2016. *Priests of Prosperity, How Central Bankers Transformed the Post-communist World*. Ithaca, NY: Cornell University Press.

Kamikawa, Ryūnoshin. 2005. *Keizaiseisaku no Seijigaku* [Politics of economic policy]. Tokyo: Tōyōkeizai Shinpo sha.

Kamikawa, Ryūnoshin. 2014. *Nihon ginkō to seiji: Kin'yū seisaku kettei no kiseki* [The BOJ and politics: Tracing financial policy decisions]. Tokyo: Chūkō Shinsho.

Karube, Kensuke. 2004. *Dokyumento Zero Kin'ri: Nichigin vs Seifu naze tairitsu suruno ka* [Document zero interest: Why do the Bank of Japan and the government come into collision?]. Iwanami Shoten.

Karube, Kensuke. 2015. *Kenshō Baburu Sissei* [Examining policy errors on bubble economy]. Tokyo: Iwanami Shoten.

Karube, Kensuke, and Tomohiko Nishino. 1999. *Kenshō Keizai Shissei: Dare ga, Nani wo, Naze machigaeta ka?* [Examination of economic policy failure: Who failed to do what, and why?]. Tokyo: Iwanami Shoten.

Katada, Saori N. 2013. "Financial Crisis Fatigue? Politics Behind Japan's Post-Global Financial Crisis Economic Contraction." *Japanese Journal of Political Science* 14 (2): 223–42.

Katzenstein, Peter J. 1996. *The Culture of National Security: Norms and Identity in World Politics*. New York: Columbia University Press.

Kaufman, Herbert. 1967. *The Forest Ranger: A Study in Administrative Behavior*. Washington, DC: Resources for the Future, Inc.

Kawai, Masahiro, and Shinji Takagi. 2009. *Why Was Japan Hit So Hard by the Global Financial Crisis?* In ADBI Working Paper 153. Tokyo: Asian Development Bank Institute.

Kawakita, Takao. 1995. *Nihon ginkō: Nani ga towarete iru no ka* [The BOJ: What is being questioned]. Tokyo: Iwanami Shinsho.

Keefer, Philip, and David Stasavage. 2003. "The Limits of Delegation: Veto Players, Central Bank Independence, and the Credibility of Monetary Policy." *American Political Science Review* 97 (3): 407–23.

Kimura, Takeshi, and Jouchi Nakajima. 2016. "Identifying Conventional and Unconventional Monetary Policy Shocks: A Latent Threshold Approach." *The B.E. Journal of Macroeconomics* 16 (1): 277–300.

King, Gary. 1991. "'Truth' Is Stranger than Prediction, More Questionable than Causal Inference." *American Journal of Political Science* 35 (4): 1047–53.

King, Mervyn. 1993. "The Bundesbank: A View from the Bank of England." *Bank of England Quarterly Bulletin* (May).

King, Mervyn. 2007. "The MPC Ten Years On." *Bank of England Quarterly Bulletin 25 June*. Lecture delivered on 2 May 2007 to the Society of Business Economists.

King, Mervyn. 2016. *The End of Alchemy: Money, Banking, and the Future of the Global Economy*. New York: W. W. Norton & Company.

King, Michael. 2005. "Epistemic Communities and the Diffusion of Ideas: Central Bank Reform in the United Kingdom." *West European Politics* 28 (1): 94–123.

Kirshner, Jonathan. 1998. "Disinflation, Structural Change, and Distribution." *Review of Radical Political Economics* 30 (1): 53–89.

Kirshner, Jonathan. 2003. *Monetary Orders: Ambiguous Economics, Ubiquitous Politics*. Ithaca, NY: Cornell University Press.

Kohn, Donald L. 2007. "John Taylor Rules." Speech at the Conference on John Taylor's Contributions to Monetary Theory and Policy, Federal Reserve Bank of Dallas, Dallas, Texas, October 12–13.

Kohno, Masaru, and Yoshitaka Nishizawa. 1990. "A Study of the Electoral Business Cycle in Japan: Elections and Government Spending on Public Construction." *Comparative Politics* 22 (2): 151–66.

Koike, Takuji. 2006. "'Zero kinri' jidai no kin'yū sesaku; seisaku suii to sono ron'ten [Monetary policy in the age of 'zero interest rate': Policy evolution and issues]." *Chōsa to Jōhō* 55: 1–10.

Kojo, Yoshiko. 1996. *Keizaiteki Sōgo izon to Kokka: Kokusai shūshi fukinkou zesei no seiji keizaigaku* [Economic interdependence and state: Political economy of international payments adjustment in postwar period]. Tokyo: Bokutakusha.

Kojo, Yoshiko. 2002. *Baburu keisei/hōkai no haikei to siteno nitibei keizai kankei: Puraza gōi ikō no kokusai shūshi kuroji zesei mondai to endaka kaihi ron* [Japan-U.S. economic relationship as a context of developing and collapsing bubble economy: The problem of correcting balance of payments surplus and opinions of avoiding appreciation of the yen after the Plaza Accord]. Edited by Muramatsu Michio and Okuno Masahiro, Heisei baburu no Kenkyū Gekan (Study on Heisei Bubble Economy, vol. 2). Tokyo: Tōyō Keizai Shinpōsha.

Komiya, Ryūtarō. 1988. "Shōwa 48–49-nen infurēshon no Gen'in" [Reasons for inflation from the 48–49 years of the Shōwa era]. In *Gendai nihon keizai* [Modern Japanese economy]. Tokyo: Tokyo Daigaku Syuppankai.

Kosai, Yutaka, Masaaki Shirakawa, and Kunio Okina. 2001. *Baburu to Kin'yū Seisaku: Nihon no keiken to kyōkun* [Bubble and monetary policy: Japan's experience and lessons]. Tokyo: Nihonkeizai Shimbunsha.

Krippendorff, Klaus. 2013. *Content Analysis: An Introduction to Its Methodology*. 3rd ed. Thousand Oaks, CA: SAGE Publication.

Krugman, Paul R., Kathryn M. Dominquez, and Kenneth Rogoff. 1998. "It's Baaack: Japan's Slump and the Return of the Liquidity Trap." *Brookings Papers on Economic Activity* (2): 137–205.

Kuhn, Thomas S. 1970. *The Structure of Scientific Revolutions*. 2nd enl. ed. Chicago: University of Chicago Press.

Kujiraoka, Hitoshi. 2017. *Nichigin to Seiji: Antō no Nijūnen shi* [The Bank of Japan and Politics: Twenty years of Silent Feud]. Tokyo: Asahi Shimbun Shuppan sha.

Kumakura, Masanaga. 2015. "Defure to Shōhisha Bukka Shisū no Hinshitsu chōsei [Deflations and the quality adjustment of the Consumer Price Index]." *Keizai Tōkei Kenkyū* 43 (1): 16–31.

Kuran, Timur. 1995. *Private Truths, Public Lies: The Social Consequences of Preference Falsification*. Cambridge, MA: Harvard University Press.

Kure, Bunji. 1981. *Nihon-no Kin'yūkai: Arubeki Sugata to Genjitsu* [Financial circle in Japan: The way it's supposed to be and the way it is]. Tokyo: Tōyōkeizai Shinpōsha.

Kuttner, Kenneth N., and Patricia C. Mosser. 2002. "The Monetary Transmission Mechanism: Some Answers and Further Questions." *Federal Reserve Bank of New York Economic Policy Review* 8 (1): 15–26.

Kuttner, Kenneth N., and Adam S. Posen. 2004. "The Difficulty of Discerning What's Too Tight: Taylor Rules and Japanese Monetary Policy." *The North American Journal of Economics and Finance* 15 (1): 53–74.

Kydland, Finn E., and Edward C. Prescott. 1977. "Rules Rather than Discretion: The Inconsistency of Optimal Plans." *Journal of Political Economy* 85 (3): 473–92.

Labonte, Marc. 2014. Federal Reserve: Unconventional Monetary Policy Options. In CRS Report for Congress.

Lam, Kwok-Chiu. 2015. "Did Abenomics' Two Arrows Hit the Bulls?" *Journal of Applied Finance & Banking* 5 (3): 47–61.

Lam, Waikei R. 2011. "Bank of Japan's Monetary Easing Measures: Are They Powerful and Comprehensive?" IMF Working Papers (11/264): 1–18.

Lambert, Frederic, and Kenichi Ueda. 2014. *The Effects of Unconventional Monetary Policies on Bank Soundness*. IMF Working Paper No. 14/152. International Monetary Fund.

Lebow, David E., and Jeremy B. Rudd. 2003. "Measurement Error in the Consumer Price Index: Where Do We Stand?" *Journal of Economic Literature* 41 (1): 159–201.

Legro, Jeffrey W. 2000. "The Transformation of Policy Ideas." *American Journal of Political Science* 44 (3): 419–32.

Lohmann, Susanne. 1998. "Federalism and Central Bank Independence: The Politics of German Monetary Policy, 1957–92." *World Politics* 50 (3): 401–46.

Lonergan, Eric. 2014. *Money (The Art of Living)*. New York: Routledge.

Lukauskas, Arvid J., and Yumiko Shimabukuro. 2006. "The Non-Linear Process of Institutional Change: The Bank of Japan Reform and Its Aftermath." *Japanese Journal of Political Science* 7 (2): 127–52.

Mabuchi, Masaru. 1991. "Nihon ginkō no sentaku: Chū ō ginkō-seido kaikaku no kokoromi to sono zasetsu" [The Bank of Japan's choice: efforts to reform the system and their setbacks]. *The Annals of Japanese Political Science Association* 42: 139–63.

Mabuchi, Masaru. 1997. *Ōkurashō ha naze oitsume rareta noka: Seikan kankei no henbō* [Why was the Ministry of Finance driven into a corner?: Change in the relationship between politicians and bureaucrats]. Tokyo: Chūkō Shinsho.

MacKenzie, Donald. 2006. "Is Economics Performative? Option Theory and the Construction of Derivatives Markets." *Journal of the History of Economic Thought* 28 (1): 29–55.

MacKenzie, Donald. 2008. *An Engine, Not a Camera: How Financial Models Shape Markets*. Cambridge, MA: MIT Press.

March, James G., and Johan P. Olsen. 1983. "The New Institutionalism: Organizational Factors in Political Life." *American Political Science Review* 78 (3): 734–49.

Marcussen, Martin. 2005. "Central Banks on the Move." *Journal of European Public Policy*, 12 (5): 903–23.

McCubbins, Matthew D., Roger G. Noll, and Barry R. Weingast. 1989. "Structure and Process, Politics and Policy: Administrative Arrangements and the Political Control of Agencies." *Virginia Law Review* 75 (431): 431–82.

McKinnon, Ronald I., and Kenichi Ohno. 1997. *Dollar and Yen: Resolving Economic Conflict between the United States and Japan*. Boston: MIT Press.

McKinnon, Ronald I., and Kenichi Ohno. 2001. "The Foreign Exchange Origins of Japan's Economic Slump and Low Interest Liquidity Trap." *The World Economy* 24 (3): 279–315.

McNamara, Kathleen R. 1998. *The Currency of Ideas: Monetary Politics in the European Union*. Cornell Studies in Political Economy. Ithaca, NY: Cornell University Press.

McNamara, Kathleen R. 2002. "Rational Fictions: Central Bank Independence and the Social Logic of Delegation." *West European Politics* 25 (1): 47–76.

Meltzer, Allan H. 2010. *A History of the Federal Reserve*. Vol. 2. Chicago: University of Chicago Press.

Metzler, Mark, and Simon James Bytheway. 2016. *Central Banks and Gold: How Tokyo, London, and New York Shaped the Modern World*. Ithaca, NY: Cornell University Press.

Mieno, Yasushi. 1999. *Ri wo mite gi wo omou: Mieno Yasushi no kin'yū seisaku kōgi* [Thinking about moral principles whenever encountering benefits: Yasushi Mieno's lecture on monetary policy]. Tokyo: Chūō Kōron Shinsha.

Mishkin, Frederic S. 2001. "The Transmission Mechanism and the Role of Asset Prices in Monetary Policy." National Bureau of Economic Research Working Paper No. 8617.

Mishkin, Frederic S., and Adam S. Posen. 1998. "Inflation Targeting: Lessons from Four Countries." NBER Working Paper (6126).

Miwa, Hironori, and Yoshimasa Maruyama. 2012. "Nichigin no 'mokuto' dōnyū ni kansuru ronten seiri to kon'go no kadai" [A summary of the issues related to the Bank of Japan's introduction of 'mokuto (goal)' and issues for the future]. In *Economic Monitor*. Tokyo: Itōchū Kenkyūjo.

Miyao, Ryuzo, and Tatsuyoshi Okimoto. 2017. "The Macroeconomic Effects of Japan's Unconventional Monetary Policies." Research Institute of Economy, Trade and Industry (RIETI).

Mori, Takeshi, and Miniko Furuichi. 2005. "Chūō Ginkō no Zaimu hōkoku no Mokuteki Igi to Kaikeishori wo meguru ronten" [The objectives and significance of central bank's financial reporting and the issues surrounding accounting measures]. *Kin'yū Ken'yū* (July): 111–62.

Nakagawa, Yatsuhiro. 1981. *Taiken Kin'yū Seisaku ron* [Theory of experiential monetary policy]. Tokyo: Nihon Keizai Shinbun Sha.

Nakahara, Nobuyuki. 2006. *Nichigin wa dare no mono ka* [Whose BOJ is it?]. Tokyo: Chūō Kōron Shinsha.

Nakakita, Toru. 2001. "Restructuring the Ministry of Finance and Revising the Bank of Japan Law." *Japanese Economy* 29 (1): 48–86.

Nakamura, Takafusa. 1971. *Senzenki Nihon Keizai Seichō no Bunseki* [Analysis of Japanese prewar economic growth]. Tokyo: Iwanami Shoten.

Nakazawa, Masahiko, and Koji Yoshikawa. 2011. "Defure ka no kin'yū seiseku: Ryōteki Kan'wa seisaku no Kenshō" [Monetary policy under deflation: Analysis of quantitative easing policy]. PRI Discussion paper (11A-3): 1–21.

Nelson, Stephen C. 2014. "Playing Favorites: How Shared Beliefs Shape the IMF's Lending Decisions." *International Organization* 68 (2): 297–328.

Nelson, Stephen C., and Peter J. Katzenstein. 2014. "Uncertainty, Risk, and the Financial Crisis of 2008." *International Organization* 68 (2): 361–92.

Neumann, Manfred J. M. 1991. "Precommitment by Central Banking Independence." *Open Economies Review* 2 (1): 95–112.

Nihon Ginkō Hyakunenshi Hensan Iinkai, ed. 1982-86. *Nihon Ginkō Hyakunenshi* [100-year History of the Bank of Japan], vols. 3, 4, 5, 6. Tokyo: Nihon Ginkō Hyakunenshi Hensan Iinkai.

Nishimura, Yoshimasa. 1999. *Kin'yū gyōsei no hai'in* [Reasons of failure in financial administration]. Tokyo: Bungei Shunjyū sha.

Nordhaus, William D. 1975. "The Political Business Cycle." *Review of Economic Studies* 42 (2): 169–90.

Oda, Nobuyuki, and Kazuo Ueda. 2007. "The Effects of the Bank of Japan's Zero Interest Rate Commitment and Quantitative Monetary Easing on the Yield Curve: A Macro-Finance Approach." *Japanese Economic Review* 58 (3): 303–28.

Ogata, Shijuro. 1996. *En to nichigin* [Yen and the BOJ]. Tokyo: Chūō Kōronsha.

Oguri, Seiji. 2000. "Chūō ginkō shinyoreggi rieki shobun shihon [Central bank seigniorage, profit management and net worth]." *Shiga Daigaku Keizai Gakubu Kenkyu Nenpo* 7: 105–18.

Ohta, Takeshi. 1991. *Kokusai kin'yū genba kara no shōgen-Nichigin kara mita gekidō no sanjyū nen* [International financial on-the-spot report: A tumultuous thirty years seen from the BOJ]. Tokyo: Chūō Kōronsha.

Okina, Kunio. 2009. "Nihon ginkō hōkaisei ni yoru seisaku kettei katei no henka" [Changes in the policymaking process due to the BOJ Law reform]. In *Henbō suru nihon seiji: 90 nendai igo 'henkaku no jidai' wo yomitoku* [Japan's transforming politics: Deciphering the 'age of changes' since the 1990s], edited by Mikuriya Takashi, 261–87. Tokyo: Keisō Shōbō.

Okina, Kunio. 2013. *Nihon ginkō* [The Bank of Japan]. Tokyo: Chikuma Shobō.

Okina, Kunio. 2015. *Keizai no daitenkan to nihon ginkō* [Major economic turning points and the Bank of Japan]. Tokyo: Iwanami Shoten.

Okina, Kunio, Shigenori Shiratsuka, and Horoshi Fujiki. 2000. "Zero kinri ka no kin'yū seisaku: chūō ginkō ekonomisuto no shiten [Monetary policy under the ZIRP:

Perspectives from the Central Bank economists]." IMES Discussion Paper Series 2000-J-10.

Organisation for Economic Cooperation and Development (OECD). 2017. Economic Survey of Japan 2017. Paris: OECD Publishing. www.oecd.org/eco/surveys/economic-survey-japan.htm.

Pang, Bo, and Lillian Lee. 2008. "Opinion Mining and Sentiment Analysis." Foundations and Trends in Information Retrieval 2 (1–2): 1–135.

Park, Gene. 2011. Spending without Taxation: FILP and the Politics of Public Finance in Japan. Stanford, CA: Stanford University Press.

Parsons, Craig. 2002. "Showing Ideas as Causes: the Origins of the European Union." International Organization 56 (1): 47–84.

Pennebaker, James W. 2011. The Secret Life of Pronouns: What Our Words Say About Us. New York: Bloomsbury Press.

Pollard, Patricia. 2004. "Monetary Policy-making Around the World." PowerPoint presentation at Federal Reserve Bank of St. Louis, February 15, 2004.Posen, Adam S. 1995. "Declarations Are Not Enough: Financial Sector Sources of Central Bank Independence." In NBER Macroeconomics Annual 1995, vol. 10, edited by Ben S. Bernanke and Julio J. Rotemberg, 253–74. Cambridge, MA: MIT Press.

Posen, Adam. 1998a. "Central Bank Independence and Disinflationary Credibility: A Missing Link?" Oxford Economic Papers 50 (3): 335–59.

Posen, Adam S. 1998b. Restoring Japan's Economic Growth. Vol. 57, Policy Analyses in International Economics. Washington, DC: Institute for International Economics.

Rhodes, R. A. W. 2008. "Policy Network Analysis." In The Oxford Handbook of Public Policy, edited by Michael Moran, Martin Rein, and Robert E. Goodin, 425–47. New York: Oxford University Press.

Rodriguez, Carlos, and Carlos A. Carrasco. 2014. "ECB Policy Responses between 2007 and 2014: A Chronological Analysis and a Money Quantity Assessment of Their Effects." In Working Paper Series: Financialisation, Economy, Society & Sustainable Development (FESSUD) Project.

Rogers, John H., Chiara Scotti, and Jonathan H. Wright. 2014. "Evaluating Asset-Market Effects of Unconventional Monetary Policy: A Multi-country Review." Economic Policy 29 (80): 749–99.

Rogoff, Kenneth. 1985. "The Optimal Degree of Commitment to an Intermediate Monetary Target." The Quarterly Journal of Economics 100 (4): 1169–89.

Rosenau, James N. 1995. "Governance, Order, and Change in World Politics." In Governance without Government: Order and Change in World Politics, edited by James N. Rosenau and Ernst-Otto Czempiel. Cambridge, UK: Cambridge University Press. Original edition, 1992.

Sagami, Takehiro. 1982. Sengo Keizaishi Saidai Ibento no Hiwa, chu [Secret Tale of the Greatest Event in Postwar Economic History, part 2]. Tōyōkeizai, 86–97.

Sakakibara, Eisuke and Noguchi Yukio. 1977. "Ōkurasyō-Nichigin Ōcyō no bunseki [Analysis of dynasty of Ministry of Finance and Bank of Japan]." Cyūōkōron 92 (8): 96–150.

Schmidt, Vivien A. 2002. "Does Discourse Matter in the Politics of Welfare State Adjustment?" Comparative Politics Studies 35 (2): 168–93.

Schmidt, Vivien A. 2007. "Trapped by Their Ideas: French Élites' Discourses of European Integration and Globalization." Journal of European Public Policy 14 (7): 992–1009.

Schmidt, Vivien A. 2010. "Taking Ideas and Discourse Seriously: Explaining Change through Discursive Institutionalism as the Fourth 'New Institutionalism.'" European Political Science Review 2 (1): 1–25.

Schonhardt-Bailey, Cheryl. 2005. "Measuring Ideas More Effectively: An Analysis of Bush and Kerry's National Security Speeches." *Political Science and Politics* 38 (4): 701–11.

Schonhardt-Bailey, Cheryl. 2013. *Deliberating American Monetary Policy: A Textual Analysis*. Cambridge, MA: MIT Press.

Shimizu, Isaya. 2004. *Nichigin wa kōshite kin'yū seisaku wo kimete iru: kisha ga mita seisaku kettei no genba* [How the BOJ decides financial policy: Policymaking as seen by journalists]. Tokyo: Nihon Keizai Shimbunsha.

Shimizu, Isaya. 2016. *Defure Saishū Sensō: Kuroda Nichigin Ijigen Kanwa no Hikari to Kage* [The last war on deflation: Bank of Japan under Kuroda and the two faces of the non-conventional monetary policy]. Tokyo: Nihon Keizai Shinbun Shuppan sha.

Shimizu, Naoki. 2005. "Defure fukyōka no Kin'yū seisaku wo meguru seiji katei: naze infure mokuhyō seisaku ha dōnyū sarenakattaka" [Political process over monetary policy under deflation: Why was inflation targeting policy not adopted?]. *Seisaku Kagaku* 13–1: 53–68.

Shirai, Sayuri. 2009. "Cross-Border Investment and the Global Financial Crisis in the Asia-Pacific Region." UNESCAP Working Paper.

Shirai, Sayuri. 2014. "Japan's Monetary Policy in a Challenging Environment." *Eurasian Economic Review* 4 (1): 3–24.

Shirai, Sayuri. 2016. *Chō Kin'yū kanwa kara no dakkyaku* [Unwinding ultra-easy monetary policy]. Tokyo: Nihon Keizai Shimbun Shuppan sha.

Shirai, Sayuri. 2017. *Mission Incomplete: Reflating Japan's Economy*. Tokyo: Asian Development Bank Institute.

Shirakawa, Hiromichi. 2014. *Kodokuna Nichigin* [Lonely Bank of Japan]. Tokyo: Kōdansha Gendai Shinsho.

Shirakawa, Masaaki. 2008. *Gendai no kin'yū seisaku: Riron to jissai* [Modern financial policy: Theory and practice]. Tokyo: Nihon Keizai Shinbun Shuppan Sha.

Shiratsuka, Shigenori. 2010. "Size and Composition of the Central Bank Balance Sheet: Revisiting Japan's Experience of the Quantitative Easing Policy." *Monetary and Economic Studies* 28 (3): 79–105.

Silberman, Bernard S. 1993. *Cages of Reason: The Rise of the Rational State in France, Japan, the United States, and Great Britain*. Chicago: University of Chicago Press.

Simmons, Beth A., Frank Dobbin, and Geoffrey Garrett. 2006. "Introduction: The International Diffusion of Liberalism." *International Organization* 60 (4): 781–810.

Simmons, Beth A., Frank Dobbin, and Geoffrey Garrett. 2008. *The Global Diffusion of Markets and Democracy*. New York: Cambridge University Press.

Suda, Miyako. 2014. *Risuku to no tatakai: Nichigin seisaku iinkai no 10 nen wo furikaeru* [The fight against risk: Looking back over 10 years of the BOJ Policy Board]. Tokyo: Nihon Keizai Shimbun sha.

Suzuki, Takaaki. 2000. *Japan's Budget Politics: Balancing Domestic and International Interests*. Boulder, CO: Lynne Rienner Publishers.

Suzuki, Yoshio. 1993. *Nihon no kin'yū seisaku* [Japanese financial policy]. Tokyo: Iwanami Shoten.

Suzuki, Yoshio. 2014. *"Horon" in Toshihiko Yoshino, Rekidai Nihon Ginko Sōsai ron: Nihon Kin'yū Seisaku shi no Kenkyū* [Chronicle of Bank of Japan governors: A study of the history of Japanese monetary policymaking]. Tokyo: Koudansha gakujutsu Bunko.

Svensson, Lars E. O. 1999. "Price Level Targeting versus Inflation Targeting: A Free Lunch?" *Journal of Money Credit and Banking* 31 (3): 277–95.

Svensson, Lars E. O. 2001. "The Foolproof Way of Escaping from a Liquidity Trap: Is It Really, and Can It Help Japan?" The Frank D. Graham Memorial Lecture, Princeton University, Princeton, NJ, April 2001.

Svensson, Lars E. O. 2006. "Monetary Policy and Japan's Liquidity Trap." Princeton University Center for Economic Policy Studies Working Paper.

Taddy, Matt. 2013. "Measuring Political Sentiment on Twitter: Factor Optimal Design for Multinomial Inverse Regression." *Technometrics* 55 (4): 415–25.

Takayama, Shin. 2009. *Koko saidai no keizai taisaku de takamaru keiki fuyou kitai to risuku* [The heightened expectations and risks arising from the largest economic measures]. In Keizai Rebyū. Tokyo: Tokyo Mitsubishi UFB Bank.

Taylor, John B. 1993. "Discretion versus Policy Rules in Practice." Carnegie-Rochester Conference Series on Public Policy 39: 195–214.

Ueda, Kazuo. 1992a. Iwata Okina ronsō wo saitei suru: mane sapurai dōkō no tadashii mikata [Arbitrating the Iwata-Okina debate: the correct way to evaluate money supply movement] Shūkan Tōyō Keizai. December 12: 114–17.

Ueda, Kazuo. 1992b. *Kokusai Shūshi Fukinkōka no kin'yū seisaku* [Monetary policy in the imbalance of international payments]. Tokyo: Tōyō Keizai Shinpōsha.

Ueda, Kazuo. 2000. "Causes of Japan's Banking Problems in the 1990s." In *Crisis and Change in the Japanese Financial System*, 59–81. New York: Springer.

Ueda, Kazuo. 2003. "Jiko shihon to Chūō ginkō [Net worth and central banks]." Paper presented at the Japan Society of Monetary Economics, Fall Convention, October 25, 2003.

Ueda, Kazuo. 2009. "Solving Japan's Economic Puzzle." *Far Eastern Economic Review* 172 (May): 49–51.

Ueda, Kazuo. 2012. "The Effectiveness of Non-Traditional Monetary Policy Measures: The Case of the Bank of Japan." *Japanese Economic Review* 63 (1): 1–22.

Ueda, Kazuo. 2013. "Ijigen no Kin'yu kanwa: Chukan Hokoku" [Super monetary easing: Mid-term report]. CIRJE Discussion Paper. CIRJE-J-252.

Ugai, Hiroshi. 2007. "Effects of the Quantitative Easing Policy: A Survey of Empirical Analyses." *Monetary and Economic Studies-Bank of Japan* 25 (1): 1.

Ugai, Hiroshi, and Keiko Sonoda. 2006. "Kin'yū seisaku no setsumei ni tsukawarete iru bukka shisū [Price indices used to explain monetary policy]." *Bank of Japan Review* 2006-J-2 (2006): 1–10.

Umeda, Masanobu. 2009. "Nihon no shōhisha bukka shisū no Sho tokusei to Kin'yū seisaku un'ei" [Various characteristics of Japan's Consumer Price Index and monetary policy management]. In *Defure Keizai to Kin'yū seisaku* [Deflationary economy and monetary policy], edited by Hiroshi Yoshikawa, 295–344. Tokyo: Keio Daigaku Shuppan kai.

Umeda, Masanobu. 2011. *Nichigin no seisaku keisei: 'Gijiroku' tō ni miru seisaku handan no dōki to seigōsei* [Monetary policymaking at the BOJ: Motivations and formation of policy judgments seen in Diet proceedings]. Tokyo: Tōyō Keizai Shinpōsha.

US Treasury Department. 2017. "Foreign Exchange Policies of Major Trading Partners of the United States." Edited by US Treasury, October 17, 2017. https://www. treasury.gov/press-center/press-releases/Documents/2017-10-17%20(Fall%20 2017%20FX%20Report)%20FINAL.PDF.

Van Overtveldt, Johan. 2011. *The End of the Euro: The Uneasy Future of the European Union*. Evanston, IL: Agate Publishing.

van Rixtel, Adrian. 2002. *Informality and Monetary Policy in Japan: The Political Economy of Bank Performance*. Cambridge, UK: Cambridge University Press.

Verdun, Amy. 1999. "The Role of the Delors Committee in the Creation of EMU: An Epistemic Community?" *Journal of European Public Policy* 6 (2): 308–28.

Vogel, Steven Kent. 1996. *Freer Markets, More Rules: Regulatory Reform in Advanced Industrial Countries*. Ithaca, NY: Cornell University Press.

Volcker, Paul, and Toyoo Gyohten. 1992. *Changing Fortunes: The World's Money and the Threat to American Leadership*. New York: Times Books.

Wakatabe, Masazumi. 2015. *Japan's Great Stagnation and Abenomics: Lessons for the World*. New York: Palgrave Macmillan.

Weir, Margaret. 1989. "Ideas and Politics: The Acceptance of Keynesianism in Britain and the United States." In *The Political Power of Economic Ideas: Keynesianism across Nations*, 53–86. Princeton, NJ: Princeton University Press.

Wendschlag, Mikael. 2016. "The Central Bank Elites—Transformations between 1950 to 2000." Working Paper.

Woolley, John T. 1985. *Monetary Politics: The Federal Reserve and the Politics of Monetary Policy*. New York: Cambridge University Press.

Yamagiwa Masamichi Denki Kankokai. 1979. *Yamagiwa Masamichi* [Masamichi Yamagiwa]. Tokyo.

Yamaguchi, Yutaka. 2015. "Intabyū; Yamaguchi Yutaka Moto Nichigin Fukusōsai ni kiku" [Interview: Yutaka Yamaguchi, former deputy governor of Bank of Japan]. Kin'yū Zaisei Bijinesu: 4–7.

Yamawaki, Takeshi. 1998. *Nihon Ginkō no shinjitsu: samayoeru tsūka no ban'nin* [The truth about the BOJ: Wandering guardian of currency]. Tokyo: Daiyamond, Inc.

Yoshino, Toshihiko. 2014. *Rekidai Nihon ginkō sōsai ron: Nihon kin'yū seisaku shi no kenkyū* [Past governors of the BOJ: Study about the history of Japanese monetary policy]. Tokyo: Kōdan sha.

Index